The Revival of Magick
and other essays

Oriflamme 2

Aleister Crowley

The Revival of

MAGICK

and other essays

Oriflamme 2

edited by

Hymenæus Beta and Richard Kaczynski, Ph.D.

with an Afterword by

Samuel Aiwaz Jacobs

New Falcon Publications

in association with

Ordo Templi Orientis International

1998 E.V.

This edition first published in 1998 e.v. by

New Falcon Publications
1739 East Broadway Road, Suite 1-277
Tempe, AZ 85252

or

320 E. Charleston Blvd., Suite 204-286
Las Vegas, NV 89104

ISBN 1-56184-133-1

Library of Congress Catalog Card Number 97-75752

Design by Spirit Vision, Inc.
Cover design by Moondog Design.
Typeset in 11.5 point Monotype Bulmer.
Printed in the United States of America.

05 04 03 02 01 00 99 98
10 9 8 9 7 6 5 4 3 2 1

The paper used in this publication meets the minimum requirements of the American National Standard for Permanence of Paper for Printed Library Materials Z39.48–1984.

Contents

EDITORS' INTRODUCTION ☆ 7

HUMANITY FIRST ☆ 9

THE REVIVAL OF MAGICK ☆ 13

THE CAMEL ☆ 40

THE SOUL OF THE DESERT ☆ 47

A HINDU AT THE POLO GROUNDS ☆ 56

THREE GREAT HOAXES OF THE WAR ☆ 58

MYSTICS AND THEIR LITTLE WAYS ☆ 64

THE ATTAINMENT OF HAPPINESS ☆ 70

AN IMPROVEMENT ON PSYCHOANALYSIS ☆ 76

BILLY SUNDAY ☆ 82

THE OUIJA BOARD ☆ 87

A LETTER FROM THE MASTER THERION ☆ 88

HOW HOROSCOPES ARE FAKED ☆ 91

ART AND CLAIRVOYANCE ☆ 96

GEOMANCY ☆ 98

GOOD HUNTING! ☆ 104

EULOGIUM UPON JEANNE D'ARC ☆ 113

WILLIAM BLAKE ☆ 115

ON THE EDUCATION OF CHILDREN ☆ 126

ON SEXUAL FREEDOM ☆ 131

DUTY ☆ 135

AN OPEN LETTER TO RABBI JOEL BLAU ☆ 145

A MEMORANDUM REGARDING THE BOOK OF THE LAW ☆ 156

THE ANTECEDENTS OF THELEMA ☆ 162

THE BEGINNING OF THE NEW WORLD ☆ 170

ON THELEMA ☆ 172

THE METHOD OF THELEMA ☆ 176

A LETTER TO HENRY FORD ☆ 184

GILLES DE RAIS ☆ 193

A LECTURE ON THE PHILOSOPHY OF MAGICK ☆ 206

THE SCIENTIFIC SOLUTION OF THE PROBLEM OF GOVERNMENT ☆ 208

AFTERWORD: FRAGMENTS ☆ 211

EDITORIAL NOTES ☆ 213

WORKS CITED ☆ 219

INDEX ☆ 233

Editors' Introduction

Aleister Crowley was a man of letters to his fingertips. He read voraciously, wrote compulsively, and when he was not writing his many books, or maintaining his voluminous diaries, he kept up a lively correspondence with his many friends both famous and obscure.

He is best known today as a great authority on Magick, and is remembered (some say unfairly neglected) as a poet. This collection is concerned with Crowley as an essayist. He had a definite gift for this literary form; it gave full range to his wit, humor, knowledge, and command of English. While many of his essays (e.g., on politics and current affairs) are now as dated as their subject matter, as many others are as fresh today as when they were first written. Some of his best are collected here, forming a curiously charming sampling of Crowley's opinions and interests.

His essay subjects are wide-ranging, including mysticism, magick, travel, humor, social satire, drugs, psychoanalysis, religious fundamentalism, "pop" occultism, art, divination, mythology, and drama. His most fertile period (in terms of work published) ran from 1909 to 1922. His first major contributions outside the pages of his own journal *The Equinox* were in *The Occult Review* and the English edition of *Vanity Fair*. After moving to New York in 1914 he became a regular contributor to *Vanity Fair*'s American edition, later becoming managing editor of the New York monthly *The International (A Review of Two Worlds)* during 1916–1917. He also contributed work to *The Bystander*, *The Open Court*, *Smart Set*, *Pearson's*, *The English Review* and other journals. For this book, his journalism has been supplemented by later essays, most previously unpublished. With the exception of the preface and the semi-autobiographical title essay (which serves as a sort of author's introduction), the essays appear in roughly chronological order.

Crowley loved and admired his father, Edward Crowley, a Protestant lay-preacher in the exclusive Plymouth Brethren, and the young Crowley often watched his father preach. He is very much his father's son as he preaches his new Law of Thelema, to good effect, in several passionate essays or "epistolatory writings." In these essays, he explains the religious philosophy of the new law given in 1904 E.V. by *Liber AL vel Legis, The Book of the Law*. Sometimes writing as Crowley the man, at other times as The Master Therion, Magus of the New Æon of Horus, the recipients range from a fellow writer (the American novelist James Branch Cabell) to an industrialist (Henry Ford) to one of his own colleagues (the German O.T.O. and A∴A∴ member Martha Küntzel). He makes doctrinal points and connections not made elsewhere, many of great relevance to the theology and social philosophy of Thelema. In other essays he explores the spiritual antecedents of Thelema, as well as the practical application of this philosophy at that great experiment in Thelemic monasticism, the Abbey of Thelema in Sicily.

Crowley owed his education to Cambridge and his lifelong curiosity. Though rarely given to stodginess or pedantry, he did love to show off his erudition; even his more popular essays are salted with references that no doubt went right over the heads of most readers when first published. With years of accumulated studies of Crowley's work available, his many enthusiastic students today are far better prepared to follow him than the average *Vanity Fair* or *International* subscriber of nearly a century ago. But as the intent of this collection is to introduce Crowley to a wider modern audience, his essays have been annotated thoroughly for this edition; no apology is offered for pedantry and stodge. Notes on sources, works cited, and an index are also provided.

We wish to thank James Banner, John Bonner, Clive Harper, William E. Heidrick, Jack B. Hogg, Jr., Marcus Jungkurth, Adam McLean, Martin P. Starr, David Tibet and Lawrence Sutin for editorial advice and research assistance. For source material we wish to thank the Warburg Institute, University of London; the George Arents Research Library at Syracuse University; the Harry Ransom Humanities Research Center, University of Texas at Austin; and Widener Library, Harvard University. We also wish to thank proofreaders Randall Bowyer and Robin D. Matthews, who also gave sound editorial advice and material for footnotes; John Bowie of Moondog Design for the cover design; and Dr. Christopher Hyatt and Nicholas Tharcher of New Falcon, for making this book possible. Oxford University Press kindly gave permission to reproduce the essay by Samuel Aiwaz Jacobs.

This book is dedicated to the architect of the revival of the O.T.O., Maj. Grady Louis McMurtry, Frater Superior Hymenæus Alpha X°.

HYMENÆUS BETA   RICHARD KACZYNSKI, PH.D.

Humanity First

It may be that one day the gold plate with its diamond inscriptions may be stripped by some vandals—Macaulay's New Zealander or another—from my sarcophagus. It may be that centuries later still the learned archæologists of some nation yet unguessed, excavating the ruins of Westminster Abbey, may find those bones and send them to anatomists for examination.

The report of these anatomists may be something in these terms: "These are the bones of a mammal, a primate, *Homo sapiens*. The skull is not prognathous; this person was probably a Caucasian."

In such a judgment I acquiesce with pleasure. It would be limitation to be described as "this German," or "this Japanese." Man is man, and in him burns the mystic flame of Godhead. It is a blasphemy to discriminate further, to antithesize the Russian against the Turk, in any matter more serious than national belief, custom, or costume.

All advanced thinkers, all men who realize the divine plan, desire and intend the solidarity of humanity; and the patriot in the narrow and infuriated sense of that word is a traitor to the true interests of man. It may be necessary, now and then, to defend one's own section of mankind from aggression; but even this should always be done with the mental reservation: "May this war be the nurse of a more solid peace; may this argument lead to a better understanding; may this division lead to a higher union."

"A man's worst enemies are those of his own household," and the worst foes of any nation are its petty patriots. "Patriotism is the last resort of a scoundrel."[1]

The deliberate antagonizing of nations is the foulest of crimes. It is the Press of the warring nations that, by inflaming the passions of the

---

[1] [Samuel Johnson, given in James Boswell's *Life of Samuel Johnson*; see Works Cited.]

ignorant, has set Europe by the ears. Had all men been educated and travelled, they would not have listened to those harpy-shrieks. Now the mischief is done, and it is for us to repair it as best we may. This must be our motto: "Humanity first."

All persons who generalize about nations: "Germans are all murderers"—"Frenchmen are all adulterers"—"Englishmen are all snobs"—"Russians are all drunkards"—and so on, must be silenced. All persons who cling to petty interests and revenges must be silenced. We must refuse to listen to any man who does not realize that civilization itself is at stake, that even now Europe may be so weakened that it may fall a prey to the forces of atavism, that war may be followed by bankruptcy, revolution, and famine, and that even within our own lifetime the Tower of the Ages may be fallen into unrecognizable ruins.

We must refuse to listen to any man who has not resolutely put away from him all limited interests, all national passion, who cannot look upon wounded humanity with the broad, clear gaze, passionless and yet compassionate, of the surgeon, or who is not single-minded in his determination to save the life at whatever cost of mutilation to any particular limb.

We must listen most to the German who understands that England is a great and progressive and enlightened nation, whose welfare is necessary to the health of Europe; and to the Frenchman who sees in Germany his own best friend, the model of science, organization, and foresight, which alone can build up the fallen temple anew. We must listen to the Englishman who is willing to acquiesce in the Freedom of the Seas; and to the Russian who acknowledges that it is time to put a term to the tyranny of arms and the menace of intrigue.

The yelping Press of every country, always keen to gather pennies from the passions of the unthinking and unknowing multitude, will call every such man a traitor.

So be it. Let the lower interest be betrayed to the higher, the particular benefit of any given country to the Commonwealth of the whole world. Let us no more consider men, but man. Let us remember who came from heaven and was made flesh among the Jews, not to lead his own people to victory, not to accept that partial dominion of the earth, but to bring light and truth to all mankind.

Had the Saviour of Humanity deigned to accept the patriotic mission of driving out the Romans, he would have united his nation, but man would not have been redeemed. Therefore, his people called him traitor, and betrayed him to their own oppressors.

Let those who are willing, as He was, to accept the opprobrium, and, if need be, the Cross, come forward; let them bear the Oriflamme of the Sun for their banner, for that the Sun shineth alike upon all the nations of the earth; and let them ever flash in the forefront of their battle this one redeeming thought: "Humanity First."

The Revival
of Magick

I

The obvious course for one who wishes to write on Magick is to invoke the God Thoth, for He is Lord both of magick and of writing.

In truth, that is the very apt slip for our leash of silence. The word used by Sir Walter Scott for Magick is "gramarye,"[1] and a ritual of magick is a "grimoire," "grimorium," or grammar; all from *gramma*, a letter.[2] Thoth, scribe of the Gods, was probably just a man called Tahuti—the Egyptian form of the Coptic word Thoth—who invented writing. Fust,[3] one remembers, who invented printing, became Faust, the "black magician."[4] The first great miracle of progress, after the conquest of fire, was this art of writing.

Magick then may be defined for our present purpose as the art of communicating without obvious means. Curiously, the new harnessing of that form of fire—I use the word in its old magical sense—called electricity to the shafts of the car of progress was followed by a new art or rather series of arts of communication without obvious means: the telegraph, the telephone, and now Hertz's discovery (exploited by one Signor Marconi) of wireless telegraphy.[5]

---

[1] [See Sir Walter Scott (1771–1832), *The Lay of the Last Minstrel*, III, xi.]

[2] [Greek.]

[3] [Johann Fust (c. 1400–1466), German moneylender and printer, did not so much invent printing as lend money to Johann Gutenburg to produce a printing press.]

[4] [Immortalized in two plays, Goethe's *Faust* (1808–1832) and Marlowe's *Dr. Faustus* (c. 1588). Some scholars hold that a German necromancer, Georg Faust (?1480–?1538), was the basis of the legend. The name Johann was given to Faust by Marlowe, but not by Goethe.]

[5] [The German physicist Heinrich Hertz (1857–1894) discovered electromagnetic waves, and confirmed Maxwell's theory of light as electromagnetic radiation. The Italian physicist Guglielmo Marconi (1874–1937) applied the work of Maxwell and Hertz and invented the first practical radio apparatus.]

Now no man doubts the existence of a supreme and illimitable power, whether he conceive of it as soulless, unconscious and mechanical, or as spirit, self-conscious, and self-willed. You may think the Sun to be God; some very ignorant and some very illuminated people have done so; but the fact is disputed by none, that the Sun, within the limits of its own system, is, physically speaking, the source of all light, heat, Energy in all its forms, as well as of the earth itself, Being or Matter in all its forms as we know it.

Now if we wish to obtain heat from the Sun, we can go and sit on Palm Beach; or we can dig up solar energy in the form of coal—and so on; in a hundred ways we can make communication with that material source of heat. Very good; magick pretends to be able to do the same thing with the Secret Source of all Being and all Form, all Matter and all Motion.

It claims to be able to draw water from the Fountain of All Things, according to its needs, by certain methods. And though ordinary prayer is a part of Magick, this point is to be considered, that in the purely religious theory, God may or may not think it fit to answer prayer. This then is the great heresy of Magick—or of religion, if you happen to be a Magician! The Magician claims to be able to force a favourable answer. If he tries to make the Elixir of Life, and fails, he has simply failed. He is a bad Magician, just as a chemist is a bad chemist who tries to make oxygen and fails. The chemist does not excuse himself by saying that it was the Will of God that he should not make oxygen that day!

The explanation is simple. What the Magician calls God is merely the divine Emanation in himself. And the reconciliation with orthodox theology follows at once. The Magician is using the formula of Hermes Trismegistus, "That which is below is like that which is above, and that which is above is like that which is below, for the performance of the miracles of the One Substance."[1] That is to say, in order to perform his miracle he must call forth his own God in the Microcosm. That is united with the God of the Macrocosm by its likeness to it; and the Macrocosmic force then operates in the Universe without as the Magician has made it operate within himself; the miracle happens. Now then it follows that unless the will of the magician be really at one with the Will of the

---

[1] [Greek name for the Egyptian god of writing, Thoth. The name literally means "Thrice Greatest Hermes." The quotation is from the "Emerald Tablet."]

Cosmos, this likeness does not exist, this identification does not take place. Therefore the Magician cannot really perform any miracle unless that be already the Design of the Universe. So that he who sets out by saying "I will impose my will on all things" ends "Thy will be done."

It is possible, indeed, to perform magic in other ways by other formulæ, but all such efforts are mere temporary aberrations from the path; at the best they are mistakes; persisted in knowingly they become black magic; and in the worst event the sorcerer is cut off by his own act from the Cosmos, and becomes a "Brother of the Left Hand Path." This truth is taught by Wagner in *Parsifal*.[1] Klingsor was unable to comply with the requirements of the Graal Knights; he could not harmonize Love and Holiness; so he mutilated himself, and was forever debarred from even a possibility of redemption.

It was because the Church misunderstood this doctrine, and saw in magic but a rival power, that she strove with all the agony of fear to suppress it. Soon only charlatans dared to practice it, because they were known to be harmless. The whole thing fell into contempt.

When I was twenty-two years of age I devoted myself to the attainment of adeptship, or whatever you like to call it. That was indeed the question: what should I call it? (For I am first of all a poet, and expert in the use of words.) I decided to call my life-work *magick*. For this very reason, that it was fallen so utterly into disuse. I cut myself deliberately off from the modern jargon "theosophy," "occultism," and so on, all words with an up-to-date connotation. I would make my own connotation, and impose it on the world. The only chance of confusion was with prestidigitation, and that not being of the same universe of discourse, hurt no more than the homonymity of "box," "game" and a hundred other words. There was something of boyish defiance, too, no doubt, in my choice of the word. However, I labelled myself with it, and I used good gum!

It has been necessary to insist that Magick is done by an identification of the magus with the Supreme in order to show how in practice one goes to work.

There are two branches of this one tree; we may conveniently call them the Catholic and Protestant.

---

[1] [German composer Richard Wagner (1813–1883) wrote *Parsifal*, his opera based upon legends of the Holy Grail, in 1877–79; see Works Cited.]

The Protestant method is that of direct prayer. As a child asks its father for a toy, so the magician asks God to cause rain, or whatever he may need at the moment. The prayer book is full of such spells, even to the extreme use of "Oh, Lord, who alone workest great marvels, send down upon our Bishops and Curates the healthful spirit of Thy grace." But there is no record of any favourable answer to this particular prayer!

In the supreme prayer of Christ in Gethsemane we find the advanced magician speaking. "*If it be Thy will*, let this cup pass from me; nevertheless not my will, but Thine, be done." [1] This ends in "My will, which is Thine, be done," for by-and-by Christ tells Pilate that if He wished He could have twelve legions of angels to defend Him. [2] But he no longer wishes the cup to pass from Him; His will is one with the Father's.

Now, in order to persuade the God addressed that it is right to grant the prayer, or in order to convince oneself that one is asking for a proper miracle, one resorts to commemoration of other miracles wrought by that God in the past.

Thus the talisman made by Dr. Dee, [3] which raised the tempest in which the Spanish Armada was destroyed, has figured upon it a symbolic image of a face blowing forth a great wind, and around it is the versicle "He sent forth His lightnings and scattered them" [4]—or some similar words. God is reminded that in the past He brought victory to His chosen people by raising a storm at the proper moment. There is, in legal phrase, a precedent for the miracle.

The conjurations of the Grimoires abound in this sort of recitation before the God of His previous exploits.

Here then is the link with the second form of magick—the "Catholic." For in Catholic magick the formula is this: the story of the God is enacted before Him; He is moved by the sight of His own sufferings or adventures, [5] and at the same time the sympathy of the actors with the God is stirred to its highest point.

---

[1] [Luke 22:42, Matt. 26:39.]

[2] [Matt. 26:53.]

[3] [Dr. John Dee (1527–1608), Elizabethan mathematician, astrologer and magician; he was the originator, with Edward Kelly, of Enochian magic. This incident is not recorded in Dee's diaries or biographies. At the time of the battle in 1588 he was residing in Bohemia; he did write Elizabeth I to congratulate her on her victory.]

[4] [See Psalms 18:14, 144:6.]

[5] Here we must remember that most Gods are deified men.

The Bacchæ of Euripides is a perfect example of this kind of ritual.[1] In fact, almost all Greek drama of the classic period is of this kind.[2] The "*deus ex machina*"[3] speech at the end marks the identification complete.

Similarly, the Eleusinian Mysteries celebrated the adventures of Demeter; those of Adonis and Osiris and Mithras tell the story of the Sun, and thus invoke his power. J. M. Robertson goes further, and says that the story of the Last Supper, Trial and Crucifixion of Christ is not a history but a scenario.[4] Nor is this view confined to rationalists and anthropologists of the type of Spencer, Frazer, and Grant Allen;[5] many Christian mystics uphold it, and say that their reverence for the *logos*[6] is not lessened but increased by the identification of the legend of His life and death with that of the Cosmos.

I must again call attention to the necessity of this formula of identification in order to show the impossibility of evil in magick. Evil is synonymous with failure.

With the low class sorcerer who sells himself as a slave to some "devil" we have nothing here to do. That is the antithesis of magick. The aim is to command the spirits. Very well; suppose we begin in a gross, selfish, avaricious way, and try to get the spirits to bring us gold. We call Hismael, the Spirit of Jupiter. Nothing happens. We learn that Hismael will not be commanded but by his proper Intelligence, Iophiel. So we call Iophiel. Equal recalcitrance on the part of Iophiel, who is only amenable to the orders of Sachiel, his Angel. Same story with Sachiel. We go to Tzadquiel the Archangel. Still no good; for Tzadquiel obeys none but El. Good; we invoke El, the God. We must then become El; and having

---

[1] [Athenian playwright Euripides (480–406 BCE) depicts the cult of Dionysus in his drama, variously titled *The Bacchic Women, The Bacchæ*, or *The Bacchants*.]

[2] [See Crowley's essay "Good Hunting," p. 104.]

[3] [Latin, "God from a machine," referring to a contrived set of events introduced into a drama to resolve an otherwise hopeless situation.]

[4] [James Mackinnon Robertson (1856–1933), *Pagan Christs: Studies in Comparative Hierology* (1903); see Works Cited.]

[5] [Herbert Spencer (1820–1903) was an English philosopher. Sir James George Frazer (1854–1941) was a Cambridge classicist and anthropologist best known for his comparative study of magic, *The Golden Bough*. Charles Grant Blairfindie Allen (1848–1899) was an English writer and scientist, and a member of the Rationalist Press Association.]

[6] [Greek, "word"; in this context, the Word of God made flesh as Jesus.]

done so, having entered into that vast divine essence, we cannot bother any more as to whether we have any money. We have left all that behind. So then we see that to perform any miracle we must show a divine reason for it. I have often asked for money and obtained it; but only when the money was really needed for some manifestly cosmic benefit.

In fact, with whatever work one begins, one is led up to the Great Work. This is a logical process, and even if one were tempted to be illogical, and turn to Black Magic, those great forces whose names one has (perhaps ignorantly) invoked are invisibly about one, and bring one into line with a jerk—and none too gentle a jerk at that!

Éliphas Lévi defines Black Magic as the result of the persistence of the will in the absurd.[1] One does not go mad on seeing the devil, because before invoking him one must be already mad.[2]

It is extraordinary how the formula of Hermes Trismegistus holds throughout; Magick is but the extension of the microcosm in the macrocosm. And as the macrocosm is the greater, it follows that what one does by magick is to attune oneself with the Infinite. "In myself I am nothing: in Thee I am All-self. Dwell Thou in me! and bring me to that Self which is in Thee!" concludes the great prayer of the Rosicrucians.[3]

This, however, explains why those who meddle with magick out of curiosity, or who try treacheries on magicians, find themselves in trouble.

The Magician is an expression of the Will of the Universe: the meddlers rebel, and suffer. To oppose a true Magician is as silly as to put your hand on a circular saw in motion. But the handless blames the saw.

---

[1] [The French occultist Éliphas Lévi (Alphonse Louis Constant, 1810–1875) was a prolific author on magick. Crowley believed himself to be Lévi's reincarnation. Lévi specified five conditions for success in the practice of black magic: "1. Invincible obstinacy. 2. A conscience at once hardened by crime and most subject to remorse and terror. 3. Affected or natural ignorance. 4. Blind faith in everything incredible. 5. A completely false notion of God." *The Mysteries of Magic*, ed. and trans. A. E. Waite, p. 215; see Works Cited.]

[2] [Lévi, ibid., states that "He who affirms the devil creates the devil." A corollary might be Crowley's "One would go mad if one took the Bible seriously; but to take it seriously one must be already mad." *Book 4*, Part II (1913), chap. 16, note.]

[3] [This is from the Adeptus Minor initiation ritual of the Golden Dawn. *The Temple of Solomon the King*, in *The Equinox* I(3), p. 173, has "In myself I am nothing, in Thee I am all self, and live in Thy Selfhood from Nothing! Live Thou in me, and bring me unto that Self which is in Thee! Amen."]

I know of one modern Master who has been often attacked. In every case the attacker has come to absolute ruin. One woman came to him, a woman old and sly, and wormed herself into his confidence. He knew her for an enemy, and trusted her absolutely. He left her his checkbook duly signed, and she embezzled his money. He left his wife in her care, and she tried to corrupt her. By-and-by it became obvious to the woman that the Master knew everything. He only smiled, and continued to trust her. So she went down with meningitis, and there was an end of her.

In such a case the only mistake the magician can make is to defend himself in the normal manner. He leaves his castle; he will be slain. You must not go onto the enemy's ground. Perfect love, perfect faith, perfect trust, and you are unassailable. But use the weapons of the flesh, and you are lost.

II

It is in this somewhat dry disquisition, bordering as it does, I am afraid, on metaphysics, that is to be sought the reason for the revival of magick. Unless this explanation were first given, it might seem a mere phenomenon of folly, an hysterical exacerbation due to over-civilization.

But assuming that irrefutable form of idealism which contents itself with the demonstration that, knowledge being a function of the mind, as the materialists not merely concede, but insist, the universe as we know it is equivalent to the contents of that mind; and assuming also that the mind contains a power able to control thought; then there is no absurdity in asserting that mind may be the master of matter. And the empirical rules laid down by the magicians of old may prove to some extent of use in practice.

Such rules are in fact the inheritance of the Magi. This is not the place to discuss the disputed cases of the Rosicrucians, of the Comte de St. Germain, of Cagliostro, and others whose names will readily occur.[1]

---

[1] [The Comte de St. Germain (c. 1710-?1780) was a semilegendary mystic who reputedly made the elixir of life and lived for centuries. Count Alessandro di Cagliostro (born Giuseppe Balsamo, 1743-1795) was a Sicilian adventurer, alchemist and (some say) charlatan; his role in the French Revolution is recounted in the elder Dumas' *Mémoires d'un médicin: Joseph Balsamo* (1846-48) and its sequel, *Le Collier de la reine* (1848). Edward George Bulwer-Lytton, 1st Baron Lytton (1803-1873) was an English novelist and playwright, and author of the occult novels *Zanoni* (1842) and *A Strange Story* (1862).]

The periods in which they lived are obscure, and the controversies sterile. But it is at least evident that some valid tradition lurked somewhere, for within the memory of living men are Éliphas Lévi and his pupil Bulwer Lytton. Now it is not philosophical to suppose that Lévi was an upstart genius, though he does claim to have "forced an answer from the ancient oracles" and indeed to have reconstituted magick. I do not believe this to be strictly true; I believe that Lévi had living masters. But that Lévi first translated ancient ideas into modern terms is undeniable. Moreover, the influence of this great master was enormous, even in spheres external to his particular orb. The revival of French Literature with Baudelaire, Balzac, Gautier, Verlaine, de Banville, d'Aurevilly, Haraucourt, Rollinat, the de Goncourts and a dozen other names of the first rank, was in a sense his work.[1] It was he that formulated the philosophical postulates that made their art possible and triumphant. Such sentences as this: "A pure style is an aureole of holiness" may pass as the very canon of art. His reconciliations of right and duty, liberty and obedience, are cardinal to the gate of modern thought. I do not hesitate to assert that very soon *The Key of the Mysteries* will be recognized as the very incarnation of the spirit of his time.[2]

In this book Lévi offered to the Church a way out of the difficulties raised by the advance of Science. That she rejected it was her suicide; just as Napoléon's disdain of his political philosophy was written large in letters of blood at Wörth, Gravelotte, Metz and Sedan.[3]

---

[1] [Charles Baudelaire (1821-1867) was a Symbolist poet; Crowley's translations of his work appeared in *Vanity Fair* and in book form (*Little Poems in Prose*; see Works Cited). Crowley included works by the novelist Honoré de Balzac (1799-1850) in his reading curricula. Théophile Gautier (1811-1872) was a poet and novelist. Paul Verlaine (1844-1896) was a Symbolist poet; Crowley translated two of his poems for *Vanity Fair*. Théodore Faullin de Banville (1823-1891) was a poet and critic. Jules Amédée Barbey d'Aurevilly (1808-1889) was a novelist and critic. Edmond Haraucourt (1856-1942) was a French poet and dramatist. Maurice Rollinat (1853-1903) was a French poet. The brothers Edmond Goncourt (1822-1896) and Jules Goncourt (1830-1870) collaborated as novelists.]

[2] [Crowley translated *La Clef des grands mystères* (1861) as *The Key of the Mysteries*, first published as a supplement to *The Equinox* I(10) (1913) and later issued in book form by Rider; see Works Cited.]

[3] [The French emperor Napoléon Bonaparte (1769-1821) reigned from 1804-1815; Crowley is listing several of his major battles.]

However, the few capable of initiation took Lévi to their hearts; and from that hour the revival of magick has never been in doubt. At the moment almost of Lévi's death the Theosophical Society was founded;[1] and Blavatsky's debt to the French Adept is the greatest of all her obligations.[2] In England Anna Kingsford—a mere megaphone for Edward Maitland—was at work; also there was Mr. S. L. Mathers, a considerable magician who subsequently fell, and was smashed beyond recognition; and, in the nineties, the giant figure of Allan Bennett.[3]

In magical literature itself we find, as is to be expected, a reflection of these facts. Ever since Christian Rosencreutz[4] there is nothing serious and first-hand, until Éliphas Lévi. The magical tradition was the basis of gracious fables like *Undine*, and of frivolities like *The Rape of the Lock* and its source the *Comte de Gabalis*.[5] Sometimes it is treated more

---

[1] [Both events occurred in 1875, the year of Crowley's birth.]

[2] [The Russian mystic Helena Petrovna Blavatsky (1831–1891) was the cofounder and principal theoretician of the Theosophical Society. Crowley considered her to have been a Master of the Temple 8°=3° of the A∴A∴. Crowley was highly critical of the Theosophical Society after Blavatsky's death, but admired Blavatsky's work. Her great debt to Lévi is usually overlooked.]

[3] [Anna Bonus Kingsford (1846–1888) was the cofounder, with Edward Maitland (1824–1897), of Esoteric Christianity and the Hermetic Society; she introduced Golden Dawn Imperator S. L. Mathers to H. P. Blavatsky. Samuel Liddell "MacGregor" Mathers was a co-founder of the Hermetic Order of the Golden Dawn; Crowley was briefly his protégé. Crowley supplanted him as Imperator of the G.D. following the revelation of *The Book of the Law* in 1904 E.V., founding the A∴A∴ around 1907 E.V. For Mathers' relationship to Crowley, see Crowley's *Confessions*, abridged ed., *passim*, and the editor's introduction to *The Goetia*, 2nd ed., ed. Hymenæus Beta (1995, 1997). The chemist and electrical engineer Allan Bennett MacGregor (1872–1923) was Mathers' protégé in the Golden Dawn, where he was Frater Iehi Aour; he may have been Mathers' adopted son. Bennett tutored Crowley in magic and yoga. He became a Buddhist monk in 1902 (taking the name Ananda Metteyya), founded the International Buddhist Society, and led the first Buddhist mission to England in 1908.]

[4] [Christian Rosencreutz is the mythical founder of the Rosicrucian Brotherhood. See Works Cited under Andrea; see also Paul M. Allen, ed., *A Christian Rosencreutz Anthology* (1981).]

[5] [*Undine* (English translation 1818) is a romance by the German writer Friedrich Heinrich Karl La Motte-Fouqué (1777–1843). *The Rape of the Lock* (1712) by the English poet and satirist Alexander Pope (1688–1744) was dedicated to the fictional Comte de Gabalis. The romance *Le Comte de Gabalis* (1670) is a well-known Rosicrucian novel by Nicolas Pierre Henri, abbe de Villars (1635–1673), named for its principal character. See Works Cited.]

seriously, as in Lewis' *Monk*, and Mrs. Shelley's *Frankenstein*.[1] There are legends of Cagliostro, too, in Dumas' *Memoirs of a Physician*,[2] and there is the *Diable boiteux* and the *Diable amoreux*."[3] Nor let ever be forgotten that terrible and true magical apologue *La peau de chagrin*.[4]

Casanova gives an admirable view of the matter, and Thackeray copies him cleverly enough in *Barry Lyndon*.[5] But it is all hearsay.

Éliphas Lévi comes up stage, and says plainly to the world: "I myself did such and such an operation of magick in such and such a time and place."

He wears a mask illegible enough, it is true; but we have at least *oratio recta* and not *oratio obliqua*.[6] For which we who remember bitter school-days thank God, and prefer Lévi to Livy![7]

In his footsteps if Bulwer Lytton did not follow, it was because of his public career. He comes near it. Everyone within even the widest ripple that is caused on the water of society when the Stone of the Wise is thrown therein knew that Sir Philip Derval's laboratory was an accurate description of Lytton's own magical cabinet. It was clear to all ripe intelligence that in *Zanoni* the author was seriously expounding his own beliefs, discussing his own problems, justifying his own career. In the *Strange Story* he recounts incidents surely seen with his own eyes.[8]

Read his account of the evocation of a demon, and his other of an ordeal, and compare them with the stories of Lévi. Observe how the

---

[1] [Matthew Gregory Lewis (1775–1818) and Mary Wollstonecraft Shelley (1797–1851) were both English Gothic novelists. See Works Cited.]

[2] [Alexandre Dumas (*père*, 1802–1870) *Mémoires d'un médicin: Joseph Balsamo* (1846–48), most of which appeared in 1847–1848 as *Memoirs of a Physician*; see Works Cited.]

[3] [The French dramatist and novelist Alain René Le Sage (1668–1747) produced the novel *Le diable boiteux* (1707), usually titled *Asmodeus* in English translation. *Diable amoreux* (translated as *The Devil in Love*) is a work by Jacques Cazotte. See Works Cited.]

[4] [Honoré de Balzac (1799–1850), *La peau de chagrin* (1831); translated as *The Wild Ass's Skin*. See Works Cited.]

[5] [Giovanni Jacopo Casanova de Seingalt (1725–1798), Italian adventurer and author; Crowley refers to his *Mémoires* (12 vols., 1826–38). *Barry Lyndon* is a novel by William Makepeace Thackeray (1811–1863); see Works Cited.]

[6] [*Lat.*, "direct (lit. 'right') speech" as opposed to "oblique speech."]

[7] [Titus Livius (39 BCE–17 CE), Roman historian.]

[8] [Edward Bulwer-Lytton's novel *Zanoni: A Rosicrucian Tale* (1842) depicts the operations of a "Rosicrucian" group. *A Strange Story* appeared in 1862. See Works Cited.]

ancient directness revives in them, and contrast them with the sneering rubbish of the courtly abbé who wrote the *Comte de Gabalis*.[1]

It is evident where the truth lies. And now let us turn to the evidence of men yet living.

III

Allan Bennett was born at the time of the Franco-Prussian war. His father, an engineer, died when he was a young child, and his mother brought him up a strict Catholic.

When he was about 8 years old he happened to hear that if you repeated the "Lord's Prayer" backwards, the Devil would come. This enterprising infant at once set himself to learn it backwards, and, when letter-perfect, went into the garden and said it. Something—the Devil or one of his angels—did appear, and the child ran screaming in terror to the house.

We hear of nothing else of the same kind for a long while, and the same startling sporadic success is true of his first step in mysticism. When he was about 18, without any premonitory symptom, he was suddenly caught up into the trance called *śivadarśana*.[2] We cannot stop here to describe this; suffice it to say that it is the highest attainment in this line, save perhaps one, possible to man.

Its effect upon him was catastrophic; he realized instantly and without any doubt that no other state was worthy of a moment's thought, and he unhesitatingly abandoned all, if perchance he might discover how to achieve of set purpose what had been thrust on him by destiny. His natural tendency to magic drew him into that line of work, and so at the age of 25 we find him already famous for his powers in this art.

He had a "blasting rod" constructed simply of the lustre of an old-fashioned chandelier, and he was always cheerfully ready to demonstrate its power by pointing it at any convenient sceptic, and paralyzing him for a few hours or days.

For more serious magical work he had a rod of almond tipped with a golden star of five points, each point engraved with a letter of the Ineffable Name Jeheshua;[3] in the centre was a diamond. With this he would trace mysterious figures in the air, and, visible to the ordinary eye, they

---

[1] [See page 21, note 5.]

[2] [Sanskrit, literally "to have sight of Śiva."]

[3] [The Hebrew spelling of "Jesus," which consists of the ineffable name of God, יהוה, combined with the letter of Spirit, *shin* (שׁ), to give יהשׁוה.]

would stand out in faint bluish light. On great occasions, working in a circle, and conjuring the spirits by the great names of the *Key of Solomon*[1] or the "Enochian Calls" of spirits given him by Dr. Dee,[2] he would obtain the creature necessary to his work in visible and tangible form. On one occasion he evoked Hismael,[3] the lowest manifestation of Jupiter, and, through a series of accidents, was led to step out of his circle without effectively banishing the spirit. He was felled to the ground, and only recovered five or six hours later. But this was simply a single untoward incident in a career of almost monotonous success.

However, he was certainly a careless person. On one occasion he had consecrated a talisman of the Moon to cause rain. (As he lived in London, I cannot imagine why he did this!) To make it work it had to be immersed in water. He would put it in a basin or tumbler, and within a few minutes the clouds would gather and the rain begin: instructive to his pupils, and beneficial to the country. But one day he lost the talisman. It worked its way into a sewer, and London had the wettest summer in the memory of man!

It was early in 1899 that I became the pupil of this great master. I say "great master," and I ask to be taken on trust, for in this account of magick it would be dull to dwell upon his true qualities; I must rather seek to amuse by recounting his misadventures. Incidentally, any magical manifestation whatever is a regrettable incident. Just as in war, even the greatest victories cost something. Every battle is an obstruction in the march of the conqueror.

In order to explain my meeting with Allan Bennett it is necessary to give a short résumé of my own magical career.

---

[1] [This probably refers to the "greater" *Key of Solomon*, or *Clavicula Salomonis*, first published in English by S. L. Mathers in 1888. See Works Cited.]

[2] [The Enochian "calls" or "keys" are invocations in the Enochian or Angelic language given by spirits to Dr. John Dee and Edward Kelly. See Meric Casaubon, *A True and Faithful Relation*, and Crowley, "Liber 84 vel Chanokh"; see Works Cited.]

[3] [Hismael is the spirit of the planet Jupiter; cf. Henry Cornelius Agrippa, *Three Books of Occult Philosophy*, bk. II, chap. 22; see Works Cited.]

IV

I was in my third year at Cambridge when the call came.[1] I had been intended for the Diplomatic Service, and had also a great ambition to be a poet. In fact, I had written many hundred thousand lines, all of which I diligently destroyed in one great holocaust of paraffin and paper a matter of eight years later. It now struck me quite suddenly that, even if I got the Embassy at Paris—why, who was ambassador a century before? I did not know, and nobody knew, or cared.

Even if I got fame like that of Æschylus—why, who reads Æschylus?[2] A few scores only, even in a University where Classics are compulsory.

And, anyhow, one day or other the earth must fall into the sun, or go dead like the moon.

I saw the Vanity of Things. I must find a material to build my temple; something more permanent than the hearts and minds of men.

This conclusion came to me reasonably enough, yet with all the force of a vision. I cannot hope to convey the quality of that despair. I rushed to the Bookseller, ordered all works ever published on Alchemy, Magic, and the like, and spent the long winter nights in ploughing those dreary sands. I had not knowledge enough even to begin to understand them.

However, the magical capacity was there, as will be seen. "In my distress I called upon the Lord; and He inclined unto me and heard my cry."[3]

This is indeed the essential quality of a magician, that he should be able, without obvious means, to send forth his will-currents to the desired quarters, and awake them to answer. It is not necessary that the reply should come magically; he should expect his will obeyed in the ordinary course of events. As an example, let me give the use I made of a talisman of Abramelin "to have books of magic."[4] When I consecrated it, I was childish enough to expect the instant appearance of a Genie with flames in his mouth and books in his hand. Instead of this, all that hap-

---

[1] [1897.]

[2] [Æschylus (525–456 BCE), Greek tragic poet. See Works Cited.]

[3] [II Sam. 22:7 and Psalm 40:1.]

[4] [The 11th chapter of the third book of *The Book of the Sacred Magic of Abramelin the Mage* contains talismans "to cause all kinds of Books to be brought to one." The second of those listed is "for Books of Magic." Crowley had a copy of this talisman in his wallet on the day he died.]

pened was that a man called to see me with just those books that I needed, for sale. The point of the story is that I had spent weeks with all the booksellers in England, trying to get just those books. And the man knew nothing of that; he had come on an impulse.

To return: one of the books that I had bought at Cambridge was *The Book of Black Magic and of Pacts*, the catchpenny production of an ignorant, dipsomaniac, half-demented scholiast named Waite, whose sole asset was a pompous jargon composed of obsolete words.[1] In his preface he said—so far as one could understand—that he was in touch with more Masters, Adepts, *mahātmās*,[2] Rosicrucians and Hermetists than had ever appeared even in pseudo-occult literature.

To him I wrote for advice and received many folios of rigmarole in return. The only intelligible sentence was one in which he recommended me to read Von Eckartshausen's *Cloud Upon the Sanctuary*.[3] This book spoke of a secret church, of a brotherhood of initiates, exactly filling the bill. I read this book over and over again at Wastdale Head in Cumberland, where I spent Easter of 1898 climbing with a splendid mountaineer, one of the three best the world has ever seen, but a terrible scoffer at all occult lore.[4] However, I sent out my S.O.S. call to the Brotherhood, and this is what resulted:

In July, 1898, I was at a camp on the Schönbühl Glacier above Zermatt, and had gone down to the village for a respite from the constant snowstorms. In the Beerhall one night, like the young ass I was, I started to lay down the law on Alchemy. To hear me, one would think I had just discharged Nicolas Flamel for cleaning my athanor badly, and beaten Basil Valentine over the head for breaking my alembic![5]

---

[1] [Arthur Edward Waite, *The Book of Black Magic and of Pacts* (1898); see Works Cited. Crowley disliked Waite's scholarship and prose, and parodied him mercilessly in *The Equinox*; he did however appreciate Waite as a poet.]

[2] [*Skt.*, *mahā* ("great") and *atmā* ("soul"), lit. "Great Soul." This was also the term for the enlightened Secret Masters of Blavatsky's Theosophical Society.]

[3] [Karl von Eckartshausen, *The Cloud upon the Sanctuary*; see Works Cited.]

[4] [Oscar Eckenstein (1859–1921), one of Crowley's best friends and his preceptor in mountaineering.]

[5] [Nicolas Flamel (c. 1330–1418) was a French alchemist famed for having accomplished the Great Work, transmuting base metals to gold and discovering the secret of longevity. "Basil Valentine" is a mythical early 15th century Benedictine monk who discovered uses for antimony and the process of distillation.]

One of the party took me seriously;[1] he saw that my bombast concealed a real desire of knowledge. We walked to the hotel together. I saw that he really knew what I pretended to know, and I dropped my "side" and became the humble learner. I had promised myself to renew the conversation in the morning: to my consternation he had disappeared. I made a vigorous search, and three days later caught him as he was walking down the valley to Viège. I walked with him and never left him till he had promised to meet me in London and introduce me to a certain Brotherhood of which he spake darkly.

The rest of the story is short. In London he introduced me to a really great magician, one known to adepts as Frater Volo Noscere, who introduced me to a true magical brotherhood.[2] It was more than a year afterwards that I found myself again at a dead-centre. Again I sent out the S.O.S. call from the City of Mexico. The next mail brought me a letter from Frater V.N., solving the questions which I had not asked! And again, two months later I sent out the call. This time a Master came from England to teach me a New Path—and who should it be but the mountaineer, who had always passed for a sceptic?[3] At the moment of my first call he had been sitting opposite me at the fireplace, had been linked to me on the precipices of Scafell by a rope—if only I had the eyes to see him!

My life has been full of such incidents; if anyone cry "coincidence," let him also admit that her long arm was very effectively pulled by my conjuration!

Now to more amusing facts of my career. The first thing I learnt was to travel in the astral body. This seems to have been a natural gift with me; in half-a-dozen experiments I was already master of the "Astral Plane." I could go where I would, see what I would, hear what I would. At that time I did not know of those higher planes to which initiation is the only key.

The next step to going out on the Astral Plane is to get it to return the visit; in other words, evocation of spirits to material appearance. It was

---

[1] [The chemist Julian L. Baker was Frater Causa Scientiæ in the Golden Dawn.]

[2] [Volo Noscere was the Golden Dawn motto of the chemist George Cecil Jones, who later co-founded the A∴A∴, in which he was Frater D.D.S.]

[3] [This was Oscar Eckenstein, who taught Crowley the elements of mind control (*dhāraṇā*) while mountain climbing in Mexico.]

just as I started on this that I found Allan Bennett. The occasion was an initiation into the order of which we were both members; but he had not been present since I joined it. After the ceremony I was led trembling before the great man, and of course, could say not a word. However, in the anteroom, an hour later, he came directly to me and began: "So, little brother, you have been meddling with the *Goetia*."[1] I protested myself unworthy even to pronounce the word! But he had spotted me as a promising colt, and when, using my opportunity, I made myself even as his familiar spirit, he consented to take me as a pupil. Before long we were working together day and night, and a devil of a time we had!

In my chambers in Chancery Lane I fitted up a temple, the walls covered by six vast mirrors, so as to throw back the force of the invocations. There were circle and triangle on the floor, and an altar in the midst of the circle.

I constructed all my magical weapons with my own hands, except the wand, which cannot be made, but must be transmitted. This, a shaft of almond cut with a single blow of the Magick Knife at sunrise on Easter morn, was transmitted to me by Frater Volo Noscere.

The effect of all this was pretty sultry.

I was attacked by a black magician in the very early days—the story is told at length and with perfect accuracy of detail in my tale, "At the Fork of the Roads"; it is too long to cite here.[2] I will only say that a woman was sent by the Black Lodge to get a drop of my blood, that she succeeded, that for ten nights following I was assailed by a succubus which I killed with my hands every time, that with the help of my master I put her out of business by sending a plague of cats to her house, and that when she came to try for more blood I punished her by sending her into my black temple—a tiny closet where I kept a skeleton which I fed on mice and birds with the idea of creating a material and living demon servant— where she was rent in pieces by the evil things she had invoked. She went to the devil, and her master fled the country.[3]

---

[1] [This took place in early 1899. The *Goetia* is part of the "lesser" *Key of Solomon*; Crowley would produce Mathers' edition in 1904. See Works Cited.]

[2] ["At the Fork in the Roads," *The Equinox* I(1).]

[3] [The artist Althea Gyles, supposedly sent by William Butler Yeats (1865–1939), Crowley's rival in the Golden Dawn. In Yeats' side of the story, "Crowley has been making wax images of us all, and putting pins in them." Yeats to Lady Gregory, June 6, 1900, in *The Letters of W.B. Yeats*, ed. Wade, p. 346; see Works Cited.]

Not bad, all this, for one's first year of magick?

One of our great exploits was the saving of the life of my master. Absolutely unselfish, he would never stir to help himself, and he was a permanent invalid from spasmodic asthma, with complications. Frater V. N. and I determined, in the name and for the sake of the Order, to save him. We evoked the spirit Buer to visible appearance.[1] This was not wholly successful; at that time we wanted things to happen as they did in books—for we were young. But we got the right leg and the foot and ankle of the left as solid as need be; and the head, helmeted, was dimly visible through the incense smoke. In those days we were too pious to use blood, or we might have done better. However, the purpose of the work succeeded. The Master recovered, and is alive to this day—fifteen years later.

Curious how dull good is, how amusing evil! Much keener in memory is one night when Frater V. N. and I were alone together working on the talismans and other necessaries for some operation or other, I entirely forget what. We went out to dinner, and before leaving the room, I noticed that the temple door was slightly open. It was locked by a Yale key of which there was but one, which had never left my possession. In those days my chief alarm was that someone would get into my magical affairs. (Nowadays I callously let them in; if they blow their heads off, that's their affair, not mine!) So I sedulously slammed and tested the door, and out we went to dinner. On the stairs was a black cat—not a real cat, either. Back we came from a perfectly temperate meal, found the outer door secure as we had left it, entered, found the temple door wide open, though with no sign of violence, and the altar overthrown, and its furniture tossed in all directions.—And then the fun began!

Round and round the big library tramped the devils all the evening, an endless procession; 316 of them we counted, described, named, and put down in a book. It was the most awesome and ghastly experience I had known.

Strange how they love to open doors! In the East of my big temple in Scotland was a secret shrine, on to which folding doors opened. These I would lock, padlock, seal, nail down, fasten (in short) by every manner of means; yet, every time I left the room, I expected to find them open. Too often to recount, I did so. I set all kinds of traps for the spirits; it was

---

[1] [Buer is an infernal president in the *Goetia* who "healeth all distempers in man."]

useless. As long as I was in the room nothing would happen; the moment I shut the outer doors behind me, the inner ones would open noiselessly. I ultimately had to perform a special ceremony to get rid of the annoyance. The demons who played this game were the 49 servitors of Beelzebub; when tamed they became exceedingly useful.

There is a manuscript in the Arsenal Library of Paris which has been translated and published under this title, *The Book of the Sacred Magic of Abramelin the Mage*.[1] It is the best and most dangerous book ever written. The translator, who lived at the other end of Paris, had to give up cycling to the library, so many were his accidents. Even afoot, he was in constant danger of his life. And he misused the book, fell from a very creditable degree of attainment as a magician to be a loafer, a dipsomaniac, a sponger, and a blackmailer; in the end he died insane.

The book is the address of one "Abraham the Jew" to his second son, Lamech, bestowing this magick upon him. The author records his research, his many travels and disappointments. At last he meets with one Abramelin in Egypt, goes with him into an oasis, and is there initiated by the bestowal of this Sacred Magick. He returns, achieves the task, and employs his powers to the glory of God and the benefit of his neighbor, "forcing even bishops to restore stolen property," winning battles for Electors by the timely creation of "artificial cavalry," healing the sick wholesale, and generally bestirring himself as a philanthropist.

The substance of the operation is as follows: Get a house in a quiet place, have a terrace opening to the North of your Oratory, have robes and a crown, a wand, and a few other not-too-Persian apparatus, and then get busy. Pray more and more every day to obtain the Knowledge and Conversation of your Holy Guardian Angel. After two months cut out all distractions and pray harder. After two months of that, pray harder still.

Then the climax. The Angel appears and instructs. Then and not till then summon the Four Great Princes of the Evil of the World and compel them to swear obedience on the wand, and order them to operate

---

[1] [By its own account, this book was "delivered by Abraham the Jew unto his son Lamech." It first appeared in German as *Die egyptischen Offenbarungen*; the title page gives Cologne: Peter Hammer, 1725, but it was probably produced in Stuttgart in 1853. An English edition (translated from a French manuscript by S.L. Mathers) appeared in 1898. See Works Cited, under Abraham ben Simeon.]

certain talismans. The next day call the Eight Sub-Princes, and the third day their servitors.

The book is written throughout in a serious and simple style. It is by far the most convincing mediæval magical document in existence. The personality of Abraham himself is evidence.

And any person who doubts magick has only to get a copy of the book, and refuse to take it seriously.[1] He will get proofs enough in standard time; place, the back of the neck!

But if you take it seriously and reverently, if you aspire with your whole will to this attainment, you are safe. The blows of the demon will fall only on those about you.

Yet every obstacle will be put in your way. For example, I had command of what was for all practical purposes unlimited money. I didn't care what I spent on this work. It took me eleven months to find a house.

In copying out on vellum the talismans, I used the breakfast-room of that house, a room chosen because it was light and cheerful and caught the early morning sun. The weather was fine. Yet I had to do my copying by artificial light. The sun could not penetrate the murk that gathered about those talismans.

One day I returned from shooting on the hill to find a Catholic Priest in my drawing room. It was to ask my permission to do what he could for my gardener, a total abstainer of twenty years' standing who had gone raving drunk.

My housekeeper vanished, unable to bear the eerieness of the place.

An adept with whom I had arranged that he should stay to be a link between me and the outer world likewise fled in terror without a word of warning.

One of the workmen employed about the place went raving mad, and tried to kill me. Others again became dipsomaniacs. All my dogs died. My cook very nearly died, and was only saved by a talisman.

Such are just a few of many incidents which averted the tragedy of dullness from my daily life. And all this, mind you, at the mere threat to perform the Operation!

---

[1] [At the turn of the last century the simple possession or handling of *Abramelin* was reputed to cause mysterious and unpredictable phenomena for the unwary.]

Time would fail me to tell of all the untoward events that happened to people who did not even go so far as this. Only to have that book on one's shelves is a more serious risk than drying dynamite on a stove!

The talismans work automatically. They are as easy to explode as Iodide of Nitrogen, and a sight more dangerous. My friend and editor, Captain J. F. C. Fuller,[1] once marked his place in the book with his butcher's bill; a couple of days later the butcher was at work; his knife slipped, pierced his thigh and killed him. As Fuller observed at the time, "It may be only a coincidence, but it's just as bad for the butcher!"

"At my initiation I was taught to be cautious" is a note in one system;[2] in another the neophyte is told "Fear is failure, and the forerunner of failure. Be thou therefore without fear, for in the heart of the coward virtue abideth not."[3]

Keep these two precepts constantly in your mind, and you should go far and fast.

Now for the third class of magical operations! It deals no longer with the brain of the magician himself, as in the case of visions and evocations; it acts upon third parties directly. I refer to the arts of "fascination" in its proper sense—the word comes from the Latin *fascinum*.[4] Love is blind: and fascination includes all arts that have this effect. You transform yourself, like Zeus into swan or bull, like Lucius into an ass,[5] like the Egyptian *magi* into an hawk, swallow, or ibis, or like the Syrian into a dove, and by this means compel the desired object to your arms. Or you become invisible—in the practical sense that you remain unseen by those whom you wish not to see you, and if you are playfully inclined, and hungry, you become a bat or a wolf and go afield for blood. These stories are not legends: they veil true powers. I only once tried vampirism, for examination purposes, and in about an hour I bled my victim white. I passed with honours and special mention.

---

[1] [John Frederick Charles Fuller (1878–1966), later Major-General. Fuller was an early member and officer of the A∴A∴, best known for his numerous works on military history and strategy.]

[2] [Ordo Templi Orientis.]

[3] [The Neophyte initiation ritual of the Golden Dawn. In *The Temple of Solomon the King*, *The Equinox* I(2), p. 256, it is given as: "Child of Earth, fear is failure: be thou therefore without fear! for in the heart of the coward Virtue abideth not!"]

[4] [*Lat.*, "witchcraft, enchantment."]

[5] [See Lucius Apuleius (c. 127 BCE), *The Golden Ass*; see Works Cited.]

Of course, the reason why one does not do these things is that in the trance *ātmadarśana*, on the threshold of masterhood[1] one loses one's Ego for ever. Thenceforth the man exists only as a vehicle for an Impersonal Master; he lives his own life, and does his own duty, but the Master in him doesn't care what happens to him.

The other day a young lady came to consult me. I gave her about a thousand dollars' worth of information. She asked me what I was going to charge. I said: "Nothing; regard me as a bank account on which you can always draw." She said: "But you must eat!" I answered: "I do not see the necessity."

I am always being asked why, if I have all these powers, I do not cause stones to become bread, and throw myself from the Woolworth Building in order to prove the truth of the Ninety-first Psalm, and obtain all the kingdoms of the earth at slight cost to self-respect.[2]

Why did Christ refuse in the Temptation on the Mount?

It is the same story: I am come to do the Will of Him that sent me. And if I have to die on the cross, that is better than living on it!

One form of fascination is the power over animals. Persuade your animal that you are not that dangerous wild beast, a man, and your task is over.

Remember St. Francis preaching to birds and fishes.[3] I have seen Allan Bennett do the same with the krait, the deadliest of the Indian snakes. We met it on a road. Before I could blow its head off with my revolver (the first duty of man) Allan interposed with his umbrella. But not to kill it. He deliberately stirred it up. It struck at the umbrella. "That," said Allan, "is anger," and went on to prove to the (I trust attentive) reptile the terrible results on character of allowing oneself to give way to anger! He also animadverted on the danger of frequenting the public highway, and, to conclude, removed the beast gently to the long grass. As a krait can strike in the fiftieth part of a second, and kill (if he does strike) in about ten minutes, and as Allan's only protection, besides his divinity, was a pair of thin white duck trousers, I think that may stand as one of the bravest acts ever done. I consider myself a bit of a hero merely to have stood by!

---

[1] [The first edition had "masterpiece"; the text gives a probable correction.]

[2] [See Matt. 4:1–11, where Satan quotes Psalm 91:11–12.]

[3] [The Italian monk St. Francis of Assisi (c. 1182–1226) founded the Franciscan Order.]

However, I learnt a few tricks of this kind myself; for example—a thing most useful in the tropics—how to prevent mosquitoes from biting one. This is done by thinking kindly of them. It must be a genuine spontaneous feeling of brotherhood, or it won't work. You can also pick up anything hot by fixing the attention on the fact that "it doesn't hurt." But that again is a matter of knack. If you think about it too hard, you can no longer do it. I believe D. D. Home had this power.[1]

Again, you can prevent things from biting you by certain breathing exercises. Hold the breath in such a way that the body becomes spasmodically rigid, and insects cannot pierce the skin. Near my bungalow at Kandy was a waterfall with a pool. Allan Bennett used to feed the leeches every morning. At any moment he could stop the leech, though already fastened to his wrist, by this breathing trick. We would put our hands together into the water; his would come out free, mine with a dozen leeches on it. At such moments I would bitterly remark that a coyote will not eat a dead Mexican, but it failed to annoy him.

With invisibility I was very successful. I made a big operation of it in the City of Mexico, and practiced daily for months in front of a mirror. I got good at it at last; and several times I have saved my life, and even things that I valued, thereby.

Another important attainment is that of traveling in the "astral body." This, too, I practiced hard. I was able in time to make my presence known to a person at a distance, by a sort of instinct. Soon I got it so that I could be both seen and heard. I have not yet been able to impress inanimate objects, for I gave up this class of work as not essential to the Great Work. For instance, when I was in Honolulu I had a long talk with a girl in Hong Kong.[2] I described the town, and her house and room, with accuracy, in great detail. She, too, saw me and wrote down my remarks correctly. But I failed to knock a vase off the mantle, as I wished.

The point is this. To "get into the astral body" really means to allow the consciousness to rest in a vehicle of fine matter, and, detaching that from the gross body, to move about. But this has its drawbacks. One is

---

[1] [Daniel Dunglas Home (1833–1886), Scottish-born mystic who achieved fame as the greatest physical medium in the history of the Spiritualist movement; his abilities withstood scientific scrutiny by investigators, including the physicist William Crookes. He was excommunicated from the Catholic Church in 1864 for sorcery.]

[2] [Elaine Simpson, Soror Donorum Dei Dispensatio Fidelis in the Golden Dawn, with whom Crowley conducted experiments in distant astral projection; see *Confessions*, abridged ed., pp. 521–525. Crowley refers to her as Soror Fidelis.]

no longer at all on the material plane, but on the astral plane, and one must not expect to see material things. This is the blunder made by "physical clairvoyants" and the cause of their constant errors. No; for physical clairvoyance, or for action at a distance, somewhere on the astral one must pick up ready material as a basis for a sort of "incarnation." Thus the girl I speak of had burnt incense specially to give me a body visible and tangible and audible. But incense is not strong enough to make a body mechanically solid. It becomes sensible to the eye and ear of a living person, as a cloud is, but not strong enough to resist pressure.

However, by offering blood one can construct a body good enough for, say, courtship and marriage. I have done this often enough; it is not at all difficult when the conditions are right. It is dangerous, though; if anything happened to the blood when you were using it, there would be a nasty mess, and if the blood be not carefully destroyed after you have finished with it, it may be seized by some vampirish elemental or demon. I think no one below the grade of Magister Templi should use blood, unless he be also an initiate of the IX° of O.T.O.[1]

Such have been only a few of very varied activities. I may remark that the methods so far employed are not altogether satisfactory. There is too much accident, for one thing. Quite recently, a disciple of mine, painting that great square of letters which synthesizes the elemental forces of water, had a tank burst and flood his house. On another occasion, at headquarters, teaching astral traveling through the Tablet of Fire, we had five fires in three days, while the disciple who was being taught went home the third night, and found his house burning, a fire having started in the coal cellar. A "natural" fire can't start in a coal cellar, especially, as in this case, in winter.[2]

---

[1] [In the A∴A∴ system, the grade of Magister Templi corresponds to the sphere of Binah (Understanding), and indicates an adept who has annihilated the ego in the Ordeal of the Abyss. See *Liber 418, The Vision and the Voice,* and "One Star in Sight"; see Works Cited. The IX° is the degree of the O.T.O. Sovereign Sanctuary wherein its central secret is preserved.]

[2] [Similar incidents resulted after the English O.T.O. member and artist Nina Hamnett agreed to paint four "elemental panels" (undoubtedly the Enochian tablets) for Crowley: "While she was painting the panel of fire, it seems that the fire element escaped and three fires mysteriously started in the studio that same day." Denise Hooker, *Nina Hamnett: Queen of Bohemia* (1986), p. 34. The Canadian novelist and magical student Malcolm Lowry had similar difficulties.]

For another thing, these methods are very tedious. A proper evocation of a spirit to visible appearance means weeks of preparatory work. Again, they do not always succeed as fully as one would like. In short, I felt the need of further initiation, and the communication of a method as safe and sane and easy as railway traveling.

I will not here detail the steps by which this came to me; enough to say that the A∴A∴, the mightiest organization on the planet, chose me eleven years ago to do a certain work, and rewarded me in no niggard spirit.[1] Then, nearly six years ago, the Frater Superior of the O.T.O. came to me, and appointed me Grand Master of the Order in all English-speaking countries of the Earth, and Special Delegate to America.[2] With this He conferred the secret of high Magick which I wanted. Easy to operate as a bicycle, and sure of results as a bottle of brandy, it only needed a little intelligent study and practice to supplant all the old methods, which became, as it were, adjutants of the real thing.

It is upon this that I am still at work, for I have not yet completely mastered it. There are two parts to every magical operation. The ancient Alchemists expressed this in their formula "*Solve et Coagula.*"[3] First, one must subtilize matter so as to be able to mould it, and then fix it again in gross matter so as to retain the desired form.

The first part of this is swiftly and surely accomplished by the method of which I write; the second part is not equally easy. The result is that one obtains always an earnest of the desired goal, a shadow of the reward, so to speak. But this does not always materialize. For example, one performs an operation "to have $20,000." A few days later a prospect of obtaining that exact sum suddenly arises, then fades slowly away. Exactly what to do in such a case is a problem of which I have not yet found the perfect answer. Fortunately, it rarely happens that this trouble supervenes. In five out of six times the desired event comes naturally to pass without further disturbance. But I confess that I should like to make

---

[1] [Crowley became the Imperator of A∴A∴ around 1907.]

[2] [Crowley was made National Grand Master General of the British O.T.O. in a ceremony in Berlin in 1912. Soon thereafter he was given a further charter (dated 1906—one of Reuss' "preformatted" charters) which gave Crowley additional authority in English-speaking countries, especially America.]

[3] [Latin terms for the alchemical metaphor to dissolve (*solve*) the base elements and reconstitute (*coagula*) them as pure gold; in Crowley's usage it has wide application as a general formula.]

that sixth time safe, and I believe that in another few months I shall have done so. Already matters have improved seventy percent, since I was first initiated in the Great Secret.

It is no great wonder, then, that Magick has revived. When I began the work of the A∴A∴ I had over a hundred pupils in less than six months. The system of the A∴A∴ is singular in many respects; in none more than in this, that it is really secret. No man except the Head and His Chancellor, and His Præmonstrator, knows more than two members; that one who initiated him, and the one that comes to him for initiation.[1] In this way the work has spread through the world with no fuss or trouble. Only now and again is any open work visible—when Isis lifts her skirt enough to show her stocking!

For instance, one hears of public ceremonies on A∴A∴ lines in South Africa, in West Africa, in Vancouver, in Sydney, in Paris and London and (maybe) New York. These appear sporadic; their simultaneity is really the mark of what is passing in the mind of the Masters of the A∴A∴.

The success of the O.T.O. is even more striking to the uninitiate, because its results are more apparent.

Part of the policy of this order is to buy real estate everywhere, to build and furnish temples, lodges, and retreats. Hardly a month passes but I hear of some new branch already financially sound, with its own headquarters, some beautiful property in the country, a fine house, large grounds, all that is needed both for initiations, and for the practice of that life, and of those works, which bring forth fruit from the seed of those initiations. And every week brings me news manifold of what is being done. There is hardly a country in the world which has not dozens of members hard at work at magick, and for the most part making progress at a rate which almost makes me jealous, although for my generation I made advance which was a miracle of rapidity and excited the envy of all the duffers.[2] But the work done by my Masters and (I think I

---

[1] [The reference here is to the external head. In the Outer College of the A∴A∴ the Imperator governs, the Præmonstrator teaches, and the Cancellarius records. When the A∴A∴ was founded Crowley (Frater O.S.V. 6°=5°) was Imperator, George Cecil Jones (Frater D.D.S., 7°=4°) was the Præmonstrator, and J.F.C. Fuller (Frater N.S.F., 5°=6°) was the Cancellarius.]

[2] [This passage was an imaginative prospectus or press release when first published in 1918, but is today becoming a reality.]

may truly say) by myself also has simplified the work incredibly for all. In *The Equinox, 777, Konx Om Pax* and a few secret documents, the whole mystery has been explained; and, for the first time in the history of Magick, a standard Encyclopedia has been published.[1] It is no longer necessary to study fifty strange tongues and wade through ten thousand obscure and ambiguous volumes. With three months' study and a year's practice any man of moderate intelligence and sufficient will-power is armed, once and for all, for the battle. Only in the O.T.O. is some knowledge kept back, and that because the great secret is so easy to learn and so simple to operate that it would be madness to entrust it to any person untested by years of fidelity.[2]

These, then, are the principal causes of the Revival of Magick. It is not possible to publish the figures, nor would it be desirable. But I can assure the public that one has only to enter the magick path to find on all sides and in the most unexpected quarters, men and women whose whole life is secretly devoted to the attainment of the Royal and Sacerdotal Art.

Already Magick is once more a World-Power; the print of the Giant's Thumb is already the amazement of the incredulous; and within five years it will be clear enough to all men Who brought about the World war and why.

We shall see science triumphant, philosophy revolutionized, art renewed, commercialism checkmated; and astride of the horse of the Sun we shall see the Lord come as a conquerer into His Kingdom.

The Revival of Magick is the Mother of the New Æon.

And who is the Father?

> Ho! for his chariot-wheels that flame afar,
> His hawk's eye flashing through the Silver Star!
> Upon the heights his standard shall he plant,
> Free, equal, passionate, pagan, dominant,
> Mystic, indomitable, self-controlled,
> The red Rose glowing on the Cross of Gold![3]

---

[1] [See Works Cited.]

[2] [Complete initiation in all degrees of the O.T.O. has been found to be an essential prerequisite to safety, sanity and success in working its highest degrees.]

[3] [Crowley, *The World's Tragedy* (1910), penultimate verses, variant reading. See Works Cited.]

Do you wish to find Him?

> Herein is wisdom; let him that hath understanding count the
> number of The Beast; for it is the number of a man; and his
> number is six hundred and three score and six.[1]

---

[1] [Rev. 13:18. Crowley writes of this quotation that "The last paragraph, a mere coxcombical flourish, though written with the quite serious idea of indicating to some person of adequate intelligence, the direction in which to seek for a Master, proved an element in an incident of the utmost complexity" (*Confessions*, abridged ed., p. 827). In response to this essay, a stranger identifying himself as Samuel Aiwaz Jacobs wrote to Crowley, indicating not only how to render the word "Therion" in Hebrew so that it adds to 666, but also providing the authentic spelling of Aiwaz (the name of Crowley's Holy Guardian Angel and communicant of *The Book of the Law*) so that it added to 93; cf. the lengthy note on this episode in *Book 4*, Part III, Appendix 3, and the account given in Crowley's "Memorandum Regarding *The Book of the Law*," p. 156 below. Crowley came to consider Samuel Aiwaz Jacobs a Brother of the A∴A∴. An essay by Samuel Aiwaz Jacobs has been appended to this collection of essays as an afterword.]

The Camel

Then Hassan bin Brahim, the camel-driver, lifted up his voice and said: "The sun is hot."

This statement gave me considerable food for reflection.

In the first place, Hassan is a number one liar. Had he not said that he was afraid to cross the desert with only one camel, and having thus induced me to pay for two, brought one of them so antique and infirm that he had to send it back to Bou Saada?

In the second place, Hassan was a fool. Had he not started on a long desert journey without money, food, or water? Had he not shivered all one cloudy night in fear that the flood would carry us away?

Clearly, no reliance could be placed upon Hassan!

So, before assenting to his proposition, I looked about for corroboration of some kind.

"By 'the sun' you mean, I take it (said I to Hassan), that glorious and beneficent luminary which is apparently a small disk in the heavens above us, but in reality a vast globe, the centre and father of our system, in diameter so many miles, in distance so many miles"—I gave him the exact figures—"around which this planet revolves in 365 days, 4 hours, 37 minutes and 28.0387541 seconds."

"No!" said the churl; "I mean that." And he pointed to the orb in question.

One could not reason with the clod! But his appeal to the evidence of my sight was far from convincing me of his integrity or of the accuracy of his observation; for he had said (in his haste), "The sun is hot," and heat, as such (I reflected at leisure), is not truly appreciable by the eye.

And then it dawned upon me! This camel-driver was a mystic! He was asserting a relation between two senses. A relation in what? In something that was certainly not either of those two senses; in something that must be a reconciler between them, a court of appeal, a … yes! a soul.

This was absurd: Hæckel has shown it to be absurd.[1] So I halted the camel and got out my sweater, and buttoned my jacket over it, and continued the journey.

Why did I feel uncomfortable? Why did I perspire? My friends, I cannot tell!

The night brought counsel. In the morning I attacked Hassan's position with horse, foot, and artillery.

"How dare you?" I said. "We have an instrument for registering degrees, the thermometer. Produce your thermometer!"

Hassan seemed abashed; he only wiped his brow.

"No!" I continued, "you are an impudent fellow, a pretender to knowledge, a sophist, a scholiast, and several other things ending in 'ast,' I dare say, if the truth were known!"

The victim hummed some rubbish about "the eyes of Arabi," which he thought superior to a gazelle's; but I did not take his point.

"Hassan!" said I, "you know absolutely nothing. You do not know that heat is a vibration of molecules, that heat is molecular motion! And is this perceptible even to feeling? Perish the thought! By feeling, who would ever have found out about molecules? Understand then, once and for all, that heat as such cannot be felt!"

The poor man was by now, metaphorically speaking, a mere pulp. The volcanic grey matter of his Arab brain sizzled under the cold spray of my intellectual acumen.

He hit the camel repeatedly and gave his wheezy whistle.

I had won; the rest of the day's march was for me a smiling silence.

Yet night found me disturbed. On what profound metaphysical conceptions (I mused) rest our simplest certainties! Think of Huxley, and the smashing blows that he delivered at "commonsense" metaphysics; how they crumbled to powder before him![2]

If I contemplate "the sun," how rapidly it becomes a mere subjective phenomenon, a puppet of the ego, or at least a strange, mystical, unknown, perhaps unknowable being. Subjective or objective, certainly

---

[1] The German zoologist Ernst Hæckel (1834-1919) was a Darwinian evolutionist whose scientific skepticism in religious matters appealed to Crowley. These questions are discussed in Hæckel, *The Riddle of the Universe*, trans. Joseph McCabe (1900); see Works Cited.]

[2] [The English biologist and writer Thomas Henry Huxley (1825-1895) was one of Crowley's main intellectual influences.]

my idea of it is dependent upon me; it is the objective school (surely!) that insists that things exist without my cooperation. Yet is not that the very proof that the object must be conjoined with my sense before it exists for me? Then "the sun" means "the relation of some unknown thing with my organs of sight."

And this relation is neither "it" nor "I." Nor is it in time or space, this relation. What is a relation? In what does it take place?

Fortunately, I stopped there. Another step and I should have had to postulate a soul, and the Rationalist Press Association might have got to hear of it—and then?[1]

The boot, and my last link with respectability snapped for ever!

The dawn broke at last, and we resumed the trudge across the sands. "Hassan!" I said earnestly, "you are concealing something! You are keeping back from me the fact that your opinion that the sun is hot (by which of course you only mean that the exposure to the rays of the sun produces effects similar to those caused by those bodies which we have agreed to describe as hot) is founded upon the fact that your experience teaches you to associate the visible appearance of yon glorious orb with sensations of heat. You are wrong! I, for example, can testify that one may be exceeding cold in bright sunshine. And, besides, your experience may be very limited."

"Forty-four yeyears, man and boy," he grunted, "ave I druv this 'ere ruddy oont." (I translate freely from his classical Arabic.)

I took no notice. "For instance," I remarked, "suppose you went to London for forty-four years more. You—who know nothing of electricity—would return to Algeria and say that in London bright stars appeared in the streets at nightfall. It would never strike you that those stars would not appear unless men kindled them, and I am just as presumptuous in supposing that the appearance of the sun would take place if (say) the sea dried up!

"You see no connecting links between the arc lamps in Picadilly and the generating station tucked away somewhere; I see no connection between the sunrise and the existence of the sea—and we both try and trade off our ignorance as knowledge!

"There was (and is) no answer to the problem of the Chinese philosopher, who dreamt that he was a butterfly, and, awaking, called his disci-

---

[1] [An English agnostic society with many noted authors in its membership; the best known was the philosopher Bertrand Russell.]

ples and said: 'I, Chuang, dreamt that I was a butterfly. Now, is it so, or am I a butterfly that has gone to sleep and is dreaming that it is Chuang?'[1]

"It is the experience of man that the appearance of the evening star heralds the darkness; but the truth is that the darkness causes the appearance of the stars. It is only in the great shadow of the earth that we may behold them, save from the darkness of a well. What a whirl of sophistry and confusion is all this babble of cause and effect! How all experience may deceive us! Hurrah!" (I broke off), "there is our oasis! How the palms wave and the minarets glitter and the waters gleam!"

"No!" said Hassan; "it is a mirage."

"Scoundrel," I retorted, now thoroughly incensed with his stupidity and falsehood, "how do you know?"

"I have been here before (says he as cool as custard), and I know there is no oasis within many days' journey. By my eyes I could not tell."

"Then you judge an optical phenomenon by treacherous memory, slave, beast, reptile, socialist that you are?

"And yet I (even I) cannot get beyond William the First ten sixty-six, William the Second ten eighty-seven, Henry the First ... and I knew them all, once!

"Why, Hassan, you are a bundle of uncertainties. Come now, confess! That remark of yours about the sun was interrogative? Or at most a feeler? You wanted to know what I thought about it? You had an intuition and wanted to test it?"

"No," said the Sahara of obstinacy; "I just passed the remark."

"Yes, I see, a mere idle frivolous bit of small-talk. A sort of joke?"

"No joke in the summer," he growled.

"Don't answer me back!" I snapped. (Something had made me irritable—not the heat of the sun, of course.) "I don't want you to speak; I'm trying to argue with you (I was on the right side of the Rationalist Press Association, that time!). But—you didn't mean that you were *sure*, did you? You sort of threw out the suggestion?"

"Dead sure," says he, and hits the camel again.

Disgusted with his brutality and Bœotian bathos,[2] I fell back, and walked alone, meditating.

He was *sure*, thought I. And Perdurabo is sure that he will endure unto The End, that his *khu* will be a mighty *khu* for ever and ever, and

---

[1] [The third century BCE Taoist philosopher Chuang-tzu (Zhuangzi) relates this story in the *Chuang-tzu*, end of chap. 2; see Works Cited under *Chuang-tzu*.]

[2] [Bœotia was a district in ancient Greece whose people were famed for stupidity.]

that he hath indeed talked with his Holy Guardian Angel and seen God face to face.[1] And Charles Watts is sure that Perdurabo is an ass, and suspends his opinion about Hassan bin Brahim until he has submitted the question to Hæckel and got a *firman* or an *ukase* about it.[2] And Aleister Crowley is sure that nobody can distinguish between Perdurabo and Hassan and Charles Watts, saying—

> On life's curtain
> Is written this one certainty—that naught is certain.[3]

What is the test? Is it the common experience of men? Then sure the sun moves round the earth, and there are no such things as molecules, and there are such things as spirits.

Is it the common experience of the instructed and competent among mankind?

The men who designed and built Luxor and Anuradhapura bore witness to gods visible and tangible.[4] Lombroso assented to Eusapia Palladino, A. R. Wallace believes in spirits, Newton thought Euclid proved the existence of God, and Kelvin relied for the same proof upon biology.[5]

---

[1] [Perdurabo (Latin, "I will endure to the end") was the motto Crowley took on his initiation as a Neophyte in the Golden Dawn in 1898. The *khu* is one of the immortal parts of the individual in Egyptian, translated as the "luminous," "the clear," or "glory," symbolized by a flame of fire, and usually given as *akh* in modern transliteration. The Knowledge and Conversation of the Holy Guardian Angel and the Vision of God Face to Face relate to stages of initiation in the A∴A∴.]

[2] [Charles Watts was a leader of the Rationalist Press Association and published Crowley's *The Star and the Garter* (1903) and *The God-Eater* (1903). The Russian *firman* and Old Persian *ukase* both mean "edict" or "decree."]

[3] [Crowley, "The Garden of Janus," *The Equinox* I(2) (1909), p. 99, which reads "on Soul's curtain / Is written this one certainty that naught is certain!"]

[4] [Luxor is, with Karnak, part of ancient Thebes in Egypt. Anuradhapura is the ancient capital of the Singhalese kings of Ceylon in Sri Lanka.]

[5] [Cesare Lombroso (1836–1909) was an Italian criminologist and psychopathologist who was persuaded of the genuineness of the Italian medium Eusapia Palladino (1854–1918). She was also studied by the British Society of Psychical Research in 1908 by investigators Hereward Carrington and Everard Fielding (both friends of Crowley's in later years), who also found for the medium. Alfred Russell Wallace (1823–1913) was a British naturalist who developed a theory of natural selection independently of Charles Darwin. The theological and occult writings of the English mathematician and physicist Sir Isaac Newton (1642–1727) are unfairly overlooked as aberrations. The Greek mathematician Euclid (c. 330–260 BCE) first systematized the elements of geometry. Baron Kelvin (William Thomson) (1824–1907) was a Scottish mathematician and physicist.]

Worse, Newman "worshipped idols and a piece of bread," [1] and I (who am hardly likely to allow that anyone is more instructed and competent than I am) believe in the Great Brotherhood, and the certain heritage of man in the Holy Kingdom. I believe in the Holy Ghost, the Holy Catholic Church (not Christianity), the communion of saints; the resurrection of the body, and the life everlasting. Amen!

This conviction is not to be shaken, for it is based upon the same rock as Hassan's conviction about the sun. It is my experience. Like any other experience, it comes through the senses; but it takes place in some unknown fortress within the five outlying towers of sense, in some secret cave of the heart and brain that even Ernst Hæckel has not dissected out.

Let him say that "as your mind decays (though I don't see how it can decay any more) you will lose this assured knowledge of your immortality."

"Yes, and I lose the sun, and the heat of the sun."

"But your Holy Guardian Angel is only a phantom of your diseased brain."

"But in that same brain is the sun."

"But other men testify to the sun."

"But other men testify to the Angel."

"But the majority of men accept the sun and deny the Angel."

"I am not a democrat. All the men whom I respect testify to the Angel, and don't care twopence about the sun."

"But I can show the sun to any man who had never seen it, and he would add his testimony to its truth."

"For 'sun' read 'Angel' and you have my exact position."

"Show Him to me! This instant!"

"Patience a moment; it requires a little trouble, even a little work."

"Ah! I have you at last. I can show the sun to any man at any moment!"

"Not if he is in England, and if it is night, and if he has cataract."

"I should remove him from England and wait for the morning and perform an operation."

"Exactly; I will arrange your moral climate, and ask you to have patience for an hour or two until the dawn, and remove the scales from your sight."

"Bah! I can't waste my time arguing with a fool."

---

[1] [John Henry Cardinal Newman (1801–1890), English Roman Catholic churchman and author of *Apologia pro vita sua* (1864).]

"I have not disagreed—so far—with anything that you have said. Why should I begin now?"

Nay, this interior certainty of Truth; this Faith in the Validity of Essential Relations; this Knowledge that stands behind and apart from Evidence; this Understanding which makes the darkness light, this Wisdom which directs the Will; are not these Children of One Ineffable Brilliance, one Selfhood beyond all Self?

And a Voice came unto me, saying—

"This Interior Certainty is the Camel that goeth ten days in the desert bearing water in his belly, as thou goest ten times seven years in the desert of life, where the Water of pure Truth is not found. And this Camel was furnished with sufficient water from the Well, yet at the end of the journey, if he be athirst, he shall drink deeply at his will from the unfailing fountains, and rest under the shadow of the never-withering palms.

"Rise up, therefore, and proceed upon thy way, for thy water is inexhaustible, and thereof shalt thou give to drink unto many men that be athirst."

The Soul of the Desert

I too am the Soul of the desert; thou shalt seek me yet again
in the wilderness of sand.

"Liber LXV" IV:61

I

The Journey

The soul is in its own nature a well, perfect purity, perfect calm, perfect
silence; and as a well springs from the very veins of the earth itself, so is
the soul nurtured of the blood of God, the ecstasy of things.

This soul can never be injured, never marred, never defiled. Yet all
things added to it do for a time trouble it; and this is sorrow.

To this language itself bears witness; for all words which mean
unhappy, mean first of all disturbed, disquieted, troubled. The root idea
of sorrow is this idea of stirring up.

For many a year man in his quest for happiness has travelled a false
road. To quench his thirst he has added salt in ever-increasing quantities
to the water of life; to cover the ant heaps of his imagination he has raised
mountains wherein wild beasts and deadly prowl. To cure the itch, he
has flayed the patient; to exorcise the ghost, he has evoked the devil.

It is the main problem of philosophy, how this began. The *rishis*,
seven that sate upon Mount Kailasha and considered, thus answered,
that the soul became self-conscious;[1] and, crying "I am That!" became
two even in the act of asserting that it was One.[2] This theory may be

---

[1] [The Sanskrit *ṛṣi* denotes a seer or *vedic* sage. Mt. Kailasha is the Tibetan mountain sacred to Hindus as Śiva's paradise and the source of the Indus.]

[2] [In Sanskrit "I am that" is "*aham-tat-asmi*"; variations replace *tat* ("that") with
prakritim ("this world") and *devan* ("the gods"); see also the *mahāvākya* ("great
sayings") *tat-tvam-asi* ("that thou art," *Chāndogya Upaniṣad*) and "*aham-Brah-
māsi* ("I am Brahmā," *Bṛhadāraṇyaka Upaniṣad*).]

found not too remote from truth by whoso returns to that tower upon the ramparts of the soul and beholds the city.

But let us leave it to the doctors to discuss the cause of the malady; for the patient it is enough to know the cure and take it. Abana and Pharpar, rivers of Damascus, are not worth the simplicity of Jordan.[1] The prophet has spoken; it is our concern only to obey: and so sweet and so full of virtue are these waters that the first touch thrills the soul with the sure foretaste of its cure.

Doubt not, brother! Reason indeed may elaborate complexities; are not these the very symptoms of the disease? Use but the rude common sense, heritage of simpler and happier forefathers, that they have transmitted to thee by the wand.

The cure of disease is ease; of disquiet, quiet; of strife, peace. And as to attain horsemanship the study of folios aids not, but the mounting of an horse; as the best way to learn to swim is to enter the water and strike out; so is it cool sense, not feverish reason, that says: To attain quiet, practice quiet.

There are men so strong of will, so able to concentrate the mind, to neglect the impressions that they do not wish to receive, that they can withdraw themselves from their surroundings, even when those are as multitudinous and insistent as those of a great city. But for the most part of men, it is best to begin in easier circumstances, to climb the mountain in fine weather before attacking it in the snowstorm.

And yet the eager aspirant will answer: Provided that the cure is complete. Provided that the sickness does not return when the medicine is stopped.

Ah! that were hard: so deep-seated is the malady that, years after its symptoms have passed, it seizes on a moment of weakness to blaze out again. It is a malarial fever that lurks low, that hides in the very substance of the blood itself, that has made the very fountain of life partaker with it in the sacrament of death.

> Has a spider found out the communion-cup,
> Was a toad in the christening-font?[2]

---

[1] [See II Kings 5:8–14.]

[2] ["Gold Hair: A Story of Pornic," in *The Poetical Works of Robert Browning* (1888–1894); see Works Cited.]

No: the remedy cures surely enough; but not often does it cure once for all, beyond relapse. But it is simple; once the symptoms have properly abated, they never return with equal force; and if the patient has but the wit to stretch out the hand for another dose, the fever flies.

What is then the essential? To cure the patient once; to give him faith in the efficacy of the remedy, so that when perchance he falls sick, and no doctor is near, he may be able to cure himself.

If thought then be that which troubles the soul, there is but one way to take. Stop thinking.

It is the most difficult task that man can undertake. "Give me a fulcrum for my lever," said Archimedes, "and I will move the earth."[1] But how when one is within, and part of, that very system of motion which one desires to stop? Newton's First Law drops like the headsman's axe on the very nape of our endeavour.[2] Well for us that this is not as true as it is obvious! For this fact saves us, that the resolution of all these motions is rest. The motion is but in reciprocal pairs; the sum of its vectors is zero. The knot of the Universe is a fool's knot; for all it seems Gordian, pull but firmly, and it ravels out. It is this seeming that is all the mischief; gloomy is the gulf, and the clouds gather angrily in monstrous shapes; the false moon flickers behind them; abyss upon abyss opens on every hand. Darkness and menace, the fierce sounds of hostile things!

One glimmer of starlight, and behold the golden bridge! Narrow and straight, keen as the razor's edge and glittering as the sword's blade, a proper bridge if thou leanest not to right or left. Cross it—good! but all this is in the dream. Wake! Thou shalt know that all together, gulf, moon, bridge, dragon and the rest, were but the phantasms of sleep. Howbeit, remember this, that to cross that bridge in sleep is the only way to waking.

I do not know if many men have the same experience as myself in the matter of voluntary dreaming, or rather of contest between the sought and the unsought in dream. For example, I am on a ridge of ice with Oscar Eckenstein. He slips to one side. I throw myself on the other. We begin to cut steps up to the ridge; my axe snaps, or is snatched from my

---

[1] [Archimedes (287–212 BCE), Greek philosopher-scientist.]

[2] [In his *Principia*, Sir Isaac Newton (1642–1727) postulated three "axioms of motion" relating to mechanics; the first deals with inertia, stating that a body remains in its state of rest unless compelled to move by a force acting upon it.]

hand. We begin to pull ourselves up to the ridge by the rope; the rope begins to fray. Luckily it is caught lower down in a cleft of rock. A *lammergeier*[1] swoops; I invent a pistol and blow its brains out. And so on through a thousand adventures, making myself master of each event as it arises. But I am grown old and weary of thrills; nowadays at the first hint of danger I take wings and sail majestically down to the glacier.

If I have thus digressed, it is to superpose this triangle on that of the task "Stop thinking." Simple it sounds; and simple it is—when you have mastery. In the meantime it is apt to lead you far indeed from simplicity. I have myself written some million words in order to stop thinking! I have covered miles of canvas with pounds of paint in order to stop thinking. Thus may it be that I am at least to be considered as no mean authority on all the wrong ways; and so perhaps, by a process of exclusion, on the right way!

Unfortunately, it is not as easy as this:—

> There are nine and sixty ways of constructing tribal lays,
> And every single one of them is right![2]

And right for A is often wrong for B.

But luckily, the simpler the goal is kept, the simpler are the means. Elsewhere in my writings[3] will be found a fairly painstaking and accurate account of the process. The present essay is but to advocate a mighty engine adjuvant—the shoulder of Hercules to the cart-wheel of the beginner whose diffidence whispers that he is incapable of following those instructions in the difficult circumstances of ordinary life, or for the enthusiast who wisely determines, like Kirkpatrick, to "mak' siccar."[4] Indeed, the cares of this world, the deceitfulness of riches, the lusts of the flesh and the eye, the pride of life, and all the other enemies of the saint, do indeed choke the word, and it becometh unfruitful.[5]

---

[1] [The Alpine bearded vulture is the largest European bird of prey.]

[2] [Rudyard Kipling, from "In the Neolithic Age," *The Seven Seas* (1896); see Works Cited.]

[3] [A deleted passage in the manuscript cites Crowley's *Book 4*, Part I. See also his later *Eight Lectures on Yoga*. See Works Cited.]

[4] [The manuscript has "like the red Comyn, to make sure." The Scottish word *siccar* means "sure," "secure," or "free from danger." Both versions allude to the death of John Cumin (or Comyn), who was given "a perilous gash" by Robert Bruce and was finished off by Roger Kirkpatrick with the words "I'll mak sicker." See G. Chalmers, *Caledonia*, vol. III, p. 79; see Works Cited.]

[5] [Mark 4:19.]

II

The Desert

As a monastery imposes the false peace of dulness by its unwholesome and artificial monotony, so is the desert nature's own cure for all the tribulations of thought.

There the soul undergoes a triplex weaving. First, the newness of the surroundings, their strange and salient simplicity, charm the soul. It has a premonition of its cure; it feels the atmosphere of home. It is sure of its vocation. Next, the mind, its frivolity once satiate with novelty, becomes bored, turns to acrimony, even to passionate revolt. The novice beats against the bars; the stranger in the desert flies to London or to Paris with the devil at his heels. A wise superior will not restrain the acolyte[1] who cannot restrain himself; but in the desert, the refugee, if he doubts his own powers—still more, maybe, if he does not mistrust them!— would wisely make it impossible to return. But how should he do so? Believe me who have tried it, the longest journey, the most bitter hardships, are as nothing, an arrow-flight of joy, when the great horror lies behind and the sanctuary of Paris ahead!

For, indeed, this is the great horror, solitude, when the soul can no longer bathe in the ever-changing mind, laugh as its sunlit ripples lap its skin, but, shut up in the castle of a few thoughts, paces its narrow prison, wearing down the stone of time, feeding on its own excrement. There is no star in the blackness of that night, no foam upon that stagnant and putrid sea. Even the glittering health that the desert brings to the body is like a spear in the soul's throat. The passionate ache to act, to think: this eats into the soul like a cancer. It is the scorpion striking itself in its agony, save that no poison can add to the torture of the circling fires; no superflux of anguish relieve it by annihilation. But against these paroxysms is an eightfold sedative. The ravings of madness are lost in soundless space; the struggles of the drowning man are not heeded by the sea.

These are the eight genii of the desert. They are the eight Elements of Fu-hsi:[2]

---

[1] [*The Occult Review* has "a probationer."]

[2] [The trigrams are added for publication; their invention is attributed to the mythical Chinese emperor Fu-hsi (Pao Hsi). Crowley's descriptions of the elements are uniquely his, as the traditional renderings of the trigrams are as follows: ☰ Chi'en (heaven). ☷ K'un (earth). ☲ Li (fire). ☵ K'an (water). ☳ Chên (thunder). ☱ Tui (marsh, lake). ☴ Sun (wood and wind). ☶ Ken (mountain).]

Male		Female	
☰	The *liṅga* (Life)	☷	The *yoni* (Space. The Stars.)
☲	The Sun	☵	The Moon
☳	Fire	☱	Water
☴	Air (Wood)	☶	Earth

In the desert all these are single; all these are naked. They are pure and untroubled; not breaking up and dissolving by any commingling or communion; each remains itself and apart, harmonizing indeed with its fellows, but in no wise interfering. The lines of demarcation are crude and harsh; but softness is incomprehensibly the result. They are immitigable, these eight elements, and together they mitigate immeasurably. The mind that revolts against them is ground down by their persistent careless pressure. It is as when one throws a crystal—say of microcosmic salt—into water: it is eaten silently and rapidly, and is no more; the water is untroubled always; its action is like Fate's, infinitely irresistible yet infinitely calm.

So the mind reaches out to think this or to think that; it is brought back into silence by the eight great facts. The desert wind suffers no obstacle to impede it; the sun shines invincibly upon the baked earth of the village; the sand invisibly eats up the oasis, save for a moment where man casts up his earthworks against it. Yet despite this, the spring leaps unexpected from the sand, and no *simoon*[1] can stifle, nor sun evaporate it; nor can the immense sterility of the desert conquer life. Look where you will, every dune of sand has its inhabitants—not colonists, but natives of the inhospitable-seeming waste. The moon itself, serenely revolving about earth, changes in appearance, as if to say: "Even so goest thou about the sun. Am I new or full? Never think it; that is but the point of view from which thou chancest to regard me. I am but a mirror of sunlight, dark or bright according to the angle of thy gaze. Does the mirror alter? Is it not always the untroubled silver? Have not I always one face turned sunward? Thou but mockest thyself when thou callest me 'The Changeful.'"

With such reflections, or their kin, it may be, shalt thou make an end of the revolt of the mind against the desert.

For life itself, here in the oasis, is a thing ordered by these elements. Night is for sleep; there is nothing whereat to wake. There is no artificial light; no artificial food—literature. There is no choice of meats; one is

---

[1] [Arabic *samūm*; a hot, dust-laden desert wind, also called the *samiel*.]

always hungry. The desert sauce is hunger, unique as, and better than, the Englishman's one sauce. Having eaten, one must walk; there is only one place to walk in. There is only one lesson to learn, peace; only one comment upon the lesson, thanksgiving. Love itself becomes simple as the rest of life. A glance in the Café Maure, a silent agreement with delight, a soft withdrawal to some hollow of the dunes under the stars, where the village is blotted out as though it had never been, as are in that happy moment all the transgressions of the sinner, and all the woes of life, by the Virtue of the Holy One; or else to some dim corner of a garden of the oasis by the stream, where through the softly stirring palms strikes the first moon-ray from the East, and life thrills in sleepy unison; all, all in silence, not names or vows exchanged, but with clean will an act accomplished. No more. No turmoil, no confusion, no despair, no self-tormenting, hardly even memory. And this too at first is horrible; one expects so much from love, three volumes of falsehood, a labyrinth rather than a garden. It is hard at first to realize that this is no more love than a carbuncle is part of a man's neck. All the spices wherewith we are wont to season the dish to our depraved palates, Maxim's, St. Margaret's, automobile rides, the Divorce Court, these are unwholesome pleasures. They are not love. Nor is love the exaltation of emotions, sentiments, follies. The stage-door is not love (nor is the stile in Lover's Lane); love is the bodily ecstasy of dissolution, the pang of bodily death, wherein the Ego for a moment that is an æon loses the fatal consciousness of itself, and becoming one with that of another, foreshadows to itself that greater sacrament of death, when "the spirit returns to God that gave it."[1]

And this great secret has also its part in the economy of life. By the road of silence one comes to the gate of the City of God.[2] As the mind is gradually stilled by the courage and endurance of the seeker, and by the warring might (that is peace unshakeable) of these Eight Elements of the Desert, so at last the Ego is found alone, unmasked, conscious of itself and of no other thing. This is the supreme anguish of the soul; it realizes itself as itself, as a thing separate from that which is not itself, from God. In this spasm there are two ways: if fear and pride are left in the soul, it

---

[1] [Ecclesiastes 12:7.]

[2] [Silence is an attribute of Harpocrates (Hoor-paar-kraat), the Egyptian god related to the Babe of the Abyss in the A∴A∴ system. Through the Ordeal of the Abyss the Exempt Adept of the A∴A∴ arrives at the City of the Pyramids (or City of God) as a Master of the Temple. See *Liber 418* and "One Star in Sight."]

shuts itself up, like a warlock in a tower, gnashing its teeth with agony. "I am I," it cries, "I will not lose myself," and in that state, damned, it is slowly torn by the claws of circumstance, disintegrated bitterly, for all its struggles, throughout ages and ages, its rags to be cast piecemeal upon the dungheap without the city.[1] But the soul that has understood the blessedness of resignation which grasps the Universe and devours it, which is without hope or fear, without faith or doubt, without hate or love, dissolves itself ineffably into the abounding bliss of God. The orgasm of orgasms whose name is peace devours it;[2] it cries with Shelley, as the "chains of lead around its flight of fire"[3] drop molten from its limbs: "I pant, I sink, I tremble, I expire,"[4] and in that last outbreaking is made one with that primal and final breath, the Holy Spirit of God.

Such must be the climax of any retirement to the Desert on the part of any aspirant to the Mysteries who has the spark of that fire in him.

He is drawn to physical quiescence (or to regularity, simplicity, unity of motion) by the constant example and compulsion of the Elements. He is obliged to introspection by the poverty of exterior impression, and through this he soon finds the sensations behind the thoughts, the perceptions behind the sensations, the laws underlying even the perceptions, and finally that consciousness which is the lawgiver. Sooner or later, according to his energy and the sanctification of his will, must he tear down the great veil and behold Himself upon the shining walls of space, must he utter with shuddering rapture: "This is I!" Then let him choose!

From this moment of the annihilation of the Self in Pan, he is "healed of the disease, self-knowledge."[5] He may return among his fellows, and move among them as a king, shine among them as a star. To him will they turn insensibly for light; to him will they come for the healing of their wounds.

He shall lift up the sacred Lance, and touch therewith the side of the king that was wounded by no lesser weapon; and the king shall be healed.[6]

---

[1] [See *Liber 418*, 10th Æthyr.]
[2] [This phrase in manuscript was omitted on its first publication in *The Occult Review*, and is assumed to have been censored; it is restored here.]
[3] [Percy Bysshe Shelley, *Epipsychidion* (1821); see Works Cited.]
[4] [Ibid.]
[5] ["Liber VII" IV:26.]
[6] [Cf. Richard Wagner, *Parsifal*. See Works Cited.]

He shall plunge the point of the Lance into the Holy Grail, and it shall again glow with life and ecstasy, giving forth its bounty of mysterious refreshment to all the company of knights.[1]

Then, should the rocks of life tear him, and its snows chill him, knoweth he not where to turn? Hath he not attained the secret? Hath he not entered into the Sanctuary of the Most High?

Is he not chosen and armed against all things? Is he not master of Destiny and of the Event? What can touch him, who hath become intangible, being lost in God? Or conquer him, who hath become unconquerable, having conquered himself and given himself up to God? As well write upon the sand, as write sorrow in his soul. As well seek to darken the Sun, as to put out the Light that is in him!

Thus I wrote in the palm-gardens of Tozeur, by the waters of its spring;
thus I wrote while the sun moved mightily down the sky,
and the wind whispered that it came no whence and went no whither,
even as it listed, from everlasting to everlasting.[2]
Amen.

---

[1] [This is implied, but not explicit, in Wagner's *Parsifal*, whose penultimate verses are delivered by Parsifal, holding the spear or lance aloft, and uttering: "The holy Spear ... which yearns to join the fountain glowing, whose pure tide in the Grail is flowing! Hid be no more that shape divine: Uncover the Grail! Open the shrine!" The symbolism is explicit in Crowley's "Liber XV, Ecclesiæ Gnosticæ Catholicæ Canon Missæ," the O.T.O. Gnostic Mass.]

[2] [John 3:8.]

A Hindu at the Polo Grounds

**A LETTER FROM MAHATMA SRI PARAMANANDA GURU SWAMIJI
(GREAT SOUL SAINT SUPREME-BLISS TEACHER LEARNED PERSON)
TO HIS BROTHER IN INDIA**

Honored Brother:

Yesterday I went with a friend to the great temple. It is an oval like the *yoni* of the most holy Bhāvanī, and the *cakras* are marked in sand. On these paths the priests run in their mystic dances. There are two kinds of priests. There are Redsox and Yanks, according to their tribes. The worshippers sit around in tiers reaching to the sky. Some of the priests are armed with clubs to slay the victims. There is also a white ball, symbolizing the sun. My friend remarked: "The Yanks will get their goat." I cannot see any goat nor is there an altar to sacrifice a goat!

Now the priests take their stations in the temple, and the ritual begins. One high-priest throws the white ball; this represents the sun travelling through the heavens. Another high-priest strikes it with the *mahāliṅga*[1] club, meaning that even the sun is tossed about by the will of God. Many priests representing other gods are stationed according to the places of the planets, as I understand, for my friend says: "It is an all-star team." The god with the club is a symbol of man, and if the sun, or ball, strike him he is dead; he throws away his club, and walks to his base, that is, he makes the next stage in his incarnations. If he strike the sun far away beyond any planets, he makes the complete circle in his sacred dance. They have an idol here—one McGraw![2] He is a *mahāthera*.[3]

The worshippers are full of religion; sometimes the sacred cry changes to a roar as if they wanted something killed. Then my friend says: "See! he sacrifices himself," but I do not see him sacrifice himself.

---

[1] [Sanskrit, the visible form of the formless deity Śiva; literally "great mark," it has the somewhat misleading connotation "great penis" in English usage.]

[2] [John Joseph "Little Napoleon" McGraw (1873–1934) was the manager of the New York Giants, winning ten pennants and three World Series championships.]

[3] [Sanskrit, "great elder."]

He only throws himself down at the feet of a god. But there is no blood; it is not good religion.

The ritual has nine parts, for the nine planets (there are nine priests of each of the two castes) and for the nine greater gods. After the seventh part all the people rise and make mystic gestures with their arms, out of reverence to the sacred number seven. And now the people disperse. They will drink of the sacred *soma*[1] of the country, the gin-rickey, or *jin-ricksha*—so called because with it they are wheeled swiftly and surely to *nirvāṇa*.

I join in this part of the ceremony also. I grasp the hand of my friend and, on gin-rickeys, we shall peacefully glide into *nirvāṇa*.[2]

Your Happy Brother.

---

[1] [Sanskrit, the sacred drink of the *vedic* Brahmin priests.]
[2] [Sanskrit, "extinction, perfection," but with various connotations in different spiritual traditions.]

Three Great Hoaxes
of the War

Blessed Are They That Have Not Seen
and Yet Have Believed[1]

On three notable occasions, since the war began, the credulity of the English people has passed all belief. The student of religious origins has probably noted that the hoaxes on all three occasions follow the generally accepted lines of demarcation, namely; legend, prophecy, and miracle.

It is now no secret that the famous legend of the "Russian Soldiers," that wonderful story of a million and a half Russian troops (with horses and artillery) smuggled through England in the dead of the night, was put about by the secret service to try to check the panic caused by the collapse at Mons. It was quite useless to point out to the English people that Archangel is served by a single line of rail, and that to ship even 10,000 troops would have strained the resources of the line for an entire summer. It was useless to ask why, having got all these troops on transports, the English did not sail them quietly down to the place where they were wanted, but went to the enormous and senseless trouble of disembarking them in England and embarking them again.

It was useless to make calculations; to show that as an English railway coach holds fifty men, and ten coaches make a pretty long train, it would have needed 3,000 trains to "flash by, with drawn blinds" for the men alone, and that the disguising of the horses, artillery, champagne and other necessary appurtenances of a Grand Ducal Russian army must have been a task worthy of Sherlock Holmes at his best.

One was always countered by the reply: "But Admiral X, or Captain Y, or Lord Z, or my Uncle Harry (as the case might be) saw them with his own eyes." The best of the joke was that the papers never printed a word of it, though the story was the sole topic of discussion for weeks.

---

[1] [John 20:29.]

58

The idea was to keep the whole thing a secret from the Germans! Ultimately, long after the yarn had been exploded—even among the semi-educated—*The Evening News* featured it as a "Strange Rumor" and one that might well be believed.

So much for legend: now for prophecy! The clairvoyants, astrologers, and psychics in England were of course besieged from the beginning. Everyone who was reputed to be able to "look into the seeds of time and see which grain will grow and which will not"[1] was immediately paid to do so.

But the clairvoyants were confronted with this difficulty: Current prophecy must always be conceded as rather a matter of faith. But if there could be found a prophecy, many years old, which had foretold the details of the war, foretold them accurately, then it would be safe to assume that the prophet who had foretold the beginning might foretell the end. This demand soon created the supply; several prophecies were discovered—Madame de Thèbes and others—but they were all lacking in satisfactory details and antiquity, until the great and glorious find—the find of the Abbot Johannes.

The Sar Péladan, a moderately good *littérateur* and a really fine critic (you can read all about him in Nordau's *Degeneration*),[2] has, in his time, contributed much to the gaiety of the French people. Years ago, someone remarked to him in a café that his name was rather like that of the Assyrian, Beladan. Péladan jumped at the idea and said that he was Beladan, in a new incarnation; after that he gave himself the title of Sar. He even conferred similar glories on his associates; hence his friends, who became Mérodach-Jauneau, Belshazzar-Dupont, and so on! Also he had announced himself to be a Rosicrucian—anything romantic and mysterious helps to work a clever trick—and published a book on the doctrines of that august Fraternity called *Le vice suprême*,[3] rather as if a learned Presbyterian divine were to preach on "Why We Believe in the Mass."

---

[1] [Shakespeare, *Macbeth* I,iii.]

[2] [Max Simon Nordau (1849–1923); his *Degeneration* appeared in English in 1895. See Works Cited.]

[3] [Joséphin Péladan (1858–1918), *Le Vice suprême* (1886); see Works Cited. Péladan was a novelist, essayist and occultist who founded the Order of the Catholic Rose Cross.]

The worthy Péladan was therefore not taken very seriously by his contemporaries in France; but England nowadays will stand for anything, even cubists and futurists and vorticists. So the English lent a willing ear to the masterpiece of Péladan. It appeared that the Sar—so he said—in going through some old papers of his father's, some ten years previously, had found a Latin prophecy of the Abbot Johannes. (There were two or three of these Abbots about 1600, but none of them were particularly prophetic!) Péladan had made a translation, but did not, of course, produce the original for the inspection of experts. The prophecy is in the best allegorical style; all about a cock, and a lion, and an eagle, and a bear. The Kaiser is described unmistakably, owing to his withered arm, and the details of the war, down to the battle of the Marne, are given with an accuracy which reflects extraordinary credit on the seership of Johannes. After this point, however, he becomes a little indefinite and less careful of detail.

The present writer warned the Editor of *The Occult Review* that anything emanating from Péladan could only be a jest, but was rebutted by the evidence of an alderman from Harrogate, who was said to have seen the original. "An alderman from Harrogate" only made it worse! [1]

However, the story "got over" and went the rounds of the press, and was swallowed by everybody. It did not last very long, though, for that part of the prophecy dealing with events subsequent to the Marne, though vague, was not vague enough to prevent even the most faithful believers from perceiving that it was totally wrong!

But all this palls before the superb story of "The Bowmen." [2] There is nothing to beat it in all the annals of mythopœia.

There is a writer in England who is not very well known over here, but who is certainly among the first half-dozen living English authors. He is saturated with the love of mediævalism and sacramentalism. His name is Arthur Machen. Falling upon evil times, he has had to write for *The Evening News.* In the course of this unhappy occupation, he read the famous *Weekly Dispatch* account of the retreat from Mons, which account was true, and caused the prosecution of the publishers. This was on Sunday morning, and he went to church later, and thought of the

---

[1] [Possible evidence for the jest is the fact that "Dr. Johannes" was a character based on Péladan's old rival the Abbé Boullan in J.-K. Huysman's *Là-Bas.*]

[2] [Arthur Machen, "The Bowmen," *Evening News,* London, September 29, 1914.]

battle instead of the sermon. By and by he wrote a story on it called "The Bowmen." In a few words, this was his yarn:

Five hundred British soldiers, the remains of a regiment, were covering the retreat from Mons. Disorganized and desperate, they saw annihilation approaching them in the shape of ten thousand pursuing cavalry. One of the men, who had been educated in Latin and the like, in the stress of emotion, found his mind wander back to a vegetarian restaurant in London where the plates had had on them a design of St. George and the motto *"Adsit Anglis Sanctus Georgius."*[1] With involuntary piety he uttered this motto. A shudder passed through him; the noise of battle was soothed to a murmur in his ears; instead, he heard a great roar as of thousands of soldiers shouting the ancient battle-cries that rang out at Crecy and Poitiers and Agincourt! He also saw before him a long line of shining shapes, "drawing their yew bows to their ears, and stroking their ell-long shafts against the Germans."

It was then observed by all that the enemy was being swept away, not in single units but in battalions. In fact, they were slain to a man; and the British rear guard strolled off quietly in the wake of their army.

It is to be noted that the author very artistically refrained from trying to lend verisimilitude to an otherwise bald and unconvincing narrative by stating that the burying-parties found arrows in the dead Germans. He thought it too much mustard!

Well, he printed the story on September 29, 1914, and thought that that would be the end of it. But no! A few days later *The Occult Review* and *Light* wrote to ask for his "authorities!" He replied that the old musty English ale at the "Spotted Dog" in Bouverie Street might know; if not, nobody did.

In a month or so, several parish magazines asked leave to reprint it; and *would* he write a preface giving the name of the soldier, and so on? He replied, "Reprint away; but as for the soldier, his name is Thomas Atkins of the Horse-Marines." The editor of one magazine replied (it was April, 1915, by now): "Pardon me, sir, if I appear to contradict you; but I know positively that the facts of the story are true; all you have done is to throw it into a literary form."

So they reprinted the story. But that was only the beginning of it. Variants began to appear. The soldier was an officer, and the picture of

---

[1] [Latin, "May Saint George stand by the English."]

St. George a canvas instead of a plate. The dead Germans, too, were now found with arrow wounds—the very detail that Machen had rejected as too absurd. Then again in some accounts a cloud appears between the armies to conceal the British. This is obviously an echo from Exodus. Sometimes the cloud disclosed shining shapes which frightened the chargers of the Uhlans. But April was to wane before the great transfiguration.

In May, Mr. A. P. Sinnett (the man who first wrote of the Blavatsky teacup fables)[1] had an article in *The Occult Review* saying: "Those who could see said that they saw 'a row of shining beings' between the two armies."

Now Machen did say "a long row of shining shapes." In this phase one may find the *raison d'être* of the last stage of the myth. Angels are still popular in England; fairies are dead, and saints are held a trifle Popish; St. George is only a name except to mediævalists like Mr. Machen. So he drops out of the story. "The Bowmen" became *The Angels of Mons* and the story fairly took the bit between its teeth, and bolted.[2] It was quoted in *Truth*, in *The New Church Weekly*, in *John Bull*, in *The Daily Chronicle*, in *The Pall Mall Gazette*, and in every case it was treated as a serious story.

Bishop Welldon, Bishop Taylor Smith (the Chaplain-General), Dr. Horton, Sir J. C. Rickett—all of them serious divines in England—preached about it. Canon Hensley Henson said he didn't believe it, but we must remember that he has quite often been near trouble for holding heterodox opinions![3]

The Evening News has been bombarded with letters on the subject; even the Psychical Research Society has got into one of its usual muddles over it. In a word, despite Machen's repeated explanations and denials, the silly fancy is taken everywhere for established fact.

The only attempt to give details of the yarn from the front has been that of Miss Phyllis Campbell, who is very young and very beautiful, but

---

[1] [See A. T. Barker, ed., *The Mahatma Letters to A. P. Sinnett from the Mahatmas M. & K.H.*; see Works Cited.]

[2] [A collection of Machen's war stories from the *Evening News* appeared as *The Angels of Mons: The Bowmen and Other Stories of the War* (1915), in which Machen refutes claims for a genuine miracle. See Works Cited.]

[3] [The novelist and author of religious books Harold Begbie (1871–1929) also argued for a genuine miracle in *On the Side of the Angels* (1915).]

who, if she had been wiser, would have given, as her authorities, soldiers who had figured on the Roll of Honor. That would have sounded better than "a soldier," or than "a wounded man of the Lancashires," or "an R. F. A. hero,"[1] or "a nurse."[2]

England believes it all, and, as faith can move mountains, perhaps it can help the Allies to force the Rhine!

---

[1] [Royal Field Artillery.]

[2] [Phyllis Campbell was a nurse who recounted first-hand reports from soldiers of a vision of St. George at Mons in *The Occult Review* in 1915.]

Mystics and Their Little Ways

ONE IS NOTHING,
WHILE TWO IS—IN REALITY—ONE

Mysticism is really quite simple. It is merely a State of Mind in which all phenomena are regarded as pure illusion. The only reality is what is called by one mystic the *plerōma*;[1] by another Iśvara, or Parabrahman, or *puruṣa*;[2] by a third, God; by a fourth, the Pure Soul; by a fifth, Being, or the Absolute—and so on, more or less indefinitely.

Mysticism is not a belief. It is a matter of direct experience resulting from interior illumination, now and then—though not often—arising spontaneously. More usually it results from persistence in certain religious practices, such as meditation, for instance.

Mysticism is entirely a matter for each individual, so that mystics rarely form sects, and when they do, the sects are never successful. However, there have been the Gnostics, the Therapeutæ, the Cathari, the Essenes,[3] and of course, farther East, the Sufis, the Taoists, and various Indian and Indo-Chinese groups.[4] But this is all a sort of accident. Every

---

[1] [Greek πλήρωμα, the "invisible spiritual fullness" that transcends manifested existence, to which Gnostics seek to return through the "perfection" of the Self.]

[2] [Sanskrit. *Iśvara* is "Lord" or "God." Parabrahman is "the Supreme Being," literally "that which is beyond Brahma." *Puruṣa* is "spirit" or "individual soul."]

[3] [Gnostics are members of any of several sects which coexisted with Christianity in its early centuries; they emphasized direct spiritual knowledge (*gnosis*) over faith. The Therapeutæ were an early group of monastic Jews in Egypt, described by Philo (c. 25 BCE–c. 50 CE). The Cathari or Cathars were a Christian sect in Provence (S. France) region around the 13th century that preserved a Gnostic and Manichæan dualism. The Essenes were an exclusive sect of Jewish mystics (c. 150 BCE) who practiced asceticism, benevolence and initiation into grades.]

[4] [Sufism is an Islamic mystical tradition that employs ecstatic practices for spiritual attainment. Chinese Taoism derives from Lao-tzu, *Tao-te Ching*, c. 600–500 BCE.]

mystic of any account is really a solitary who, thinking to bring all men to his own perfection, merely succeeds in founding a new cult, or religion.

Most of the original disciples of such a man have had probably some mystic experience. Then arises some worldly, ambitious person who exploits the crude (and, failing to understand them, glosses over the subtle) elements of the Master's teaching. All "teaching" is cardinally false, as nothing matters so much as teaching each man how to destroy the illusion which is keeping him from perfection.

Many mystics have, of course, realized the fatuity of founding a religion, and so have left themselves to a small circle of disciples. Such were Porphyry, Plotinus, Joachim of Fiora, Hildegard of Bingen, Elizabeth of Schönau, Amalric of Bèna, Meister Eckhart, Suso, Tauler, Van Ruysbroeck, Gerhard Groot, Thomas Münzer, Nicholas of Cusa, Sebastian Franck, Paracelsus, Valentine Weigel, Jacob Bœhme, St. Teresa, Mme. Guyon, John of the Cross, J. G. Gichtel, Henry More, Poiret, Dr. Dee and Sir E. Kelly, William Blake, Bernard of Clairvaux, Hugh and Richard of St. Victor, Novalis, Bonaventura, Éliphas Lévi, Victor Benjamin Neuburg, and our own Emerson.[1] Of many of these men we have little trace. We can only rely upon their occasional treatises and letters. It would be impossible to give any account of the Asiatic mystics. In Asia every man realizes that mysticism is the soul of religion, and seeks a direct mystical experience.

Of mystics who have founded or attempted to found cults we have more famous names: Socrates (and Plato), Zoroaster, Dionysus, Ignatius Loyola, St. Francis of Assisi, Apollonius of Tyana, Issa bin Jusuf, William Law, Claude de St. Martin, George Fox, Swedenborg and H. P. Blavatsky.[2] Perhaps Andreas, and his successors, and many others who have preferred to work through the medium of secret societies, should also be mentioned.[3] Often in such cases their names and deeds are lost, although their work may have secretly revolutionized the spiritual life of whole continents.[4]

---

[1] [See note on following page.]

[2] [See note on following page.]

[3] [Johann Valentin Andreas (or Andrea or Andreæ) (1586-1654) was a German Lutheran pastor, mystic and author, whose early Rosicrucian works *Fama Fraternitatis R.C.* (1614) and *The Chymical Wedding of Christian Rosencreutz* (1616) helped give rise to that movement. See Works Cited.]

[4] [See Crowley's *The Heart of the Master* for a treatment of this theme; see Works Cited.]

[1] [Most of these mystics are discussed in Evelyn Underhill's classic survey *Mysticism*, which gives a historical summary and a good bibliography; see Works Cited. The Greek Neoplatonic philosopher Porphyry (233-304 BCE) was the student and biographer of the Egyptian philosopher Plotinus (c. 205-270). Joachim of Fiora (1132-1202) was a Benedictine abbot (the original text gave Joachim of Flons). The great visionary, musician and reformer St. Hildegard of Bingen (1098-1179) was a Benedictine nun, as was St. Elizabeth of Schönau (1138-1165). The French theologian Amaury or Amalric of Bèna (d. c. 1206 CE) developed a pantheism found heretical by Rome (the original text gave Ameluc of Bena); see also p. 118, note 1. The great theological scholar Meister Eckhart (c. 1260-1328) was the teacher of the German mystic Heinrich Suso (1295-1365) and the German quietist Johannes Tauler (1300-1361); all were Dominicans. Eckhart was a major influence on the great Belgian mystic Jan van Ruysbroeck (the Blessed, 1293-1361) and his disciple Gerhard Groot (1340-1384). Thomas Münzer or Müntzer (c. 1490-1525) was a German Protestant reformer. Cardinal Nicholas of Cusa (1401-1464) was a mathematician, natural scientist and Neoplatonist who drew on the work of Ruysbroeck. The German Sebastian Franck (c. 1499-1543) was called a "devil's mouth" by Martin Luther. Phillipus Aureolus Paracelsus (1493-1541) was a Swiss physician, alchemist and natural philosopher. Valentine Weigel (1533-1588) was a Protestant mystic. The great German mystic and philosopher Jacob Bœhme (1575-1624) was a prolific author influential in Germany and England. St. Teresa (1515-1582) was a Spanish Carmelite nun. Madame Guyon (1648-1717) was a French mystic and quietist. John de Yepes or St. John of the Cross (1542-1591) was a Catholic poet and contemplative. The German mystic Johann G. Gichtel (1638-1710) edited Bœhme's works posthumously. Henry More (1614-1687) was an English Platonist. Peter Poiret (1646-1719) was a French quietist and bibliographer who edited Mme. Guyon's writings. For Dr. John Dee see note to p. 16. The clairvoyant and alchemist Edward Kelly (1555-1593) was a colleague of Dr. Dee. For William Blake (1757-1827) see Crowley's article on p. 115; he was influenced by Bœhme and Swedenborg. St. Bernard of Clairvaux (1091-1153) was a French Benedictine. The Augustinian scholastic philosopher Hugh (1097-1141) and his student Richard (d. c. 1173) were both of the Abbey of St. Victor in Paris. Novalis was the pseudonym of the German poet Friedrich von Hardenberg (1772-1801). The Italian Franciscan theologian St. Bonaventura (1808-1889) was called "the Seraphic Doctor." For Éliphas Lévi see note to p. 18. Victor Benjamin Neuburg (1883-1940) was a poet and A∴A∴ member who was a gifted visionary; see *Liber 418*. Ralph Waldo Emerson (1803-1882) was an American contemplative philosopher.

[2] The Greek philosopher Socrates (469-399 BCE) was the teacher of Plato (c. 427-347 BCE). Zoroaster or Zarathustra (?c. 700 BCE) founded the Iranian religion Zoroastrianism. Pseudo-Dionysus the Areopagite (c. 500 CE) is a pseudonymous author (probably a Syrian Greek) with a profound influence on mediæval European mysticism; Crowley may instead mean the Greek deity Dionysus, which he believed was a deified man. The Spaniard St. Ignatius of Loyola (1491-1556) founded the Jesuit order. For St. Francis of Assisi see p. 33, note 3. Apollonius of Tyana was a 1st c. CE Greek Neopythagorean philosopher and thaumaturge. Issa bin Jusuf is an Arabic form of Jesus, son of Joseph (Jesus Christ). The English theologian William Law (1686-1761) popularized the works of Bœhme in England. The French mystic Marquis Louis Claude de Saint-Martin (1743-1803) is known as "the Unknown Philosopher," and his teachings are carried on by the Martinist Order. The English theologian George Fox (1624-1691) founded the Society of Friends (Quakers). For Emanuel Swedenborg see p. 119, note 4. For H. P. Blavatsky see p. 21, note 2.]

The method of a mystic in proclaiming his "Law" is always the same. He takes one single, simple, fundamental, revolutionary remark, and makes the Universe obey it. Thus Mohammed with his "There is one God."[1] The rest is but the harvest of that seed. So also Buddha with his denial of the *ātman*, the cardinal doctrine of the Hindus; he puts his finger on the one essential of the system which he seeks to destroy, and the whole system explodes.[2] A modern instance is the saying "Do what thou wilt shall be the whole of the Law. Love is the law, love under will."[3]

For mysticism at its best may be defined as Genius on a Religious plane. And all genius consists of two parts: one, the capacity to see, hear and feel everything in the world with accuracy; and two, the power to distill this impression to a quintessence, and pour it forth as a perfume. Now the mystic mind can, by definition, do both of these things. It interprets every phenomenon as a direct dealing of God with the soul, and it creates from each phenomenon an image of glory, radiates it and spreads it over the universe.

Shelley has voiced the portrait of a true mystic in a single stanza:

> He will watch from dawn to gloom
> The lake-reflected sun illume
> The yellow bees in the ivy-bloom,
> Nor heed nor see, what things they be
> But from these create he can
> Forms more real than living man,
> Nurslings of immortality![4]

This is the keynote of all mystics, that their analysis of the Universe ultimates in Deity. The consciousness is no longer human, but divine. Country and language hardly vary the very expression.

Manṣūr,[5] the Persian mystic, was stoned for saying "I am The Truth, and within my turban I wrap nothing but God." His blood is said to have

---

[1] [From the Arabic *lā ilaha ill' Allāh*, "there is no God but God." Crowley would later write that Mohammed's "true Word was LA ALLH that is to say: (There is) No God." *Liber CXI vel Aleph*, chap. 74.]

[2] [Gautama Buddha (c. 563–483 BCE), Indian spiritual teacher and founder of Buddhism. *Ātman* is Sanskrit for "self," the basis of individual reality. Buddhism instead posits *anātman* (literally "without substance" or "not-self"), referring to the non-existence of the soul.]

[3] [*Liber AL* I:40, 57. See Crowley, *Liber CXI vel Aleph*, chaps. 68–75, for a discussion of these Magi and their Words.]

[4] [Percy Bysshe Shelley, *Prometheus Unbound*, lines 743–749; see Works Cited.]

[5] [Manṣūr al-Ḥallāj was a Sufi mystic, executed in 922 CE for heresy.]

traced *ana 'l-ḥaqq*—"I am the Truth"—upon the sand. The usual greeting of the Hindu is almost identical. "Thou art That," he exclaims reverently on meeting a man, and places his hands together as a sign that Two are in reality One.[1]

The Gnostics, the Neoplatonists, the Christians, all possess this same inner consciousness. There is only one further step, and that is to identify this One with Nothing. The Chinese were the first to express this clearly in words; their conception of the *tao* is still unequaled for clarity on this point. But Indian and Christian have outdone them in detail and in intellectual demonstration. In the famous *Book of Lies*,[2] one of the best modern treatises on mysticism, by Frater Perdurabo, the author fills his first page with a question-mark, and the reverse of it with a mark of exclamation, signifying that the Universe has two phases, scepticism and mysticism, and that these two are equal and opposite, and therefore One.[3] His first chapter he calls "The Chapter which is not a chapter,"[4] and begins it with the sign: 0!

He means, by the 0, the infinitely large; by the ☉ the infinitely small; and by the straight line, the manifested universe, the result of the interplay of the first two. He then descends to our inferior understanding by using mere words, and describes "The Ante Primal Triad which is NOT-GOD" in these simple but elegant terms:

> Nothing is.
> Nothing becomes.
> Nothing is not.

Of course, when Nothing is not, Something is; so we reach "The First Triad, which is GOD," which begins "I AM."

There are many other chapters to excite wonder in this little volume. Here are some additional phrases: "It is not necessary to understand; it is enough to adore."[5] The God may be of clay; adore him and he

---

[1] [Sanskrit, *tat-tvam-asi*, "that thou art," from the *Chāndogya Upaniṣad* of the *Sāma Veda*.]

[2] [Frater Perdurabo was the magical motto chosen by Aleister Crowley as a Neophyte in the Golden Dawn. *The Book of Lies* was published c. 1913, and with commentary in 1962; see Works Cited.]

[3] [Crowley called these the soldier (!) and the hunchback (?) in his essay "The Soldier and the Hunchback," *The Equinox* I(1) (1909); see Works Cited.]

[4] [This is a translation of the Greek title of Chapter 0 of *The Book of Lies*.]

[5] [Ibid., chap. 21.]

becomes GOD. We ignore what created us; we adore what *we* create. Let us create nothing but GOD! That which causes us to create is our true father and mother; we create in our own image—which is theirs. Let us therefore create without fear; for we can create nothing that is not GOD.

And this is from the chapter called "Phæton":

> No.
> Yes.
> Perhaps.
> O!
> Eye.
> I.
> Hi!
> Y?
> No.
> Hail![1]

This chapter needs no explanation; it is evidently a perfect synopsis and solution of the great Philosophical, Mystical and Ethical Problem which has always, and will always, baffle MAN.

---

[1] [Ibid., chap. 76.]

The Attainment of Happiness

A RESTATEMENT OF THE PURPOSE
OF MYSTICAL TEACHINGS

The best and wisest of men are always seeking a solution of the problem of human sorrow. There is one which the wandering ascetics of the world have always known. Whoever said "The kingdom of heaven is within you"[1] certainly knew the best solution of the problem. Man is, in reality, only a very little lower than the angels.[2] He is far more independent of circumstance than most people are aware. Happiness is not so utterly beyond his reach as those who do not climb spiritual mountains suppose.

But there are remedies nearer than the mighty pyramid of Chogo Ri, and the tented pavilion of the massif of Kanchenjunga.[3]

You can woo the butterfly—the poppy bud. You can float, like a butterfly in the enchanted air. You have only to draw a little of the hydrochloride of cocaine into your nostrils, and you become full of intense virility and energy, a devourer of obstacles. To smoke a few pipes of opium, and you rise to the cloudless and passionless bliss of the philosopher. To swallow a little hashish and you behold all the fantastic glories of fable, and those a thousandfold; or to woo a flask of ether—breathing it as if it were the very soul of your Beloved—and you will perceive the heart of Beauty in every vulgar and familiar thing.

Every one of these drugs gives absolute forgetfulness of all misfortune; nay, you may contemplate the most appalling catastrophes imminent or already fallen upon you; and you care no more for them than does Nature herself.

---

[1] [Luke 17:21.]

[2] [Psalm 8:5, Hebrews 2:7.]

[3] [The Himalayan mountains Chogo Ri (better known as K2, Dapsang, or Mt. Godwin Austen, 28,250 ft.) and Kanchenjunga ("Five Peaks," 28,146 ft.) are the second and third highest mountains in the world. Crowley attempted to climb both some 50 years before they were successfully scaled in 1954 and 1955.]

⟨•••⟩

The only drawback to the use of drugs is that the phenomenon of *toleration* is so soon set up, and the effect diminished; while for weaklings there is always the danger of the formation of a habit, when the treacherous servant becomes master, and takes toll for the boon of his ephemeral heavens by the bane of an abiding hell.

These remarks have only been introduced to emphasize the fact that happiness is an interior state; for every one of these drugs gives happiness supreme and unalloyed, entirely irrespective of the external circumstances of the individual. It would be folly to fill the apartment of an opium-smoker with the masterpieces of Rembrandt or Sotatsu,[1] when a dirty towel or a broken chair suffices to flood his soul with more glories than it can bear; when he realizes that light itself is beautiful, no matter on what object it may fall, and when, if you asked him what he would do if he were blind, he would condescend, from Heaven, to reply that darkness was more lovely still, that light was but a disturbance of the serenity of the soul, a siren to seduce it from the bliss of the contemplation of its own ineffable holiness.

⟨•••⟩

But why should we talk of drugs? They are only the counterfeit notes, or at best the fiat notes of a discredited government, while we are asking for purest gold. This gold can be ours for the asking.

We may begin by reassuring ourselves. The gold is really in the vaults of every man's treasury. The mystic quest is not a chimæra. The drugs assure us of that. They have not put anything supernatural into us; they have found nothing in us that was not already there. They have merely stimulated us. All the peace, the joy, the love, the beauty, the comprehension that they gave us; all these things were in us, bone of our bone, flesh of our flesh, and soul of our soul.[2] They are in our treasury, safe enough; and the chief reason why we should not burglariously use such skeleton keys as morphia is that by so doing we are likely to hamper our locks.

---

[1] [Rembrandt Harmenszoon van Rijn (1606–1669), Dutch painter. The Japanese painter Tawaraya Sotatsu (d. 1643) founded the Rimpa school of painting.]

[2] [Gen. 2:23.]

We seen, then, that we are but so little lower than the angels that the most trifling stimulus raises us to a plane where we enjoy—without consideration even of what it is that we enjoy! Our trouble is due entirely to the law that action and reaction are equal and opposite. We have to pay for the pleasure with pain. We sat up all night, last night, and so tonight we must go to bed early; we drank too much champagne at supper, and now, in the morning, it is the turn of Vichy. The question then has always been whether we can overcome this law of duality, whether we can reach—one step—to that higher plane where all will be ours.

⊂⊛⊃

Mysticism supplies the answer. The mystic attainment may be defined as the Union of the Soul with God, or as the soul's realization of Itself, or—but there are fifty phrases to define the attainment. Whether you are a Christian or a Buddhist, a Theist or an Atheist, the attainment of this state is as open to you as is nightmare, or madness, or intoxication. Religious folk have buried this fact under mountains of dogma; but the study of comparative religion has made it clear. One has merely to print parallel passages from the mystics of all ages and religions to see that they were talking of the same thing. One even gets verbal identities, such as the "That *tao* which is *tao* is not *tao*" of the Chinese,[1] the "Not That, not That" of the Hindu,[2] the "Head which is above all Heads, the Head which is not a Head" of the Qabalist,[3] and the "That is not, which is" of a modern atheistic or pantheistic mystic.[4]

Mysticism, unless it be a mere barren intellectual doctrine, always involves some personal religious experience of this kind; and the real strength of every religion lies, consequently, in its mystics. The conviction of truth given by any important spiritual experience is so great that although it may have lasted for a few seconds only, it does not hesitate to

---

[1] [Lao-tzu, *Tao-te Ching*, chap. I. Crowley translated this passage as "The Tao-Path is not the All-Tao. The Name is not the Thing named." See Works Cited.]

[2] [The Sanskrit "*neti neti*" is also translated as "neither this nor that."]

[3] [*Zohar*, "The Lesser Holy Assembly" §63. Crowley gives a slight paraphrase of S. L. Mathers' translation of portions of Knorr von Rosenroth's *Kabbalah Denudata* (1677–84), *The Kabbalah Unveiled* (1887), p. 265. See Works Cited.]

[4] [See the epigram "*Nur Nichts ist*" (attributed to a Comte de Chevallerie) that opens Chapter 0 of the revised second edition of Part III of Crowley's *Magick (Book 4, Parts I–IV)* (1994, 1997).]

pit itself against the experience of a lifetime, in respect of reality. The mystic doubts whether he, the man, exists at all, because he is so certain of the existence of him, the God; and the two beings are difficult to conceive intellectually as co-existent!

♔

Now the extreme state of Being, Knowledge and Bliss,[1] which characterizes the intermediate stages of mystic experience, is a thousandfold more intense than any other kind of happiness. It is totally independent of circumstance. We could bring a cloud of witnesses[2]—to swear to this truth—from the ends of all the earth; but one, the Persian bard El Qahar, whose masterpiece is the *Bagh-i-Muattar*, must suffice.[3]

> [W]hether Allah be or be not is little odds so long as His devotees enjoy the mystic rapture [...]
> Whether He exist or no, whether He love him or no, El Qahar will love Him and sing His praises."[4]
>
> The perfect lover is calm and equable; storms of thunder, quakings of the earth, losses of goods, punishment from great men, none of these things cause him to rise from his divan, or to remove the silken tube of the rose-perfumed *huqqa* from his mouth.[5]

It is, therefore, unnecessary to fret over earthly problems and all the trials of a merely earthly experience. The root of the cause is duality, the antithesis of the Ego and the Non-Ego; and the cure is Realization of the Unity. Socialism, and religion, and love, and art, are all fantastic things, good to lull the ills of life: dreams pitted against dreams. But the only real way of going about the problem of happiness is to attack the cause of all our troubles, the illusion in us of a duality of being.

Every great mystic has taught us that a singleness with God is the prime desideratum.

---

[1] [Sanskrit *sat, cit, ānanda.*]

[2] [Hebrews 12:1.]

[3] [El Qahar is a fictitious name used by Crowley in his *The Scented Garden of Abdullah the Satirist of Shiraz (Bagh-i-Muattar)* (1910), an invented Persian mystical treatise imbued with sexual and homoerotic imagery; most copies were destroyed as obscene by British Customs. See Works Cited.]

[4] [*The Scented Garden*, chap. 11.]

[5] [Ibid., chap. 18.]

⟨⁂⟩

The Saviour's instructions to his disciples to "take no thought for the morrow,"[1] to "abandon father and mother and all other things,"[2] "not to have two cloaks,"[3] "not to resist evil,"[4] are merely the ordinary rules of every eastern and western mystic. The disciple must have nothing whatever to turn his mind to duality, or to divert his mind from concentration. The whole secret of "Yoga" is given in Matthew 6:22. "The light of the body is the eye; if therefore thine eye be single, thy whole body shall be full of light." This is a perfectly simple statement of the virtue of what the Hindus call "one-pointedness."[5] The gospel of John, too, is full of praises of mystic practice. "I and my Father are one."[6] "I am the Way, the Truth, and the Life";[7] "I am in my Father, and ye in me, and I in you."[8] *Kappa tau lambda.*[9]

The Evangelists have been very stupidly accused of copying such passages from Chinese and Indian classics, on the grounds of absolute identity of idea, and even close verbal parallelism. It might be difficult to rebut such a charge if the passages were illustrative of remote, abstruse or even nonsensical doctrines.

⟨⁂⟩

For instance, if I happen to begin a poem by saying that: "The purple pigs lament the music of Madrid; They cook the nightingale with limping eyes of kid" it is fair to assume that I am plagiarizing the classic lines: "*Les cochons rouges pleurent un musique espagnol; leurs yeux de suède boîtent à cuire le rossignol*,"[10] because it is highly unlikely that two such

---

[1] [Matt. 6:34.]

[2] [Mark 10:28–30, Matt. 19:29, paraphrase.]

[3] [Matt. 10:10. Mark 6:9, Luke 9:3, paraphrase.]

[4] [Matt. 5:39, paraphrase.]

[5] [Sanskrit *ekāgrata.*]

[6] [John 10:30.]

[7] [John 14:6.]

[8] [John 14:20.]

[9] [The Greek abbreviation κ.τ.λ., equivalent to "et cetera" or "and so on."]

[10] [Crowley's version of this French nonsense-rhyme is close to the original. In *Liber 888, Jesus*, Crowley again quotes this and jokingly cites "Missinglink," i.e., Maurice Mæterlinck (1862–1949), whose work Crowley otherwise respected. These lines do not appear in Mæterlinck's *Serres chaudes.*]

complex pieces of pure nonsense should occur to any two independent thinkers—unless indeed they were German metaphysicians. But fifty men may observe independently that still water reflects images and record the fact with all due solemnity. No question of copying arises from the restatement of any great truth. There is, it is true, a universal tradition as to the means and of the end of mysticism, and we may perhaps think that Jesus had His teacher; but there is no necessity for any such supposition.

During an experiment made by me with a certain drug in an English midland hospital, the matron, who was one of my subjects, had not even a smattering of the history or even of the terminology of mysticism; yet she passed through trance after trance in the traditional order, and described her experiences in almost the same language as Lao-tzu and Bœhme, and Śrī Sabhapaty Swāmi,[1] and all the rest, of whom she had never so much as heard the names. One remedy for the ills of life is to make the subjective mind—by training—independent of all the senses. To cleanse the soul of the contamination of illusion; of the belief in duality; of the fear of even earthly misery.

Let us, by meditation and by all the true mystical practices, learn that the light of the body is the spiritual eye, and that the eye must be single, devoid of every thought of duality, to the end that the body and mind and soul shall be full of light. That is certainly a wise way to go about the attainment of happiness but, whether we think this is the best way, or the only way, there can be no reasonable doubt in the mind of any student of comparative religion that this is the way pointed out by at least one of the authors of the Gospel.

---

[1] [For Lao-tzu see p. 64, note 4. For Jacob Bœhme see p. 66, note 2. Śrī Sabhapaty Swāmi (b. 1840) was an Indian poet and *yogin*, and author of *Vedantic Raj Yoga*; see Works Cited.]

An Improvement on Psychoanalysis

THE PSYCHOLOGY OF THE UNCONSCIOUS
(FOR DINNER-TABLE CONSUMPTION)

Psychoanalysis, the investigation of the nature of the mind, is an old diversion. But science—if it really be science—has found a new method for such analytical parlour games. By it the reactions of a man to various impressions, through the nerves, are measured. The quickening of his pulse, when the professor suddenly shouts the word "Muriel" at him; the depressed expression when he whispers the words "income tax"; all these can now be weighed in the scales of science.

After a labourious research of months the whole nature of the soul is laid bare, and the reasons of a preference for Cherrystones over Little Neck clams, unmasked. Even the character of a man's dreams is supposed by this school to reveal his hidden nature.

Professor Freud of Vienna is the best known of those who have been developing this line of study, but recently Professor Jung of Zurich, has challenged his teaching and his supremacy alike with a book called *Psychology of the Unconscious.*[1]

There is, in short, a split in the psychoanalysis camp. This essay will give in outline the main doctrine of psychoanalysis, and explain the

---

[1] [Sigmund Freud (1856–1939) was the founder of psychotherapy, a branch of clinical psychology which viewed neuroses as springing from the suppression of sexual impulses. Carl Gustav Jung (1875–1961) entered Freud's circle around 1906 and became his heir-apparent as leader of the movement, but by 1914 they had split over fundamental differences in theory and therapeutic practice. Freud favored his sexual theory of the unconscious, while Jung developed a religious and mythic interpretation. Jung's *Wandlungen und Symbole der Libido* (1912, English translation, 1916) examines the mythic nature of neurosis, and marks his break with Freud; the German title means *Transformations and Symbols of the Libido.* Jung issued a revision in 1952, published in English as *Symbols of Transformation*; see Works Cited.]

nature of the quarrel between Freud and Jung. The subject is quite a fascinating one, and will probably be discussed at every dinner-table during the coming social season.

Our grandmothers, before we had finished teaching them to extract nutriment from ova (by suction),[1] were wont to spend the hours of night-lights with divines—or rather, with their Works. They would interpret their own dreams by the aid of a variety of theological works. *Mais nous avons changé tout cela.*[2] Today our grandmothers dance the hula-hula at Montmartre, or at the Castles in the Air, until the dawn breaks, and they now interpret their dreams by the aid of Professor Freud or Professor Jung, for Joseph and his ilk have been tried and found wanting.[3]

Psychoanalysis has been but ill understood by the average man. Most of us, however, will acquiesce in the necessity for an inquiry into the cause of dreams—and of the poet's dreams, dreams which are in reality the myths of a race. For all effects have psychic or hidden causes.

The Victorian age was distinguished by its mechanical interpretation of all phenomena. Not only did it destroy our ideas of the divine nature of the soul, but it would not even permit us to be human. A live man only differed from a dead one as a machine in motion does from one at rest. The only exception to this analogy was that we did not know how to restart a man that happened to have stopped.

Dreams, therefore, were regarded as undigested thoughts. I made a small research of my own in this matter, recording the dreams of a month. All but two of some fifty of my dreams were clearly connected, either with the events of the previous day, or with the conditions of the moment. Rainfall on my face would start a dream of some adventure by water, for example. Or a battle royal with a man at chess would fight itself all over again, with fantastic additions, in the overtired and overexcited brain.

I am bound to say that the theory that dreams come from natural causes in our everyday life seems to me perfectly an adequate and satisfactory one. I conceive of the brain as an *édition de luxe* of the wax cylinder of a dictograph. I imagine that disturbances of our blood currents (intoxications, and the like) reawaken some of these impressions at ran-

---

[1] [I.e., suck eggs.]

[2] [French, "But we have changed all that."]

[3] [See the account of the Biblical interpreter of dreams Joseph, son of Jacob, in chapters 37–50 of Genesis.]

dom, with the same result, more or less, as if you started a victrola, and kept on jerking it irregularly. Our thoughts are normally criticized and controlled by reason and reflection and will; when these are in abeyance they run riot, combine in monstrous conspiracies, weave wizard dances. Delirium is but exaggerated nightmare.

But since the Victorians, the universe is conceived more as dynamic than kinematic, more as force than as motion; and the will has at last become all-important to philosophy.

We ought not to be surprised to learn that Dr. Jung of Zurich balked at some of Freud's conclusions. Instead of relating will to sex, he related sex to will.[1] Thus, all unconsciously, he has paved the way for a revival of the old magical idea of the will as the dynamic aspect of the self. Each individual, according to the initiates, has his own definite purpose, and assumes human form, with its privileges and penalties, in order to execute that purpose. This truth is expressed in magical language by the phrase "Every man and every woman is a star"[2] [in] *Liber Legis*, which stands at the head of all hieratic writings.[3] It follows that "The word of Sin is Restriction"; "Do what thou wilt shall be the whole of the Law."[4] So, once more, we see Science gracefully bowing her maiden brows before her old father, Magic.

Dr. Jung has, however, not reached this high point in conscious thought. But he sees clearly enough that neuroses and insanities spring from repressions, from internal conflicts between desire and inhibition; and he does apparently accept fully the definition of "libido" as Will, in the magical sense.[5] Bergson's "*élan vital*" is very much the same,[6] if a

---

[1] [Freud's theory was that our behavioral impulses come from the Id, the unrestrained sexual nature. Inappropriate behaviors were modified and sublimated by the superego into their ultimate expression in the ego. Jung was dissatisfied with relating everything to a sexual impulse. While acknowledging that both a key and a battering ram could be sexual symbols in a dream, he was interested in why one would be chosen over the other.]

[2] [*Liber AL vel Legis* I:3.]

[3] [This passage was corrupted and was edited here for clarity.]

[4] [Ibid., I:41, I:40.]

[5] [Crowley, in his later writings, would equate Freud's Id (which is closely related to the libido) with his own concept of Will.]

[6] [The French philosopher and Nobel laureate Henri Bergson (1859–1941) was the brother of Golden Dawn matron Mina Mathers. His theories were very influential when this article was written. His *Creative Evolution* (1907, trans. 1911) defines the mind as pure energy or vital force (*élan vital*); see Works Cited.]

shallower conception. At any rate, let us rejoice that the tedious and stupid attempt to relate every human idea to sex has been relegated to oblivion; or, if you prefer to put it that way, that we must now interpret sex in vaster symbols, comprehending and achieving the ancient and modern worships of Pan as embracing the universe more adequately than almost any other conception. The charge of anthropomorphism still lies; but this is necessary. "God is man"[1]—the third and secret motto of the Knights of the Temple—is, after all, for humanity at least, a proposition of identity, and relative only in so far as all Truth is relative.

The main practical issue of Jung's acquiescence in magical theory is, as explained above, his interpretation of myths. The myth is the dream of the race. He sees that Freud cannot sustain his thesis that every dream is a picture of unfulfilled desire; but he seeks to prove that the great myths of the race, being really the poems of the race, are the artistic and religious expression of the will of the race. For the will of the world becomes articulate in the true poet, and he is the incarnation of the spirit of the times (the *Zeitgeist*). He was of old limited by the frontiers of his own civilization and time, but today his footstool is the planet,[2] and he thinks in terms of eternity and of infinite space.

Now Jung's great work has been to analyze the race-myths, and to find in them the expression of the unconscious longings of humanity.

We cannot think that he has been particularly happy in selecting wooden, academic exercises like *Hiawatha*,[3] which has as much inspiration as the Greek iambics of a fourth-form boy in a fourth-rate school; and he is still obsessed by the method and also by the main ideas of Freud. Much of his analysis is startling, and at first sight ridiculous.

Can we close our eyes to the perpetual contradictions in his alleged symbolism? Jung regards a serpent on a monument as desire, or the obstacle to desire, or the presence of desire, or the absence of desire, just as suits his purpose. There is no consistency in the argument, and there is no serious attempt to bring all cognate symbols into parallel. He brings many, it is true—but he omits certain important ones, so that one is bound to suspect that all his omissions are intentional!

---

[1] [In Latin, *deus est homo*; a doctrine preserved by the O.T.O.]

[2] [See Isaiah 66:1.]

[3] [The American poet Henry Wadsworth Longfellow (1807–1882) wrote a narrative play, *Hiawatha*, which has been frequently adapted and parodied.]

However, the main point of this paper is to illustrate the prime line of reasoning adopted by Jung. This understood, the reader can ferret out his own explanations for his own dreams, desires and myths!

Jung is a determinist. The Victorians—especially Herbert Spencer—denying "free will," would argue that a man ate an egg not because he wanted to do so, but because of the history of the universe. The forces of infinity and eternity bent themselves in one herculean effort, and pushed the egg into his mouth! This is quite undeniable; but it is only one way of looking at the egg question.

Now Jung treats literature in just this way. He will not admit that an author has any choice of material. If Rupert of Hentzau[1] wounds somebody in the shoulder, it is because of the story of Pelops and Hera,[2] in which the shoulder is a sexual symbol. If the other man ripostes and touches Rupert in the ear, it is because Pantagruel was born from the ear of Gargamelle.[3] So the ear is a sexual symbol. If the hero of a novel goes from Liverpool to New York, it is the myth of "the night journey by sea of the sun." If he goes on to Brooklyn, it is the Descent into Hades of Virgil, or Dante, or anybody else![4] There is no evasion of this type of argument; but all arguments that prove everything prove nothing! If I prove that some cats are green, it is interesting; but if I go on to show that all cats are green, I destroy myself. "Greenness" becomes included implicitly in the idea of "cat." It is senseless to say that "all bipeds have two legs."

However, Dr. Jung does not mind this at all. He definitely wishes to reduce the universe of will, which we think so complex and amusing, to a single crude symbol. According to him, the history of humanity is the

---

[1] [*Rupert of Hentzau* (1898) was the sequel to *The Prisoner of Zenda* (1894) by British novelist and playwright Sir Anthony Hope (Hawkins) (1863-1933); see Works Cited.]

[2] [In Greek mythology, Pelops was killed by his father and served as food to the gods; he was returned to life, but with an ivory shoulder to replace the one eaten by Demeter (not Hera).]

[3] [Pantagruel the giant was the son of Gargantua in Rabelais' *Pantagruel* (1532); see Works Cited. See also "Antecedents of Thelema," p. 162.]

[4] [Virgil or Vergil (70-19 BCE) is considered classical Rome's greatest poet, and is remembered for *The Æneid*. The Italian poet Dante Alighieri (1265-1321) is best known for *The Divine Comedy*.]

struggle of the child to free itself from the mother.[1] Every early need is met by the mother; hunger and fatigue find solace at her breast. Even the final "will to die," the desire of the supreme and eternal repose, is interpreted as the return to earth, the mother of us all.

It will occur to the reader that there is much in this; for instance, the myth or religion of the race tends to disappear with its emancipation from the mother and family system.

But we cannot conquer one's revolt against what seems the essential absurdity of the whole Jung argument; that, considering—let us say, the importance of the horse to man, with so many horses to choose from, Jung can see nothing in a story of a man on horseback but a reference to the "symbol of the stamping horse," which has something to do with the dreams of one of his neurotic patients on the one hand, and the mythical horse in the *Rg-Veda* on the other![2]

We almost prefer the refinement of modesty evidenced by the young lady who always blushed when she saw the number "six"—because she knew Latin![3] However, we should all study Jung. His final conclusions are in the main correct, even if his rough working is a bit sketchy;[4] and we've got to study him, whether we like it or not, for he will soon be recognized as the undoubted Autocrat of the 1917 dinner-table.

Just ask your pretty neighbour at dinner tonight whether she has introverted her Electra-complex;[5] because it will surely become one of the favourite conversational gambits of the coming social season!

---

[1] [Compare this to Freud's Œdipal Complex, wherein the son struggles to overcome his desire to kill his father and marry his mother. When Freud was 64, he wrote his landmark *Beyond the Pleasure Principle* (1920, trans. 1922), in which he deals with religion, the repetition compulsion, and the death instinct, many years after Jung first broached these topics.]

[2] [The *Rg-Veda* is one of the four *vedas* or sacred scriptures of Hinduism. The other three are the *Yajur-veda*, *Sāma-veda* and *Atharva-veda*.]

[3] [The numeral six in Latin is "sex."]

[4] [Jung's psychological system was still in its early stages of development in 1916; key concepts such as personality types, the anima, the persona, and the collective unconscious, were not yet fully formulated.]

[5] [A corollary to the Œdipal complex in which the daughter desires to kill her mother and marry her father.]

Billy Sunday

> The wild man went his weary way
> To a strange and lonely pump.[1]

The feelings of the Albert Memorial having been wounded by the criticisms of artists, I thought it only kind to bring back a photograph of the City Hall of Philadelphia, on the same principle as the association of Count Guido and Judas by Caponsacchi.[2]

I repaired accordingly to the Quaker City for this purpose, and being strayed amid the various nuts, herbacea, and other vegetables after which the foxy folk name streets, came suddenly upon a large low wooden tabernacle.

Like Blind Bartimæus, I enquired why, in view of the fifteen thousand people then just coming out, there should be fifteen thousand more obviously waiting to go in. My informant replied that it was a preaching. A preaching, in my system of metaphysics, postulates a preacher. I asked about the preacher. "Billy Sunday" was the answer, and I felt like the man at Melbourne who was told that the people were all going to see the race for the cup, and, an instant before his extermination, asked "What cup?"[3]

But I am not the Pride of the Bench, and I did not continue "Who is Billy Sunday?" For this preacher is certainly the most often discussed

---

[1] [Lewis Carroll, from "Poeta Fit, Non Nascitur," first published in *Phantasmagoria and Other Poems* (1869); see Works Cited.]

[2] [Count Guido Franceschini and Fra. Caponsacchi were historical opponents in the 17th c. Italian marriage and murder tragedy that formed the basis of Robert Browning's *The Ring and the Book*; see Works Cited.]

[3] [William Ashley (Billy) Sunday (1862–1935) was a former undertaker's assistant and professional baseball player who became the most sensationalistic Revival-meeting evangelist of his day. Although ordained as a Presbyterian minister in 1903, Sunday was a Fundamentalist who preached the literal truth of the Bible, one of the first to combine staging, music and showmanship. Total attendance at his revival meetings for his career has been estimated at 100 million.]

man in the United States today. Opinion varies between the widest of extremes. Some think him a grafter and hypocrite like Comstock;[1] others do not hesitate to compare him to the Saviour. Some say his talk is all profanity, blasphemy, and slang, and revile his antics. Others, admitting the slang, say that he has to reach his hearers. Booth's excuse for his brass band, sweat-shop, graft game was the same.[2]

However, I took Hamlet's advice, and went to see for myself. I did not wait in the queue; I went and lunched and came back to find him in full swing on the subject of The Moral Leper. Of course he did not mean that; he meant The Immoral Man, whom I compare with a leper on account of his immorality.

I need hardly say that his text was from the story of Naaman.[3]

Let me describe his person. It will clarify matters. First, one sees a striking resemblance to that other atheist, Charles Bradlaugh.[4] But this is facial only. Billy Sunday lacks Bradlaugh's "steadfast and intolerable eyes," and his noble brow, and his giant cranium. There is force in the face, but it is only courage combined with cunning in the proportions of about 3 to 5. Intellect is obviously altogether lacking. The body is athletic; Sunday being a "converted" baseball player. His enemies say "translated" for "converted." He has some facility of coarse repartee, learnt in the bar-room in the old days. If you raise a point in argument, he is apt to reply wittily "I can smell the liquor off your breath." He did so reply to someone that afternoon, and maybe sincerely thought that he had answered him.

He has also a number of American slang phrases, probably prepared for him by a newspaper man; many of these have some epigrammatic force.

He suits the action to the word, and the word to the action. In saying "I take my stand on the Bible," he does so with both feet.

---

[1] [Anthony Comstock (1844–1915) led the Society for the Suppression of Vice, which lobbied for the American "Comstock Law" of 1873 by which 3,500 individuals would be prosecuted (less than 10% convicted) and 120 tons of literature destroyed. Rabelais' *Gargantua* was banned; they failed with Cabell's *Jurgen*.]

[2] [William Booth (1829–1912), founder of the Salvation Army.]

[3] [II Kings 5.]

[4] [The English M.P. Charles Bradlaugh (1833–1891) was repeatedly denied his seat in Parliament for his refusal to be sworn in on the Bible; finally seated in 1886, he secured the Affirmation Act of 1888 which permits atheists to "affirm."]

His theology is of the crass Evangelical order. He believes that the human race sprang from two people named Adam and Eve. Apparently he has never heard it doubted, except by "rum fiends in *delirium tremens*" and the like. He would be astounded if one told him the plain fact that the Bible never made itself responsible for so idiotic an hypothesis.

But all this you were prepared to hear. What no American has seen— or could see—is just what I saw. Billy Sunday, for all his extravagances, is just a common Bible-banger of the first class. He does not stand out at all. I tell of what I know; I was brought up in the air of revivals. It is not the preacher, but the crowd, that makes the hysteria. I have heard Rowland Edwards, and my own father, addressing larger meetings, getting more enthusiasm, more "conversions," with far less effort, and not a line in the newspapers. Here Billy Sunday fills columns in half the newspapers of the district every week. There is no just cause for this. There is not nearly so much hysteria in his audiences as I have seen at Dr. Barnardo's meetings,[1] and the Salvation Army, and the Children's Special Service Mission. Billy Sunday is three parts yellow journal fake. I cannot say whether this is spontaneous; I suspect a mastermind somewhere with a profit and loss account, and an arm long enough to lever the composer's stick. For whether one cries "graft" or not—and here everyone who gets a dollar at all is called a grafter by the man who grabbed at it and missed—there is, no doubt, a pile of money in the business. It is said that he cleared $100,000 last year; and the free-will offerings this weekend are expected to reach a similar amount.[2] For Billy is going away; he sighs for new worlds to conquer. I understand that the negotiations for his going to New York fell through. I suspect that he knew he could do nothing there, "because of their unbelief,"[3] and also perhaps that the newspapers there have more expensive columns.

After all, the real reason of his success in Philadelphia is this: You can't buy a drink on the Sabbath. One must be either a Rabelaisian genius or a toad just come out of the Lower Silurian Strata to find anything amusing in Philadelphia between Saturday and Monday, or indeed anything amusing but to get drunk between Monday and Saturday. So

---

[1] [The British physician and social reformer Thomas John Barnardo (1845–1905) founded numerous homes for poor and orphaned children.]

[2] P.S. They actually did reach $57,136.85.

[3] [Matt. 13:58.]

Sunday is Sunday's chance to be heard. As the tract of my childhood's happy days said, "Man's extremity is God's opportunity."

In New York the crowd gapes to be amused as the hart panteth after the water-brooks,[1] but the slightest rustle in the leaves, and it tosses its horns, and is off.

Philadelphia is serious. Philadelphia would turn a lark into a raven in six weeks. People get religion in Philadelphia because there is nothing else to get except dollars—and religion helps to get those! Whenever a Philadelphian thinks of the time when he was somewhere else, and beings to smile, his eye catches the City Hall, and gloom again shrouds him in its nightshade pall.

I am rather in hope that a really great humorist may arise in Philadelphia. Ordinary humorists depend on circumstances; the first-rate man (like Lewis Carroll) must dig it all out of his own mind in the midst of a milieu like *The City of Dreadful Night*.[2] And now I come to think of it, perhaps Billy Sunday is the humorist in question. There is a certain unholy joy in getting money from the pious for your piety in proportion to the shamelessness of your blasphemies. Think of the morning when he said to his wife, "My dear, I'll bet you a pair of gloves I smash the chairman's hat over his eyes, and they'll only laugh and cheer" (to illustrate how the devil blinds sinners). On another occasion, in an address to women only, he asked them to place their knees together, and then exclaimed "The gates of hell are closed." All right in Boccaccio and d'Haraucourt and Rabelais![3] Oh, yes, it is true humour! Think of the Christian revivalist delivering a sermon of Ingersoll's almost verbatim![4] And that was one of Billy Sunday's jokes. The freethinkers took him seriously, and proceeded to expose him!

Observe: the religious man has always had license to play antics. In fact, the "fool" or "natural" has always been considered inspired. And it has always been the secret joy and power of the religious man to go

---

[1] [Psalm 42:1.]

[2] [A work by the Scottish poet James Thomson (1834–1882) first published in 1874. Thomson was a close friend of Charles Bradlaugh.]

[3] [The Italian poet Giovanni Boccaccio (1313–1375), author of the *Decameron*. For Haraucourt see p. 20, note 1; for Rabelais see p. 163, note 1.]

[4] [Robert G. Ingersoll (1833–1899) was an American lawyer, public official, and author. Known as "the Great Agnostic," he remarked that "an honest God is the noblest work of man," and "with soap, baptism is a good thing."]

through some meaningless mummery, and get paid for it. But most religious men have been scholars, and their jokes have had a certain fruity flavour as of ripe old port. Now, deliver that secret into the hands of a professional baseball player, accustomed to the horseplay of the tap-room, and what will he do?

What Billy Sunday is actually doing.

The Ouija Board

A NOTE

Suppose a perfect stranger came into your office and proceeded to give orders to your staff. Suppose a strange woman walked into your drawing room and insisted on being hostess. You would be troubled by this. Yet, people sit down and offer the use of their brains and hands (which are, after all, more important than offices and drawing rooms) to any stray intelligence that may be wandering about. People use the Ouija Board without taking the slightest precautions.

The establishment of the identity of a spirit by ordinary methods is a very difficult problem, but the majority of people who play at Occultism do not even worry about this. They get something, and it does not seem to matter what! Every inanity, every stupidity, every piece of rubbish, is taken not only at its face value, but at an utterly exaggerated value. The most appallingly bad poetry will pass for Shelley, if only its authentication be that of the planchette! There is, however, a good way of using this instrument to get what you want, and that is to perform the whole operation in a consecrated circle, so that undesirable aliens cannot interfere with it. You should then employ the proper magical invocation in order to get into your circle just the one spirit that you want. It is comparatively easy to do this. A few simple instructions are all that is necessary, and I shall be pleased to give these, free of charge, to anyone who cares to apply.

It is not particularly easy to get the spirit of a dead man, because the human soul, being divine, is not amenable to the control of other human souls; and it is further not legitimate or desirable to do it. But what can be done is to pick up the astral remains of the dead man from the *ākāśa* and to build them up into a concrete mind. This operation, again, is not particularly profitable. The only legitimate work in this line is to get into touch with the really high intelligences, such as we call for convenience Gods, Archangels, and the like. These can give real information as to what is most necessary to our progress. And it is written in the *Oracles of Zoroaster* that unto the Persevering Mortal the Blessed Immortals are swift.[1]

---

[1] [*The Chaldæan Oracles of Zoroaster*, §158, ed. Westcott.]

A Letter from
The Master Therion

To the Editor of *The International*.

Sir:—

In answer to the question, "Can you tell us anything of the Great White Brotherhood, known as the A∴A∴," Mr. Chas. Lazenby, of the Theosophical Society, made the following remarks after his public lecture on Magic, at the Vancouver Labor Temple, July 31, 1917 e.v.

> The A∴A∴ is an Occult order having a definite purpose, and was started by a man of immense power,[1] perhaps the greatest living. The place of this great Being in the Occult Hierarchy is a profound mystery, and he and his mission are causing a great amount of speculation at the present time.
>
> Judged by any ordinary standard, he is absolutely and entirely evil; he has broken his occult vows and all codes of morality, openly stating that he has done so and will continue to do so. He may have a very great purpose in view.
>
> No living person perhaps has had such an influence on occult thought, and wrought so much change therein. He has knowingly taken upon himself a tremendous *karma*, but what will be the ultimate result it is impossible to judge. To all appearance, as I remarked, he is the personification of evil.

Later, during private conversation, Mr. Lazenby continued:

> He is a very wonderful being; an ordinary man like myself has no possible means of judging what his ultimate motive is.
>
> Looked at from known standards he is evil, but from a distance, in perspective, one may imagine that he is taking this great *karma* for some definite end; he may be the Savior of the World.

---

[1] The Master Therion. [Crowley's magical motto as a Magus 9°=2□ of A∴A∴]

In any case 300 years from now he will be looked upon as one of the greatest of the World's geniuses.

I should not care to have any part in his work myself. You have this to remember, however, that you are connected with a genuine Occult order, not a pseudo-occult one such as Heindel's and others which are worthless.[1]

What has the Master Therion to say about this?

C. S. J.

⊂€♦୨⊃

Mr. Lazenby has so long and so laudably labored upon the production of canned soup that he has neglected that of the wine of Iacchus. But I think he only needs to be shown. It is something to be hailed as a possible Savior of the World by one's avowed and bitter enemies.[2] *Nunc dimittis!*[3] Anyhow, to be called the "Personification of Evil" is not exactly a precise charge. If I wished to attack Mr. Lazenby, I should define my accusation. I should say that under Alpine conditions, the Lentil Soup Squares dissolve too slowly.

I believe that H. P. Blavatsky was a great adept.[4] I judge her by her highest, *The Voice of the Silence*,[5] not by any mistakes that she may have made in other matters. I consider that her work has been treacherously ruined by Mrs. Besant, the street corner atheist, socialist, and advocate

---

[1] [Max Heindel was the pen-name of Carl Louis van Grashof (1865–1919), who wrote numerous works on astrology and Theosophy and led the Rosicrucian Fellowship in California. Crowley was always openly critical of any organization that made public claims to be Rosicrucian.]

[2] [This sentence, underlined by Crowley in his set of *The International*, is highly significant in light of his later efforts to oppose Annie Besant's spiritual protégé Jiddu Krishnamurti as the "World Teacher," and put himself forward in his stead; for a brief account of this episode, see *The Heart of the Master*, 2nd ed., editor's introduction. It appears that the original impetus for Crowley's position may have been external, i.e., Charles Lazenby, a Theosophical Society member.]

[3] [Latin, lit. "now you disband/dismiss," i.e., permission to depart.]

[4] [For Madame Blavatsky see p. 21, note 2.]

[5] [Crowley rarely cited Blavatsky's best-known works, *Isis Unveiled* (1877) and *The Secret Doctrine* (1888), but he had high regard for *The Voice of the Silence* (1889). He wrote an extensive commentary, published in *The Equinox* III(1) (1919), and in *Commentaries on the Holy Books*, *The Equinox* IV(1) (1996).]

of abortion.[1] Of this offense she was actually convicted. Mrs. Besant's whole object seems to have been to prevent disciples from making those bold experiments which open the gates of the higher planes. I do not believe that any man or woman can come to ultimate harm by a passionate will to seek truth. They may go insane. They may be slain. They may be damned. These are only ordeals which do them good. If they can stick it out, they will get through. Mrs. Besant wants to be like conscience, to make cowards of us all.[2] In my first initiation I was told, "Fear is failure. Be thou therefore without fear, for in the heart of the coward virtue abideth not. Thou hast known me; pass thou on."[3] To prevent men from confronting the unknown, to sidetrack them with petty drivel about minor ethics, to deck them out with the stolen regalia of orders of whose secrets they are profoundly ignorant: these are the works of the Brothers of the Left Hand Path; and of these I believe Mrs. Besant to be the greatest now alive.

Therion 9°=2□ A∴A∴.

---

[1] [Annie Besant 1847–1933) became the president of the Theosophical Society after Blavatsky's death. Crowley treated her as a rival, primarily for her efforts to establish Co-masonry and the Liberal Catholic Church, as well as her campaign to promote Krishnamurti as the world teacher. Besant was also an early feminist and birth control advocate, and author of *The Ancient Wisdom* (1897) and other works. Crowley became increasingly feminist (after his own fashion) after his American period. While he never changed his views on abortion, he clearly supported women's ethical right of choice; see *Liber Oz sub figura* 77. For a fictional account of Annie Besant and the workings of the Black Lodge, see his *Moonchild* (1929), chap. 19.]

[2] [Shakespeare, *Hamlet*, act III, scene i.]

[3] [See the Golden Dawn Neophyte Ritual, *The Temple of Solomon the King*, in *The Equinox* I(3) (1910).]

How Horoscopes
are Faked

I have always been opposed to the receiving of money for anything which has in any way to do with the occult sciences. Because they are so important and so sacred, one ought to be particularly on one's honour with regard to them. As the Scripture says: "Avoid the appearance of evil."[1] The more serious one is about the subject, the more careful one should be to do nothing which can make anyone justified in calling you a humbug.

The laws of the State of New York are supposed to prohibit fortune-telling, and they are, indeed, applied with great severity so far as the little fish are concerned. But the big fish, the most conscienceless swindlers of all, seem to dodge the police. A lot of bluff has been put up about "scientific" astrology. I propose to show how the game is really worked.

Let us pay a visit to one of the best known of them. We find an expensive apartment in one of the best parts of the city. We are not very much impressed by the furniture. There is a good deal of muddle, a good deal of junk, a complete absence of taste. The spider of this web is a grey-haired old woman of exceedingly shrewd expression. She explains to us by pamphlets and by word that she is a really "scientific" investigator. In setting up a horoscope, for example, she is very careful to calculate the places of the planets, not only to degrees, but to minutes and seconds. That sounds wonderfully accurate, doesn't it? However, when it comes to making the real calculations upon which astrology is based, an error of ten or twelve degrees is of no account at all. Which is rather like announcing that a man took 2 hours, 33 minutes and 14.25 seconds to run *several* miles. The alleged accuracy is quite meaningless. It is only a sham to impress the client. It is also to be observed that owing to the pressure of business she has these calculations made by her chauffeur! This, I suppose, is a point of war economy.

---

[1] [I Thess. 5:22, paraphrase.]

She is grotesquely ignorant of the first principles of astronomy. She has no conception, for example, of the Solar System as a Disk, but imagines that the planets are all over the place, like the raisins in a plum-pudding. She calls her country house the Zodiac—and doesn't know what the Zodiac is!

One word more on the "scientific accuracy" business. If astrology is to be done at all, if there is any sense in it whatever, which I do not for one moment deny, the calculations depend upon a fairly close approximation of the hour and minute of birth. For example, the Seventh house, the place of the setting sun, refers to marriage, so that if a person is born with an unfortunate planet like Saturn setting, he may expect an unfortunate marriage. It is obviously of vital importance for the inquirer to know whether Saturn was setting or not. There is a certain amount of latitude, from about one to two hours, for Saturn would remain in that house for about that period. But where the birth hour is not known within about an hour the horoscope becomes worthless. If the time were six hours earlier, Saturn would be in the mid-heaven and bring misfortune in business or reputation rather than in marriage. However to the fashionable astrologer this must not matter. She has to get the dollars from the people who do not know in the least at what hour of the day or night they were born. She has the impudence to assure them that it doesn't matter, all the time insisting upon her wonderful scientific accuracy.

There is no need to cast any doubt upon the sincerity of the belief of the woman. She talks astrology day and night. She dreams of it. She sets up a horoscope for her vast family of cats and dogs, and is scared out of her life when some planet threatens her horoscope.

But the people who deceive themselves most effectually are also those who deceive others most effectually. Whether it is knavery or folly does not matter very much. What I want to do is to explain to the people who are paying five dollars that they are not getting genuine astrology at all. It may be said that a horoscope (granting for a moment the genuineness of the science) is a complete map of the life and character of the native. To read one properly would mean at least a week's continuous work. But the demand is for 5 dollar and 10 dollar horoscopes; and obviously no more than a few minutes can be given to each one if the lady is to clear her forty or fifty thousand a year. It is also necessary to give a good deal of *apparent* value for the money. There are only 12 signs and 9 planets to be considered.[1] For the influence of the rising sign, therefore, one only needs twelve multigraphed pages. As each planet can be in any sign we shall need 9 times 12 multigraph pages to cover the action of the planets. Each planet can be, roughly speaking, in fortunate or unfortunate aspect, and 162 more pages will be needed. These pages need not be prepared right away. A new one can be dictated as each aspect turns up in practice. These pages are all pigeon-holed, and by means of a chart the astrologer can tell her secretary which paper to pick out for any horoscope that comes along. The secretary can then pick them out and pin them together in a very few minutes, and there is your horoscope.

The objection to this proceeding is fairly obvious. In practically all horoscopes there are indications which clash with each other. To judge such a horoscope properly, the whole thing should be taken into individual consideration, and a reconcilement obtained. With the "reach-me-down" method all this is necessarily ignored, and the client may be surprised to find on page two of the horoscope, that she is kind and considerate, and on page four, that she is selfish and inconsiderate. There is further a great theoretical objection; which is that a horoscope, to be a horoscope at all, must be a live thing. To get them out in this mechanical fashion is to offer a corpse instead.

It is true that the astrologer sometimes condescends to look upon a horoscope as a whole, and dictate one or two pages at the end, but this is not always done. There is no guarantee that it will be done.

It is probably difficult to take legal exception to this branch of the business, but it is only a very small branch. It is the thin end of the wedge. The fortune-telling, pure and simple, comes afterwards. The astrologer issues a series of so-called monthly forecasts which explain how the actual position of the planets in the heavens at the time should react upon any given horoscope. Another set of multigraphed pages is of course required for this. These pages are carefully examined by a lawyer, for we are now getting into the danger zone.

The phraseology is very carefully chosen, for nothing must be said which would be indictable as a prediction. Thus, instead of saying, "You will be lucky in speculation during the first week of October," the phrase is "Financial conditions seem to be operating favourably during the first week in October." These monthly forecasts are received at $24 a year, and as they require a good deal of trouble in preparation, it is evident that

---

[1] [This article was written before the discovery of Pluto in 1930.]

the cheapness has something behind it. These forecasts are what you may call bait, and the fish to be caught is the "personal consultation."

Suppose I am told in my forecasts that financial conditions are favorable for a certain period, I am going to ask for more. I want to know exactly how to make the best use of the opportunity; so I ring up the lady and get an appointment. This appointment may ostensibly be a $5 or a $10 one; but in reality I may have to pay much more for it. I may have to let the lady in on a percentage of profits on the gamble in "war babies." Similarly, if I am an actress, or other easily exploitable person, I may have to pay a great deal extra. Once the fly is in the web, the spider can dictate its own terms.

Women are particularly foolish with astrologers. They tell all their love affairs. Again, even cautious Mrs. A will tell one side of a story; prudent Miss B next day, the other side. The astrologer becomes mistress of these women, body and soul. Perhaps she does not blackmail them; but she is in a position to do so if she wishes. At the very least, the victims realize their position, and are careful to do anything the astrologer may ask.

Then, again, there is the matrimonial agency graft; and the highly profitable business of *entremetteuse*.[1] (We do not assert that, in the particular case we are discussing, these things are done, but they could be done. It is immoral to permit the existence of a secret power of this kind.)

It is all done under the cloak of astrology. Mr. C calls, and looks for a soul-mate; the astrologer soon finds some woman, "whose Venus is on his Sun," and arranges a little dinner party. All in the sacred cause of astrology—scientific astrology; the old lady would be genuinely shocked if you called her by her real name. But she takes her commission all the same, and superstition is so extraordinarily strong that when faith is established, there is no limit to the amount of which the victim can be fleeced. This being the really dangerous part of the work, the astrologer is extraordinarily careful about making appointments. One has to have very good introductions. Word quickly goes round as to what the police are doing. For example, a few months ago it was rumoured that a redhaired detective had been engaged, and all women with red hair, unless previously known, had to pass the 33rd degree before they reached the centre of the web. There is no doubt in the mind of the astrologer that

---

[1] [French, "procuress."]

she is breaking the law. She lives in continual terror of the police. She knows well enough that it was only a fluke that she was not convicted at her previous prosecutions. However, she boasts openly of her "pull" with certain society leaders who can protect her from the police. Properly managed, evidence is easy to obtain. Will not Mrs. Isabel Goodwin look to it?

Art and Clairvoyance

The power of clairvoyance has replaced the faith boosted by St. Paul as "the evidence of things not seen."[1] It is comparatively easy to obtain the inner sight. The mistake which has been made is that people have expected to see the material world with their astral eyes; and this cannot be done unless the astral body is rematerialized, that is to say, brought back to the same plane as it started from. If you want to find out what is happening elsewhere you have first to form the astral body and travel in it to that place. When you are there you must find sufficient material to build a physical body. This being done, you can see very nearly as if you had travelled there in the body. Then by reversing the process you come back to your own body with the information desired. It cannot be too clearly understood that the astral world is a place with laws of its own just as regular as those pertaining to what we call the material world. In reality one is just as material as the other. There is merely a difference in the quality of the material. We cannot say, therefore, that the colour and form perceived by the clairvoyant is really identical in its nature with that perceived by the physical eye. Yet there is a certain analogy or similarity; and there is no particular reason why the astral world should not be represented plastically. Attempts to do this have been made by clairvoyants from the beginning of history. The most successful have on the whole been of purely hieroglyphic or symbolic characters. Geometrical patterns and sacred words and numbers have been used by the best seers to represent—perhaps not exactly what has been seen, but the truth of what has been seen. Attempts to make a direct representation have not been successful, but the reason for this has not been the impossibility of the task. It has not been the lack of good clairvoyants; it has been the lack of good artists. We cannot say that there is any actual incompatibility between the two powers. In fact, the greatest artists have nearly always

---

[1] [Hebrews 11:1.]

possessed a touch of mysticism. One might even go so far as to say that even art itself is of a mystic character, since even the most realistic of painters transmutes the physical facts before his eyes into a truth of beauty. A good picture is always a picture of more than the model.

In the exhibition held last month by Mr. Engers-Kennedy,[1] we have a very definite attempt to portray that which is seen by the spiritual sight, and the result may be described as extremely successful because the artist is a good artist. These pictures can be looked at with pleasure from the purely æsthetic standpoint. There is no *ad captandum*[2] effort to interest people in the subject of the picture. They stand on their own merits as pictures. But it would be useless to deny that a supreme interest is superadded by the representation of the character or mood of the sitter by the simple means of using the symbolic colors and forms perceived by the spiritual eye as background. We need not go in detail into the nature of the method employed. These pictures must be seen to be appreciated at their full value. But it is certainly possible to predict a great vogue for these portraits. Everyone must naturally wish a representation in permanent form of their inner as well as their outer body.

---

[1] [The portrait painter Leon (or Lionel) Engers-Kennedy IX° O.T.O. was Grand Secretary General of the Antient and Primitive Rite (a precursor to the O.T.O.), and Frater $To\ K\alpha\lambda ov\ \tau'\alpha\lambda\eta\theta\eta\ \tau'\epsilon\nu$ (Greek, "the beautiful, the true, the one") in the A.·. A.·.. Crowley dedicated his poem "The Disciples" in *The Equinox* I(10) to him, and his portrait of Crowley as The Master Therion appears in *The Equinox* III(1) (1919) (credited to Frater T.A.T.K.T.A.). See *Confessions*, abridged ed., pp. 778–779.]

[2] [*Lat.*, "for the sake of pleasing."]

Geomancy

BY ONE WHO USES IT DAILY

Robert Browning says "one truth leads right to the world's end,"[1] and in the Gospels we read "Not a sparrow that falleth to the ground but your Heavenly Father knoweth it."[2] What do these things mean if not that there is nothing in Nature too small to be significant? The fall of an apple sets Newton on the road to the Law of Gravitation, and the whole theory and practice of the steam engine was started by Watt's observation of a kettle.[3]

Further, we know from Newton's First Law of Motion[4] that the Universe is a whole in which even the slightest tremor is echoed by an equilibrating tremor equal and opposite. As the poet says:

> I bring
> My hand down on this table-thing
> And the commotion widens—thus!—
> And shakes the nerves of Sirius.[5]

An earthquake in Calabria may be recorded in California. Even disturbances in the photosphere of the sun may be detected these 93,000,000 miles away by methods other than optical. It is all a question of the sensitiveness of the recording instrument. And so the right interpretation of even the smallest phenomenon may be the clue to great events. Just, therefore, as by sensing present causes we can anticipate their effects in the future, there is nothing unreasonable in supposing the possibility of a science of divination. It is, however, a great step from admitting a possibility to admitting an actuality.

---

[1] ["Mr. Sludge, 'The Medium'"; see Works Cited.]

[2] [Matthew 10:29.]

[3] [For Sir Isaac Newton see p. 44, note 5. The Scottish instrument-maker Charles Watt (1736–1819) invented the steam engine.]

[4] [Inertia; see p. 49, note 2.]

[5] [Crowley, *The Sword of Song*, "Ascension Day," 411–414. See *Collected Works*, vol. II, p. 154. Crowley edited the quotation slightly.]

Now when I am asked about these matters, I say that on the whole the simplest, the most reliable, the most readily tested, the most easily learnt of all these sciences is Geomancy. It requires too, the least possible apparatus. The name means "divination by earth," and the requisites are a staff and a desert—which of course every Chaldæan had ready to his hand! But in New York we use a pencil and a piece of paper, instruments which (thanks to the Free Institutions of America!) are within the reach of a majority of people.

There are several systems of Geomancy, but all depend on the simplest possible basis; thus:

A number is either odd or even.

The first system is then to make one row of dots at random, and count them. Odd means yes; even means no. But one cannot work out problems in detail on so crude a system. So Fu-hsi, the great Chinese philosopher, invented his system of 8 trigrams.[1] (It will be obvious that by combining two sets of odd and even one can obtain 4 figures; by combining 3 one gets eight; 4 gives 16; 5 makes 32 and so on.) King Wên and Duke Chao, during years of prison, passed the time by inventing a system, in which they combined the 8 trigrams of Fu-hsi with themselves, thus obtaining 64 hexagrams. The book in which their system is explained, the *I Ching*, is probably the oldest book in the world.[2]

Before I leave this part of my subject I must refer to the Taoist system of that Master of the Temple whom some of us know as V.V.V.V.V.[3] He joined to the odd and the even, the *yin* and the *yang*, as the Chinese call them, the male and female principles, a third principle, neither odd nor even, neither male nor female. Thus his "Liber Trigrammaton" has 27 trigrams, and this amazing book is not only an atlas and a history of the Universe, but a compendious hieroglyph of the most secret forces of nature.[4]

---

[1] [Fu-hsi (Pao Hsi) is a legendary figure in Chinese prehistory. See p. 51, note 2.]

[2] [King Wên (c. 1150 BCE) and his son, the Duke of Chou, developed the divinatory meanings of the *I Ching*. Crowley produced his own translation of this work (*Liber 216*), and left extensive notes and commentaries; see Works Cited.]

[3] [Vi Veri Universum Vivus Vici, Crowley's motto as a Magister Templi 8°=3□ of the A∴A∴.]

[4] ["Liber Trigrammaton sub figura XXVII" was first published in volume 3 of Θελημα [*Thelema*] (1909), known as *The Holy Books*, and is included in *The Holy Books of Thelema*, *The Equinox* III(9) (1983); see Works Cited.]

In pure divination, however, there is a seven-fold scheme of 128 figures,[1] invented by that mysterious Grand Master of the Order of the Temple who hides his identity under the name of Baphomet.[2] It is far too elaborate even to outline in this brief account.[3]

The common and generally received system is four-fold, and has therefore 16 figures. Its source is very ancient; it was first properly explained in public by Henry C. Agrippa, or by someone who found behind that great name a convenient shelter.[4] The figures with their titles are as follows: I tabulate them for convenience, and give their attribution to, or sympathy with, the planets and signs of the Zodiac. But they have a certain individuality all their own, and they are governed by special "intelligences" (a higher order of "elemental spirits") whose duty it is to give true answers.[5] I may here interpolate that the mighty Baphomet not only invented a new and superior system, but actually went to the trouble of creating a new hierarchy of demons to subserve it![6] However, here is the ordinary system.

---

[1] [$128 = 2^7$. There are thus 128 figures in a "septagram."]

[2] [Baphomet was Crowley's name as Grand Master X° of the British O.T.O.]

[3] [This work is "Liber 49, Shih I Ch'ien," described in the notice in *The Equinox* III(1) (1919) as "an account of the divine perfection illustrated by the seven-fold permutation of the Dyad"; this paper is not believed extant.]

[4] [Henry Cornelius Agrippa von Nettesheim (1486–1535); his *Three Books of Occult Philosophy, or of Magic* (1531), bk. II, chap. 48, has a brief account of Geomancy, but Crowley's explicit doubt as to the authorship of his reference suggests that he intends the spurious *Fourth Book of Occult Philosophy*, trans. Robert Turner (1655), a posthumous English compilation that relies in part on Agrippa's Latin *Opera* and contains a more detailed explanation from his work *Of Geomancy*. For a useful survey see Agrippa, *Three Books of Occult Philosophy*, ed. Donald Tyson (1993), app. 8; see Works Cited. Many attribution systems exist, and some works (such as Franz Hartmann's *Geomancy* (1889) introduce deliberate "blinds"; Crowley's attributions are closest to those of Agrippa's *Of Geomancy* in the *Fourth Book*, although with four transpositions; for comparative purposes Agrippa's are given beside Crowley's in the table.]

[5] [See the tables of geomantic figures and genii in "Liber Gaias sub figura 96, A Handbook of Geomancy," *The Equinox* I(2) (1909). A prefatory note suggests that this paper introduced "blinds" to prevent abuse of the system, possibly the transpositions discussed above. See also Crowley, *Magick (Book 4, Parts I–IV)*, rev. ed., ed. Hymenæus Beta, chap. 18 ("Concerning Divination") and app. 5; see Works Cited.]

[Geomantic Figure]	[Latin Name]	[English Translation of Name]	[Astrological Attributions Crowley	Agrippa]
⸬	1121	Puer	A Boy	♂ in ♈	♂ in ♈
⸫	1212	Amissio	Loss	♀ in ♉	♀ in ♎
⸬	2212	Albus	White	☿ in ♊	☿ in ♊
⸬	2222	Populus	The People	☽ waxing in ♋	☽ in ♋
⸬	1111	Via	The Way	☽ waning in ♋	☽ in ♋
⸬	2211	Fortuna Major	Greater Fortune	☉ in North Declination in ♌	☉ in ♌
⸬	1122	Fortuna Minor	Lesser Fortune	☉ in South Declination in ♌	☉ in ♌
⸬	2112	Conjunctio	Conjunction	☿ in ♍	☿ in ♍
⸫	1211	Puella	A Girl	♀ in ♎	♀ in ♉
⸬	2122	Rubeus	Red	♂ in ♏	♂ in ♏
⸬	2121	Acquisitio	Gain	♃ in ♐	♃ in ♓
⸬	1221	Carcer	Prison	♄ in ♑	♄ in ♑
⸬	2221	Tristitia	Sorrow	♄ in ♒	♄ in ♒
⸬	1222	Lætitia	Joy	♃ in ♓	♃ in ♐
⸬	2111	Caput Draconis	The Dragon's Head	☊ ♄ ♂	☊ in ♑
⸬	1112	Cauda Draconis	The Dragon's Tail	☋ ♃ ♀	☋ in ♏

In order to work this system, the proper influences are first invoked in a proper manner, and the questioner then takes a pencil that has never been used for any other purpose, and a piece of paper equally pure. He

---

[6] [In holograph annotations to "Liber 96" in his copy of *The Equinox* I(2), Crowley drew sigils in the margins along both sides of the table of geomantic figures and genii that may relate to this; only the sigils survive. However, the reference to a "new system," and the authorship ascription to Baphomet, suggests that Crowley may be continuing to refer to "Liber 49," discussed on p. 100, note 3.]

makes 16 rows of dots at hazard. These are then counted, and their total number is noted. Its meaning is discovered by reference to the book called "Sepher Sephiroth."[1] Each line is then counted and marked as odd or even. These are divided into four sets of four, and these figures are called the Four Mothers. The Four Mothers are then read horizontally, and four more figures called the Four Daughters are thus found. From these eight we form Four Nephews by combining each pair. Now we have twelve figures, which are placed according to a certain secret plan in the twelve Houses of Heaven, as in an ordinary Astrological chart.[2] The Four Nephews are again combined to form Two Witnesses, and these again combine to form One Judge.

The figure is now ready for judgment, and this is the moment which calls forth intuition, and tests the knowledge and experience of the diviner.

I will here state only that problems can be worked out in the greatest detail. First a general question may be asked, and the minor points filled in by subsequent figures. Care must be taken to put the question in such a form that a clear answer is possible, and that ambiguity or even punning is not possible; for the intelligences serve unwillingly, and are always ready to match their wits against yours. Woe to you if you are not as alert as they!

I will conclude this too brief sketch with an actual verifiable example of how this method may be used.

A friend of mine,[3] at that time a chartered accountant practicing in Johannesburg, learnt this science from me, and, being able to devote much time to it, the disciple rapidly outstripped the master. One day he was called in to examine the books of a firm, and, appalled at the size of

---

[1] [A Qabalistic reference dictionary listing Hebrew words by numerical value; see Works Cited under "Liber 500."]

[2] [I.e., "ordinary" by the older system that arranges the houses of a horoscope in a square with twelve divisions. The usual arrangement (and that used by Crowley) is illustrated at right; for other historical house arrangements see J. D. North, *Horoscopes and History* (London: Warburg Institute, 1986), figure 1, p. 2.]

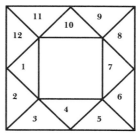

[3] [James Thomas Windram (1877–1939) was an accountant. He was Frater Semper Paratus 6°=5□ A∴A∴ and Mercurius X° of the South African O.T.O.]

the task—for the suspected error might have been anywhere in a number of years—he determined to try Geomancy. He set up a series of figures; and after only three hours went to a particular book, opened it, and put his finger on the falsification he was seeking—a saving of three months' onerous work. This, it is to be understood, is only one of many remarkable successes.

One day it struck him that, living as he was in the centre of gold and diamond fields, he might as well use his powers to discover one. He formulated the question as concerning "mineral wealth"; for he did not mind very much whether he got gold or diamonds! The intelligences directed him to ride out from the city in a certain direction, which he did. Far and fast he rode, and found never a hint of anything to reward his search. At last, toward sunset, he drew rein in despair as a line of low hills sprang into view before him. And then he bethought to him that a certain figure in his divination might be taken to mean "beyond the hills." I will ride another quarter of an hour, he said, for luck. He came to the hills; still no trace of that auriferous quartz outcrop or that blue clay formation which he had hoped to find. On the contrary, in front of him stretched an unbroken plain. I will return, said he, and curse the hour when I first took up Geomancy. But, a pool of water lying a few yards ahead, he decided to give his pony a drink before he turned. The pony refused the water; and at the same moment he perceived that it was fetlock deep in mire, and ready to sink. He dismounted hastily, and dragged the beast from the quagmire. He slipped in doing so; the mud splashed his face, and at that moment he found that it was bitter.

He had discovered the biggest alkali deposit in South Africa! "Mineral wealth," right enough; and today, in spite of the war, he is well on the way to his first million sterling.[1]

---

[1] P.S. He lost it all again through errors in O.T.O. IX° working.

Good Hunting!

AN ESSAY ON THE NATURE OF COMEDY AND TRAGEDY

I

Do what thou wilt shall be the whole of the Law.

> Bye, Baby Bunting!
> Daddy's gone a-hunting ...[1]

Such is the sole stuff of art, as it was the sole occupation of primitive man. Hunting is the one real passion of man. Love, the desire of wealth or power, are only branches of the sport. For it is directly related to the first of all passions, hunger; and it is an exciting sport; it is gambling for the highest of all stakes. Now, art is primarily the celebration of excitement, the record of some stimulus of the soul. Dramatic art, which represents drama, action, consequently concerns itself with hunting—and with nothing else.

When daddy came back with a deer, there was great rejoicing in the tribe. Everyone filled himself with meat; the cockles of his heart grew warm; he began to laugh. You can do the same today with a very hungry man, without the aid of alcohol. This expansive state being clearly associated causally with the killing of the deer, and the sportsman excitedly recounting his exploit, the story itself was food for laughter. And the key of the jest soon discovered itself as contempt for the foolish victim. "What a fine stag he was, how proud and swift! Nothing could catch him, and, if he wished, how sharp were those great branching horns of his! And all the while there was I tracking him with my little flint axe—ha! ha! ha!"

All these points were seen and seized on by the old comedians. They would always accentuate the self-esteem of the victim. They would dress him up as a king or a God, and hunt him down. A still funnier elaboration of the joke was to persuade him that he was the hunter. "Come," say they to Pentheus in *The Bacchæ*,[2] "come, great king, adorn thyself accord-

---

[1] [A nursery rhyme.]

[2] [Euripides, *The Bacchæ*, lines 777–860, paraphrase.]

ing to thy dignity; come, arm thyself, slay these wild creatures!" and aside: "And when we've got him there his own mother shall kill him in her madness, and run about with his head under the impression that it is a lion's!" This further development of humor was doubtless due to Dionysus; even the hungriest man could hardly think that out on mere venison.

I read my *Agamemnon* through the spectacles of Dr. A. W. Verrall,[1] and it seems to me that the play is a comedy. The incident of the carpet is very like adornment of the victim. Agamemnon, however, is not taken in the snare; he does not show "Hubris," but modesty; and this makes the play more serious. Still, no doubt, it ends on the comic note—Ægisthus chuckling over the success of his clever stratagem. This Hubris hated of the Gods is the root of many a proverb. "At the hour of triumph sacrifice the dearest thing thou hast to the Infernal Gods"—the case of the play *Jephthah*.[2] "Beware of the moment of success." Think of Ajax flattered into the madness wherein he kills the sheep—what a superlative jest for the onlooker! Alternative themes lead surely to anticlimax. Consider Abraham's sacrifice—what a typically inartistic ending! The whole passion and beauty of the drama is destroyed by the sneaking subterfuge of the substitution of the ram for the heir of promise.

Let us glance now at the Crucifixion. Here we have comedy in its fullest flower. "Hail, King of the Jews!"[3] Triumphal entry into the capital; robing in purple, crowning in mockery, barbarous murder at the close. The ritual is that of all ancient comedies of initiation, with mere local variations. Now why do not we laugh? They did at the time. "Let us see whether Elias will come to take him down!"[4] "He saved others, himself he could not save."[5] The answer follows easily, and we shall see incidentally why we are a little doubtful as to whether Agamemnon is a comic figure.

When Daddy goes a-hunting he does not always bring home a deer. Sometimes he meets a diplodocus, and does not come home at all. Then, what do the tribe do? They squat and hug their empty bellies. There is no laughter. There is one long wail. There is no food, and the

---

[1] [The Greek scholar Arthur Woolgar Verrall (1851–1912) was professor of classics at Cambridge, where he was the author of *The 'Agamemnon' of Æschylus* (1889); see Works Cited. Jane Ellen Harrison dedicated her *Prolegomena to the Study of Greek Religion* (1903) to him.]

[2] [A dramatic work by Crowley (1898).]

[3] [Matt. 27:29; Mark 15:18; John 19:3.]

[4] [Mark 15:36.]

[5] [Matt. 27:42; Mark 15:31.]

man who used to get it has been eaten alive. This is no joke, no joke at all. Presently the wail becomes articulate; someone recounts the heroic deeds of the dead hunter. How skilful he was! How cunning! How swift and strong! How accurately he swung the axe! And now "he is gone on the mountain, he is lost to the forest!" He died fighting heroically against enormous superiority of force ... and so on. Anyhow, he's dead, and we're without food, and what can we do but weep? It is a tragedy!

Just so; that is the definition of tragedy. The primitives of the next tribe probably are laughing to split their sides. Their hunter has brought in a wild bull, and they are having a glorious time. "And that fool across the valley who fancied himself so at hunting went out after rabbits and got a diplodocus—ha! ha! ha!"

It is all a question of our sympathies. The event described is always the same. Whether it is a tragedy or a comedy depends on the point of view. The *Agamemnon* is a tragedy for the family man; for the young sport who wants to beat him out of his wife and his kingdom, it is a romantic comedy.

So when we come to consider plays about Hecuba and other people that in no wise concern us personally, we judge by our own sympathies, and laugh or cry accordingly. Thus the sympathy of mankind has been secured, in the case of the crucifixion, for the figure of Jesus, so we call the story a tragedy. We have been told to identify him with Everyman, who is doomed to suffer a barbarous death sooner or later. It is the same with the stories of the murders of Osiris and of Hiram.[1]

In other words, man began to think of himself no longer as a hunting animal, but as a victim. In the second stage of human thought, man is the sufferer.[2] Man has begun to fear Nature, to wail over his own fate sym-

---

[1] Observe, dear brother, the hunter's ritual in this later story; the stationing of the hunters, and the way they head off the game in turn.

[2] Compare William James, and his remarks on the once-born and the twice-born. [The American psychologist William James (1842–1910) was the first to examine the psychology of religion. Although the terms "once-born" and "twice-born" were coined by Francis W. Newman, James extends them: "In the religion of the once-born the world is a sort of rectilinear or one-storied affair, whose accounts are kept in one denomination.... Happiness and religious peace consist of living on the plus side of the account. In the religion of the twice-born, on the other hand, the world is a double-storied mystery. Peace cannot be reached by the simple addition of pluses and elimination of minuses from life.... There are two lives, the natural and the spiritual, and we must lose the one before we can participate in the other." *The Varieties of Religious Experience*, Lecture 8; see Works Cited.]

bolically in lamenting the deaths of the great heroes of the past. It no longer seems funny to us to adorn a man as a God, and eat him, for that is just what life is doing to all of us.

To recover the comic spirit, therefore, we must acquire a new view of death.

II

In certain previous essays of the writer it has been pointed out that desire or love must be held to include such phenomena as chemical change.[1] All true acts of love produce or consume energy in some form, [so] that we have explosive disintegrations and violently rapid oxidations which disengage heat, light, electricity, and other forms of matter and of motion—regard them as you please—which are (on the surface) of a different order of Nature to the ingredients of the operation. Similarly, by putting the right pair of featherless bipeds together, there are explosions and emotion, poetry, perhaps spiritual growth, as well as the phenomenon which is obviously of the same order—a baby.

In all such acts, chemical or physiological, there is a true transmutation, therefore, and we may class these things as genuinely partakers of the Ineffable Mystery of Godliness. In mere admixture we do not get this transmutation. Mix hydrogen and oxygen; they remain the same; nothing at all happens. Combine them and you get not only a transformation of the very nature of the molecules, but numerous physical phenomena—flame, heat, moisture—which were not there before.

Now let us take another issue. All conscious, self-willed motion implies life, and, all such motion being accompanied with chemical change and (as Buddha insisted) with the partial disintegration of the individual, we must define life as something quite beyond the crude conception which is usually formed of it. Every true phenomenon, whether it be the hæmoglobin-oxyhæmoglobin-carboxyhæmoglobin cycle in the blood, or the changes in the brain which we call philosophy from a consideration of their effects, may be thought of as a form of copulation, atom seeking atom, and producing molecule, just as woman seeks man and produces offspring. Now every such act of copulation involves the

---

[1] [Crowley seems to refer to *Liber CXI vel Aleph* (1962, 1991), written in the winter of 1917–1918 and completed in the month this essay was published. His later "new" commentary to the first chapter of *Liber AL vel Legis* treats of this theme; cf. Crowley, *The Law is for All*, ed. Louis Wilkinson and Hymenæus Beta (1996). See Works Cited.]

death of the partakers. True, the hydrogen can be recovered from the water; ultimate simplicities are in some sort immortal, but (again we quote Buddha) all complexities perish and are not recoverable in their integrity. We cannot suppose that by recombining the recovered hydrogen and oxygen into water each atom in the original water will find the self-same mate. We cannot recover the father in the child, though we may perceive many traces of him; and the persistence of the father himself is due to the fact that only a minute percentage of his life is used in the production of the child. His quintessence vivifies any amount of other matter and transmutes it to his likeness; this is the Alchemical miracle, to produce some such process in the mineral kingdom. If one possessed the quintessence of gold, the unknown "seed of gold," that which makes gold gold and not silver, it might impregnate other elements and make them grow into its own nature. This at least was the theory evolved by the fathers of chemistry, and (I doubt not) will be the practice of their descendants in a year not distant.

Now, to return, since every copulation may be considered as involving death, we may say (at the risk of appearing to convert an *A* proposition) that every death may be considered as a form of copulation. The chemical changes of disintegration are in no way distinguishable from those of life. We cannot call one set synthesis and the other analysis, even. We merely make a false distinction on account of the fact that our personal prejudices are involved … just as we were in doubt whether to laugh or to cry at the *Agamemnon*.

Now, it is to be noted that certain people take the sexual view of death. To this day the peasants in some parts of Greece regard the death of an individual as his marriage to that deity, Artemis or Aphrodite, to whom he was most devoted during life. Mohammed taught that death was the key to the enjoyment of the *ḥūr al-'ayn*.[1] Even in Christian mysticism we find the death of the saint equivalent to his marriage with the Saviour. We are "waiting for the Bridegroom." In fact, this idea is almost universal in all true religion.[2]

Now, we have no means of telling what occurs in the "soul" at the time of death. Whatever may be the approaches to the pylon, we have no evidence with regard to the Door itself. But we have certain analogies in

---

[1] [The eternal virgins of Paradise (*houris*) promised in the *Qur'ān*.]
[2] Buddhism, an exception, is more a philosophy than a religion.

the experience of mystics. We have the "Dark Night of the Soul" break-ing in the "Dawn of the Celestial Bridal." And we have in physical life an exact counterpart in the fear of Love which is characteristic of the Virgin. This is especially marked in the case of boys. There is an instinctive fear, repulsion and anxiety, which must be overcome before the soul swoons in bliss. Is it racial experience that tells him that love is the twin brother of death? Love and Death are the levers of that universal life which we saw to be the Name of the Universe. Each is an annihilation of an indi-vidual in the interests of universal Energy. Thus, as we have seen in a slightly different shape, when referring to the quintessence of comedy, Love and Death are the sole preoccupation of the artist, whose subject is Life. There is no other real interest, for there is nothing else in which to delight.

If, then, we can take the view that Death is an intense form of Love, in which the individual is permanently destroyed, as he is temporarily destroyed during the act of love, then this Life is universal Joy, a Divine Comedy, whose soul is Laughter. We can even explain the joy of cruelty as a deeper realization of the nature of cruelty, as a piquancy, a sting, in what would otherwise be a detestably sweet wine.

But if we fail to grasp this view, then we are forced to the alternative that Love is only a form of Death. The universe is an abyss of agony. "The mystery of the cruelty of things" is as terrible as Swinburne's "Anactoria" makes it.[1] Everything is sorrow;[2] we are Buddhists, and only in utter cessation is there peace. Buddha himself recognized this clearly enough; his intense distaste for sex is our witness. He saw that it was playing the game of Life to love; it was allowing oneself to be dragged deeper and deeper into the mire of Existence. A monotheism with any perception of the facts of nature—hard nowadays to escape some such perception!—may make its God in the image of the Marquis de Sade. The whole of organic nature is an orgy of murder and lust. There is only one escape from this position; to accept the unity of Love and Death, and to regard Death as mere Delight. Such a realization avoids the snare of Dualism, lays its axe to the root of the problem of the Origin of Evil, and renders Existence possible and desirable for the thinker as well as for the sensualist.

---

[1] [For "Anactoria" see *The Poems of Charles Algernon Swinburne* (1905). See Works Cited.]

[2] [The first "noble truth" of Buddhism.]

III

To the blessed ones who have accepted the Law of Thelema these words will hardly have been necessary. The doctrine is plainly stated in *The Book of the Law.*

> For I am divided for love's sake, for the chance of union.
>   This is the creation of the world, that the pain of division is as nothing, and the joy of dissolution all.

> Now let it be understood: If the body of the King dissolve, he shall remain in pure ecstasy for ever.

> Aye! feast! rejoice! there is no dread hereafter. There is the dissolution, and eternal ecstasy in the kisses of Nu.

> Thrill with the joy of life & death! Ah! thy death shall be lovely: whoso seeth it shall be glad. Thy death shall be the seal of the promise of our agelong love.

> Strive ever to more! and if thou art truly mine—and doubt it not, an if thou art ever joyous!—death is the crown of all.[1]

This, then, is the will of the Universe; Life eternal and universal, not petty, individual and transient; Life of which we are only conscious when in trance; Life whose consciousness is gained perfectly and permanently by the adept in virtue of his trance in proportion as he becomes fixed therein and makes his daily life partake thereof; Life that works inexorably and deliciously through Love and Death, which are Love. And this is expressed simply, succinctly, perfectly, in that transcendent phrase, the greeting wherewith we close our writings:

> Love is the law, love under will.

Note

Taking a few plays at random, we see in every one the description of a hunting. Note that the strongest dramas are those in which the hunt is keenest. Where the hunting interest is weak or masked, the play becomes frivolous and lacking in the stuff of greatness.[2]

---

[1] [*Liber Legis* I:29-30, II:21, 44, 66, 72.]

[2] [This list was rearranged slightly, sorting the titles by author. See Works Cited for sources. See also Crowley, *Golden Twigs*, ed. Martin P. Starr (1988), a collection of mythological short stories derived from Sir J. G. Frazer's *The Golden Bough*.]

[Sophocles]

Ajax—The hunting of Ajax by Ulysses.

Œdipus [*Rex*]—Œdipus by Fate. *Karma* is very frequently taken for the hunter. The man's being hunted by himself is particularly funny!

[Æschylus]

Agamemnon—Agamemnon by Ægisthus.

Orestes trilogy—Orestes by Fate. [The trilogy includes *Agamemnon*, q.v.]

[Euripides]

Bacchæ—Pentheus by Dionysus.

[William Shakespeare]

Hamlet—Claudius by Hamlet. Here the motive is weakly carried out, and so the play is only interesting for the revelation of Hamlet's soul.

[*King*] *Lear*—Lear by Madness.

Macbeth—Macbeth by his conscience, or by the Witches.

Othello—Othello by Iago.

Twelfth Night—The Duke by Viola (note hunter's disguise).

As You Like It—Orlando by Rosalind (ditto).

Romeo and Juliet—Love by Heredity.

Coriolanus—Coriolanus by the mob-spirit.

Julius Cæsar—Cæsar by Cassius.

[Henrik Ibsen]

Ghosts—Oswald by Heredity.

Hedda Gabler—Hedda by Breck.

Rosmersholm—Rosmer and Rebecca by the wife's ghost.

A Doll's House—Nora by her nascent individuality. (The lack of personal struggle makes this a weak, silly play.)

The Master Builder—The Builder by Hilda.

An Enemy of Society [*An Enemy of the People*]—Society by Stockmann. (He conquers it, so this is a comedy.)

Brand—Brand by the Hawk.

Peer Gynt—Peer Gynt by Solveig. (Note the way she lurks silent throughout the play. Other exciting episodes are all huntings.)

[Aleister Crowley]

Mortadello—Mortadello by Monica. (Note disguise at banquet.)

Snowstorm—Nerissa by Eric; Eric by Maud. (Observe hunters' disguises again.)

The Scorpion—Laylah by Rinaldo; their love by the Scorpion. (This is a romance, and neither comedy nor tragedy in the best sense.)

Household Gods—Crassus by Alicia. (Note supreme disguise.)

The Mother's Tragedy—Cora by *karma*.

The Fatal Force—Ratoum by S'afi (disguise again).

Jephthah—Jephthah by Jared. (Crude and undeveloped form of the idea.)

The World's Tragedy—Fate by Alexander.

The Blind Prophet—The Prophet (individual life) by Universal Life.

The Argonauts—Jason by Ares.

Adonis—Adonis by Psyche.

[Lord Dunsany]

A Night in an Inn—The Thieves by the Idol.

The Gods of the Mountain—The Beggars by the Gods.

[Algernon Charles Swinburne]

Atalanta in Calydon—Meleager by Circumstance. (Here the hunter is not personified, and so the play is weak. But note the comedy of the hunter hunted.)

Eulogium upon Jeanne d'Arc

JEANNE! Eternally as now named excellent, robed of beatitudes, eleutherian, royally throned, found only supreme to excite reverence, how dare I name thee?[1] Hail, immaculate love and religion incarnate, one name not to be surpassed in the long story of heroism, virtue and grace that deify the word Woman.[2]

Now blessed above all trees be the olive beneath whose shadow thou wast nurtured! A mountain village, a lonely hut; no palace gleaming above the splendours of a mighty city; the Spirit of Liberty knows not these bonds. The sky is its dome; the sun its lamp; the flowers its tapestries.

JEANNE, thou was born with the Spring; and July set its seal of gold upon thy forehead. The sun himself coloured thy hair; and Mars and Venus blended their rays to gild thine eyes. Fearless and free wast thou, and knewest not thy destiny. For when thou wast come to hours of knowledge, thou didst find thy sacred land in the power of a monster. Monstrous and terrible, threatening hell's envy, with fire of Satan, tyrannous, evil, remorseless.[3] Beneath the holy mountain, the fair springs, fringed with their ashen aspens, were befouled. Sorrowfully brooding, thou didst seek light and life and liberty and love—not upon earth but in

---

[1] [The French heroine and mystic Jeanne d'Arc (St. Joan of Arc, c. 1412–1431) is known as the "Maid of Orléans" for her role in raising the seige of that city. A mystic since childhood, she had visions urging her to deliver France from English occupation. She rallied the French forces and persuaded Charles VII to be crowned, restoring the French monarchy and its sovereignty. She was tried for witchcraft and heresy by an ecclesiastical court and burnt at the stake. The Roman Catholic Church canonized her in 1920. Most of this sentence is an anagram for "Jeanne Robert Foster," Crowley's lover during this period.]

[2] [The beginning of this sentence spells out "Hilarion," Jeanne Robert Foster's magical motto in the A∴A∴.]

[3] [This sentence spells out "Matthew Foster," Jeanne Robert Foster's elderly husband and Crowley's rival.]

the heavens! Thou didst call, and the Lord answered thee, a Lord eternal, invisible, strong tower, eternal refuge, crowned, radiant, omnipotent, white lion, eternal youth![1]

The snowy summits of the Alps, witnesses of God's will that man be free, rejoiced as on that glorious morning of July, the rod of the Divine Will was laid upon thee first. It penetrated all thy being, that glowed and quickened as the first outpourings of the Holy Spirit flooded thee. From such initiation there is no escape, no turning-back; so holy an hour is the Fiat of the Fate of the Chosen of the Lord Most High.

Thus vision after vision came upon thee; Saint Francis saw the heavens no clearer; the angels themselves surprised thee not, folding their wings upon their faces before the Glory of the Lord. Soon or late, thou must take up thy burden; the monster must be slain; the fair land must be freed.

And so didst thou, as it was given thee to do. Victory sat upon thine helm; the land was free.

I have no heart to say more. Must it ever be thus that treason and superstition and tyranny should have force to destroy the vehicle of the Spirit of Freedom? Nay, it shall not be so. America, answer it!

Whether in this great city,[2] where the Atlantic thunders, the vision come upon us, or in Chicago where the wide waste of Michigan is the silence of the tameless waters, or in Buffalo where Niagara roars his battle-slogan, or where the pines of Oregon answer the palms of California, "Skyward to sun and light" (yea! or even in Canada, from Erie to Vancouver), let it inspire us to preserve and to enlarge that liberty—of which thou, Jeanne, wast the protagonist of thine age.

This wreath of green and white speak to us of freedom and of purity; a talisman consecrated by almighty power; a symbol of the victory she won for us not only over tyranny, but over time. And these letters of crimson, be they our sacrifice, that man should no more have to die—as did this maid—for what should be his heritage unchallenged.

JEANNE, golden rose of earth, white lily of heaven, Jeanne, true sister and true bride of every poet's and every free man's heart, I salute thee. I bid thee not farewell; nay, be thou ever with me till the hour of death bring me to that greater freedom that flowers not upon earth.

---

[1] [The initial letters of part of this sentence spell out "Aleister Crowley."]
[2] [New York City.]

William Blake

BY A MENTAL TRAVELLER

The Road of Excess, said William Blake,
    To the Palace of Wisdom leads one.
Open a bottle, for Wisdom's sake!
    And I am the boy that needs one!
It's the only possible step to take—
Open a bottle for Mister Blake! [1]

Verily, Omar Khayyám was not the first, nor Alcofribas Nasier the last, of the Angelical Doctors of the Theological Schools of Dionysus.[2] The Word of the Oracle was in the beginning, is now, and ever shall be, this most arcane monosyllable of the Adepts: TRINC.[3] For Dionysus is he whose sire is Zeus made manifest to Earth in the form of golden rain from Heaven; and the child, threatened by the malice of Respectability, conceals himself beneath the paternal purple, within that hollow reed wherein Prometheus brought down Fire from Olympus. This reed is also that of Pan; and it is Aaron's Rod that budded, the Sacred Lance of Parzival, the Sword that pruned the vine of John the Baptist, filling the charger of Herod with his perfumed and prophetic blood.

It is Charles Baudelaire who urges us: "One must be always drunk,"[4] adding this scholion, that the means of intoxication may be absinthe for one and music for another. Each man must discover for himself the method most suitable in his own case whereby he may attain to cry "It is finished,"[5] so that the Veil of the Temple may be rent from the top to the

---

[1] ["The Moralist," in Crowley, *Temperance: A Tract for the Times* (1939). The first two lines paraphrase Blake's "Marriage of Heaven and Hell." See Works Cited.]

[2] [Omar Khayyám (d. 1123) was a Persian astronomer and poet, best known for his *Rubáiyát*. Alcofribas Nasier is an anagram-pseudonym of François Rabelais.]

[3] [See the concluding chapters of Rabelais' *Gargantua and Pantagruel*, where the High Priestess Bacbuc reveals the mystery of TRINC; see also Crowley's *Liber CXI vel Aleph* and "The Antecedents of Thelema," p. 162 infra.]

[4] [This quotation is from Crowley's own translation of Charles Baudelaire's *Little Poems in Prose*, chap. 33, "Intoxicate Yourself!" See Works Cited.]

bottom.[1] Hark! this is the moment of the death of the Man-God to his earthly life, the birth of the God-Man to Life immortal. Destroy this temple, and within three days I will raise it up—a Temple not made with hands, Eternal in the Heavens![2]

Because "Every thing that lives is holy,"[3] and because the Mystery of Ungodliness consists simply in the fact that there is a mystery at all before the face of Truth; therefore a "genius" may be defined as one who is able to express the genius—the *daimon* of Socrates, the *augœides*, *ādibuddha*, the "Holy Guardian Angel" of a Man—which is in him.[4] "I am the flame that burns in every heart of man, and in the core of every star."[5] It is theoretically possible for all of us to split the valve of our muddy, weed-covered, calcareous husk, and reveal the Pearl of Great Price which we secrete.[6] The common failure of mankind to do so is due to the fear of exposing to destruction that slimy succulent life of humanity which we foolishly seek to preserve, forgetting that Death the Oysterman will surely wedge his steel in our shell, that the harlot Babalon,[7] on whose forehead is written "Mystery,"[8] may devour us!

For this cause, when first the Candidate for Initiation is restored to Light for a moment, his eyesight tells him of a dreadful God, sable and scarlet, and, thunder to that levin,[9] he hears the words of awe

> Fear is failure, and the forerunner of failure: be thou therefore without fear, for in the heart of the coward Virtue abideth not. Pass thou on![10]

Instantly the hoodwink is replaced; instantly silence swoops like an hawk upon a sparrow; instantly he is dragged fiercely forward through the voiceless darkness ——

---

[5] [Greek τετέλεσται ; see John 19:30. See also *Liber 418*, 9th Æthyr.]

[1] [Matt. 27:51; Mark 15:38.]

[2] [John 2:19; Mark 14:58; II Cor. 5:1.]

[3] [Blake, "The Marriage of Heaven and Hell"; see Works Cited.]

[4] [*Augoeides* (Grk., αὐγοειδής), a term from *De Mysteriis* by Iamblicus of Apamea (d. c. 330 CE) meaning "of the nature of light." In Sanskrit *ādi-buddha* has the sense of "first [i.e., promordial] Buddha." See *Book 4*, Part III, chap. 2.]

[5] [*Liber AL* II:6.]

[6] [Matt. 13:46.]

[7] [See *Liber 418*, 12th Æthyr, and "Liber 156."]

[8] [See Rev. 17:5.]

[9] [An archiac word for lightning.]

[10][From the Neophyte initiation ceremony of the Golden Dawn, *The Temple of Solomon the King*, in *The Equinox* I(3) (1910).]

It is not given to many of the sons of men to tear the bandage from their brows with ruthless rage, demanding to face the Reality of the Universe, even should they have succeeded in striking the fetters from their hands and feet. Few know, will, dare, to force an Oracle from the Silence, even though the Speech of the Sphinx be the one Word of Power to avail them in their souls' sore need. Yet the Vision shews always ΘΕΛΗΜΑ, and the Voice says always: TRINC.

Some there are who achieve "genius." A man there may be who hath wrought his own Nothung,[1] hath smitten on the spear of Wotan, and with his own right arm hath gotten himself the victory, passing through Loki's fires to the Virgin Valkyrie of the World, his own immaculate Soul. But the natural "genius" is one to whom that fatuous circle is congenitally apparent as phantasmal, and by whom it is more or less easily dissoluble at the will of either party.

The Universe being a coherent whole, each item thereof is equal and opposite to the sum of the remainder. The corollary is obvious: "Every number is infinite; there is no difference."[2] So also: "Every man and every woman is a star."[3]

Anglo-Saxon hypocrisy has charms which only the most deplorable lack of taste would care to criticize; but historians are notoriously defective in the sense of propriety. They have abused their privileges, in the present issue, by observing that the Little English matrimonial conventions which support the Equilibrium of the Solar System hoped to conceal the illuminating fact—the devastating fact—that William Blake was an O'Neil.[4] The artists' curious devotion to places with such names as Felpham,[5] and his attempted identification of London with Jerusalem—a task nobly seconded and ably executed in later days on different lines—mask still more indecipherably the Celtic face of him. The soul of Eire is

---

[1] [The name of the sword in Richard Wagner's *Siegfried*.]

[2] [*Liber AL* I:4.]

[3] [*Liber AL* I:3.]

[4] [Crowley claimed Irish extraction and was passionately pro-Celtic, and accepted the claim of E. J. Ellis and W. B. Yeats for Blake's Irish origins: "James Blake, or, as he was called in childhood, James O'Neil, the father of the poet, was of Irish extraction. John O'Neil, James' father, had got into debt and difficulties in his own country. He married Ellen Blake … at Rathmines, Dublin, and took her name." *The Works of William Blake* (1893), vol. I, pp. 2–3. Arthur Symons soundly refuted this in *William Blake* (1907), pp. 23–26; see Works Cited.]

[5] [The coastal village in Sussex where Blake lived for three years in the employ of William Hayley; this was his only period of residence outside London.]

visible only in those eyes like coals of fire of the Most High, and her voice in the melancholy yet enraptured melody of that mystical mouth, that vivid, that virginal vessel of Musick!

It is not the traditional Catholic Ecstasy of the Isle of the Saints that quickens his pulse, but the almost mechanical rhapsodies of a Teutonic-Scandinavian visionary, which form the intellectual lens of his manifestation in art.

His is nevertheless the most authentically Gælic spirit in history, the more essentially so, it may be, for the very reason that it is emancipated so completely from the formal warrants of ethnology; the absence of racial stigmata guarantees the noumenal validity no less of its creative Wisdom than of its transmissive Innocence.

Like all true artists, William Blake is a Pantheist.[1] To him the Holy Ghost is immanent in the All, equally in its every part. We find him therefore a partisan of the legendary Jesus who rebuked the exclusiveness and restrictions of the Pharisees, and of the Miltonic Satan who fulminates against the same qualities as they appear in Christianity. He is, in brief, the Master of the Temple who is vowed to understand, to love, to control, and to harmonize all things; finally "to interpret every phenomenon as a particular dealing of God with his soul."[2] His only opponents are the "Brothers of the Left-Hand Path," that is, the representatives of the spirit that resists change, defies "love under will",[3] and endeavours to shut itself out from the operation of the universal flux; that seeks to make a difference "between any one thing & any other thing", whereby "cometh hurt."[4] (How admirable is the choice of this word "hurt," from *heurter*, "to jostle"!) That is the only evil, the only illusion; the conflict

---

[1] [Pantheism in this context refers to a theological school that holds that God is the universe. Crowley also alludes to immanence, a related doctrine sometimes characterized as more spiritual than pantheism, which some argue implies materialism. The French mediæval theologian Amalric of Bèna (d. 1206) was a pantheist, and the Amalricans (a sect that grew up after his death) rejected transubstantiation (as God was already present in the sacraments), advocated knowledge of nature over faith, and denied the absolute reality of good and evil.]

[2] [This is a paraphrase of part of the A∴A∴ Oath of the Abyss. See "Liber 860, John St. John," *The Equinox* I(1), supplement, pp. 10–11 and *Eight Lectures on Yoga*, part II, lecture 1, §5. For an account of the A∴A∴ Grade of Magister Templi see "One Star in Sight"; see Works Cited.]

[3] [*Liber AL* I:57.]

[4] [*Liber AL* I:22.]

and division between any two things which refuse to recognize their identity, to assert it and enjoy it by means of "love under will."

The comprehension of this attitude, intuitively certain as it was in him, is the Master-Key to his Art. He has been neglected abominably for his merits, and praised undiscerningly for his defects. Neither Swinburne nor Yeats, still less the chorus of caterwauling critics which have beset him in this present century, have been capable of the Master's simplicity; or, perceiving it from Pisgah, have been content to leave it as it is.[1] Yet all his serious poems are variations on this Theme, and all his symbolic pictures hieroglyphs of this Arcanum!

Whether he is with the burning Tyger in the forests of the night, or in the Crystal Cabinet, or with Sultan-Jesus in the Porch of Pythagoras, his sublimely single Experience is the Identity of Contraries.

In him, from the beginning, the barrier between the conscious and Unconscious is tenuous—almost too tenuous, for the surge of the latter washes over into the former so mightily that the intellectual machinery of his mind was never brought to perfection. His natural tendency to skepticism saves him indeed from the serfdom of gross sectarianism in its more fatal forms, but there are times when one cannot but feel irritated at his insistence on a symbolism which does not even possess, like that of the Hebrew Qabalah, a traditional instrument of interpretation. It may well be, of course, that the abominable crime of the dastard who destroyed the bulk of Blake's manuscripts was successful to the extent of depriving us of some general key to his formal modes of thought.[2] We are aware indeed that the Tree of Life in the Chokmah Nesethrah[3] framed the code of his thought in some respects, that the ideas of Emanuel Swedenborg[4] dominated his early development, and that the full fruit of his genius was ripened by the Sun of the Fraternity A∴A∴, although the secrecy to which he was pledged by that Holy Order forbade him to employ Its symbols openly or even organically. There is also the influence of the more mystical sections of the Bible, interpreted skeptically

---

[1] [See Deut. 3:27.]

[2] [Frederick Tatham.]

[3] [Hebrew נסתרה חכמה, "the secret wisdom," a name for the Holy Qabalah.]

[4] [Emanuel Swedenborg (1688–1772) was a Swedish scientific polymath and visionary theologian whose *Arcana Cœlestia* (1749–56) emphasized the allegorical and symbolic interpretation of the Bible, and denied the Trinitarian doctrine of Jesus Christ as the Son in favor of a humanistic interpretation. He spent his last years in London, where the New Church was founded around 1787.]

and diabolically. This method is decidedly untidy and dangerous, owing to the absence of any philosophical unity in the divers books of that heterogeneous encyclopedia of unscientific material.

The spontaneity of Blake's genius is thus, for ourselves, his most serious defect. It is necessary to build the Temple of Intellect with extreme accuracy before it is safe to invoke the Holy Spirit to indwell its sanctuary.

What then is the supreme significance of the work of the Master? It is, to speak plainly, absurd to pretend that his existing remains are in themselves so super-excellent and unique either for matter or for form. They are unfinished on the one hand, and in ruins on the other. Many of his ideas are totally unintelligible to us; others appear mere fads. There is no single masterpiece to which we can point as supremely perfect, as satisfying any of our deepest instincts to the uttermost. It is the existence of the man himself which compels us. For he is "a man of like passions as we are," exercising two arts with abundant ability; yet his subject-matter is not the Universe of the common tailless primate, chief of the mammals and placental amniotes. His Reality is that of the philosopher, but it is an object of direct sense-perception. Instead of proclaiming the actuality of the "invisible world," and proving it by syllogisms, he relies upon the direct appeal to sense: "I see it." The man who does not "believe in fairies" is not an unphilosophical man, but a man with cataract. Varley tells us that Blake, asked to sketch Edward III or some such historical character, "as he exists in the other world," might have to wait for the model to take the pose.[1] Once, when he was drawing Corinna the Theban, Isis of Corinth[2] stepped in front of her and insisted on her portrait being executed before allowing the completion of the other.[3]

---

[1] [John Varley (1778-1843) was an English painter of watercolor landscapes and a friend of Blake's for some nine years. The incident cited involved Edward I.]

[2] [According to Varley's account, the interloper was not Isis but Lais the courtesan: "with the impudence which is part of her profession, she stept in between Blake and Corinna, and he was obliged to paint her to get her away." See Cunningham, *Lives of the Most Eminent British Painters and Sculptors* (1831), ii, pp. 145-8.]

[3] There seems no valid reason for interpreting this as a mere matter of mental concentration or an "imaginary" form. Hamilton's Law of Parsimony forbids this to any observers who have practical acquaintance with the Astral Plane. [The law of parsimony relates to "Ockham's Razor," that the simplest explanation of the facts tends to be true. The Scottish philosopher and historian Sir William Hamilton (1788-1856) applied it to thought, emphasizing that knowledge is relative and only attained with reference to known properties.]

To us Blake is therefore rather the great man of science than the artist in idea or in form. He demonstrated an extension of human faculties no less than did Röntgen and Bell.[1] The objectivity of his visions, the degree of validity of his clairaudience, the interpretation of his statements from an ontological point of view: these are minor matters. What is important is the fact that he himself took all that he saw and heard *au pied de la lettre*[2] without losing touch with the world of the man in the street. He was not hallucinated in the sense in which the alienist[3] uses the word; for his "other world," while interpenetrating that of ordinary sense-perception, did not supplant it or even distort it. His conversations with Elijah did not interrupt his communications with his earthly friends. He strove to discover the laws of the spiritual world and to measure its relations with the material world, as a physicist should; and the reality of that did not diminish, but increase, that of this, any more than the establishment of the electromagnetic properties of steel makes it any less fit to forge into a sword.

Every new Christ demands a John Baptist; every Renaissance is preceded by its proper prophet. This prophet is commonly himself an artist—Elias Artista, as Paracelsus calls him—of pantomorphous achievement.[4] Thus the Child born at that Renaissance of French art which

---

[1] [The German physicist Wilhelm Conrad Röntgen (1845–1923) discovered x-rays. Alexander Graham Bell (1847–1922) invented the telephone.]

[2] [French, "at the foot of the letter," or literally.]

[3] [An obsolete word for a psychiatrist.]

[4] [In his treatise on minerals, Paracelsus gives a personified Elias Artista with a prophetic and eschatological connotation: "God revealed lesser things, but the most important thing is still wrapped in darkness, and will remain so until the coming of Elias Artista," trans. Adam McLean (personal communication); A.E. Waite has a variant (giving "Elias the Artist") in *The Hermetic and Alchemical Writings of Paracelsus* (1894), vol. I, p. 27. This theme recurs in the literature of alchemy, giving variants of a Biblical interpretation concerning Elias (the prophet Elijah) appearing before the world's end. A technical definition of *Elias artista* attributed to Von Helmont is given in W.-E. Peuchert's glossary to Paracelsus' *Werke*, vol. 5 (1968): "the *sal artis* which enhances the color [tinge, i.e. *tinctura*] in the Gold and Silver." This was specified by Paracelsus as the prerequisite to the preparation of the *tinctura*, the final stage of the Great Work; the *sal artis* is "like the *rebis*—the bisexual creature—which transmutes silver and other metals into gold; it 'tinges,' i.e., it transforms the body, removing its harmful parts, its crudity, its incompleteness, and transforms everything into a pure, noble, and indestructible being." Paracelsus, *Selected Writings*, ed. J. Jacobi, trans. N. Guterman (1951), p. 148. See also I Kings 17, where Elijah is the lord of rain and dew.]

found twin sister in our own Pre-Raphaelite movement was brought into the light by that successor of Merlin, Alphonse Louis Constant, or (as he chose to translate his name) Éliphas Lévi Zahed.[1] This great, neglected, misinterpreted man was not only the most famous magician of his generation, but a writer whose prose would be recognized as worthy of Apollo but for the oracular darkness with which he veiled his utterance. The Israelites did not comprehend the Sinaitic glooms and splendours of Moses; they continued to adore the golden Calf; but they went forward to the Promised Land. So also Lévi was a curious draughtsman, not for the sake of the work, but as a medium for his ideas. "Maker of hieroglyphs" were a better term. But his supreme importance to us is that in saying—two generations ago!—"a fine style is an aureole of holiness,"[2] he made Baudelaire, Verlaine, Swinburne, Manet, Whistler[3] *et hoc genus omne*[4] possible in a world which had neglected manner for matter.

The Italian Renaissance had similarly its own prophets. Luther, Andrea, and—*precipue*[5]—Pope Alexander VI stood Satanfathers to that Child.[6] Rabelais, once more, laid down the philosophical principles which determined the destiny of Shakespeare in literature and Bacon in science.[7] We find the inscrutable shadow of Maximinus looming behind

---

[1] [For Éliphas Lévi see p. 18, note 1. Crowley seems to refer to the French Symbolists, who considered the Pre-Raphaelites to be their æsthetic precursors.]

[2] [Lévi, *The Key of the Mysteries*, trans. Crowley, in *The Equinox* I(10) (1913), special supplement, ch. III, p. 191; see Works Cited.]

[3] [For Baudelaire and Verlaine see p. 20, note 1. The English poet and writer Algernon Charles Swinburne (1837-1909) was a major influence on Crowley, and first brought Blake to wide attention. Edouard Manet (1832-1883) was a French painter. James Abbot McNeill Whistler (1834-1903) was an American-born painter who lived in England.]

[4] [Latin, "and all this kind."]

[5] [Latin (mediæval), "especially, particularly, chiefly."]

[6] ["Satanfathers" is a pun on "godfathers." Pope Alexander VI was Roderic Borgia (1431-1503), who weakened the Roman Catholic Church's hold on Europe from within. For Andrea see p. 65, note 3. Martin Luther (1483-1546) was a German Protestant theologian and founder of the Lutheran Church. Crowley's thesis seems to be that they inaugurated the Reformation—Luther openly through the Protestant movement, and Andrea secretly through the Rosicrucian movement.]

[7] [Sir Francis Bacon, Baron Verulam (1561-1626) was an English lawyer, scientist and philosopher.]

Julian,[1] that of Weishaupt whispering wisdom to the revolutionary spirit which culminated in '48.[2] Thus then stands the terrific Titan, Blake, as Hierophant of those Mysteries whose Neophytes were Coleridge, Shelley, Keats, Byron, even Wordsworth.[3] For he came at the end of that Eighteenth Century of artificiality and arrogance which, while indeed it had ground into powder the false gods, had left the people prone before profaned and crownless pedestals. The *Zeitgeist*[4] appears simultaneously in Protean phases to innumerable individuals, each of whom perceives but one facet. They need not know their prophet, or communicate consciously with each other, in order to fulfil the Word of the Lord. But the Pantheism of William Blake created the comet of Byron, the evening star of Poe, the sun of Shelley, and the moon of Keats. He is responsible equally for *Kubla Khan* and for the "Intimations of Immortality";[5] for it is he whose attitude to life made transcendentalism the formula of Art, whose magical gesture destroyed the god of the Firmament Shu, or Zeus, whose strength had sundered Seb from Nuit. With the fall of Jehovah the heavens fell; so (did not the proverb tell us?) we were able to catch skylarks![6]

It was the Swinburne who wrote the pantheistic pæan "Hertha," and announced the antinomian atonement, the formula of "Salvation by Sin," that discovered the Daimon Blake.[7] It was the Yeats who wrote *The Tables of the Law* and other secret books, proclaiming fearfully the dispensation of the Holy Ghost, so fearfully that he suppressed them, that analyzed the mighty seer who talked with Satan and Elijah as familiar

---

[1] [The Roman Emperors Julian (Flavius Claudius Julianus, called "the Apostate," c. 331–363 CE) and Maximinus (Galerius Valerius Maximinus, d. 313 CE) opposed Christianity and restored official paganism in the Roman Empire.]

[2] [Adam Weishaupt (1748–1811), professor of law at the University of Ingoldstadt, philosopher, political theorist, and founder of the Order of Illuminati of Bavaria. Crowley refers to the widespread European revolutions of 1848.]

[3] [These are all well-known English poets. Coleridge and Wordsworth transformed English poetry with their *Lyrical Poems* (1798).]

[4] [German, "spirit of the age."]

[5] [Samuel Taylor Coleridge, *Kubla Khan* (1816) and William Wordsworth, *Ode: Intimations of Immortality* (1903); see Works Cited.]

[6] [The traditional proverb is that if the sky falls, we shall catch larks.]

[7] [Algernon Charles Swinburne, *William Blake: A Critical Essay* (1868). For "Hertha" see *The Poems of Charles Algernon Swinburne* (1905). See Works Cited.]

friends.[1] But the dull world has failed to grasp the hilt of this atrocious *yataghan*.[2] We have sleepily acquiesced in Blake as a craftsman in words and forms; we have overpraised him idly for the qualities that he would himself have scorned to claim, being in truth unimportant to him, and of secondary value to the world.

The Unconscious surged furiously through the frail dyke of his spiritual diaphragm, and expressed itself in terms which are for the most part utterly inadequate, incomplete, unpolished, and unintelligible. As a technician, Blake was overweighted by the omniscience of his omnipresence. In him the Idea was too portentous; the wizard could not control the tempest evoked by his enchantments; his command of Form was shaken by the energy of his enthusiasm. There is in fact no Work of his extant to which we can point with serene confidence, and say: *Ecce Homo*![3] What can we put against the "Ode to Psyche," the "Ancient Mariner," *Prometheus Unbound*, or even *The Monk*?[4] We stultify ourselves, and blaspheme Blake, when we emphasize his attainment as an artist. What went ye out into the wilderness for to see? A prophet, and more than a prophet. Otherwise, he is but a reed, albeit the reed of Pan, shaken by the wind, the wind of the Spirit of Pan![5]

There has been at no time any true critical genius of the first rank in England; the national character is fatal to its development.[6] We must be always praising away, and blaming *à propos de bottes*.[7] As a tragedian, Shakespeare was the brain of the barnstormers of the Surrey Side;[8] as a

---

[1] [William Butler Yeats, *The Tables of the Law: The Adoration of the Magi* (1897); in 1893 Yeats co-edited the first collected works of Blake, as discussed in note 4 on p. 117. See Works Cited.]

[2] [Turkish; a hiltless sabre with a double-curved blade.]

[3] [Latin, "behold the man!" See John 19:5.]

[4] [John Keats, "To Psyche," in *Lamia and Other Poems* (1820); Samuel Taylor Coleridge, "The Rime of the Ancient Mariner," in *Lyrical Ballads* (1798); Percy Bysshe Shelley, *Prometheus Unbound* (1820); Matthew Gregory Lewis, *Ambrosia, or the Monk* (1795). See Works Cited.]

[5] [See Matt 11:7,9; Luke 7:24,26.]

[6] Arthur Machen in *Hieroglyphics* is our first stirring. [See Works Cited. Crowley considered Machen "one of the most original and excellent minds of England."]

[7] [French, literally "speaking of boots," i.e., without regard for the subject.]

[8] [I.e., of the Thames.]

theologian, Milton was a superstitious pedant;[1] yet we concur in the verdict of the "Chorus of Camberwell Costermongers" and the "Consistory of Cold Boiled Calvinists."

But—shall not the judge of the whole Earth do right?[2] Assuredly; and his name is Perspective, graduate of the devil's school whose presiding genius is the Muse of History. The time has come for the children of Wisdom to justify their mother:[3] we can see the members of this Revolutionary group in their true aspect as antagonists of the atrophying influence of the "glories" of George the Third,[4] exactly as Swinburne and Whistler were antitoxins to the sleeping-sickness of Victorian complacency.

No task is more important to the philosopher than this identification of the *Zeitgeist* through inspection of the Coat of Many Colours which he wears; we can place the men of genius of a period as we can place the elements in the spectrum. Our analysis of the galaxy which burst out so suddenly and spontaneously nearly a century and a half ago—though it seem to us as yesterday—nay! as yesterday, today, and forever!—shows the Light of William Blake as almost wholly in the ultraviolet. He is the highest and holiest vibration of that Light; but for this very reason, he is not wholly appreciable by our optical apparatus as human beings. He operated obscure chemical changes in the soul of the epoch; we wrong him when we try to assign to him definite lines in the blue, green, or orange. But without the invisible higher vibrations there can be no manifestation of those visible lower vibrations which we perceive as Art, still less of those sombre and viewless tremors beyond the red which we know only as religious and political revolution. As a reformer, in the vulgar sense of the word, we may call Blake negligible; as an artist, in the technical sense of the word, we may call him imperfect; but as a spiritual current of the highest potential we must call him absolute. The "limit velocity" is that of the Light of the Unconscious which initiated William Blake.

---

[1] [The English poet John Milton (1608–1674) was a Puritan who expressed his unconventional religious beliefs in works such as *Paradise Lost* (1667). Milton was a primary influence on Blake, who illustrated several of his works.]

[2] [Genesis 18:25.]

[3] [See Matt. 11:19; Luke 7:35.]

[4] [Blake's radical political views included support for the American Revolution and opposition to the British monarchy, then headed by King George III.]

On the Education of Children

I

Each child must develop its own Individuality, and Will, disregarding alien Ideals.

At Cefalù's Abbey of Thelema its resources and originality are matched against divers environments.

It is confronted with such problems as swimming, climbing, housework, and left to solve them in its own way.

Its subconsciousness is impressed by reading literary masterpieces, which are left to infiltrate its mind automatically without selective stress or asking conscious comprehension.

Nothing is taught except How to think for oneself.

It is treated as a responsible and independent being, encouraged in self-reliance, and respected for self-assertion.

II

Education is assisting a soul to express itself. Every child should be presented with all possible problems and allowed to register its own reactions; it should be made to face all contingencies in turn until it overcomes each successfully.

Its mind must not be influenced, but only offered all kinds of nourishment. Its innate qualities will enable it to select the food proper to its nature.

Respect its individuality! Submit all life for its inspection, without comment.

Truth teaches understanding, freedom develops will, experience confers resourcefulness, independence inspires self-confidence. Thereby success becomes certain.

III

Every child is God of its own Universe. Education develops control thereof.

It must be taught nothing except how to govern its environment. Truth is the first condition; it must behold all facts scientifically.

Courage, the second; it must grapple all facts resolutely.

Organization, the third; it must integrate impressions and ordinances.

It must be allowed absolute authority over its reactions, but its tendency to deceive itself or evade actuality must be cauterized by insistent confrontation with the repugnant realities.

It must know cloudlessly, dare dauntlessly, will integrally, and keep silence sublimely.

IV

Education fits individuals to encounter environment.

From infancy children should face facts, unadulterated by explanations.

Let them think and act for themselves; let their innate integrity initiate itself!

Make them explore all life's mysteries, overcome all its dangers.

Falsity and fear are their only foe-men.

Let them witness birth, marriage, death; let them hear poetry, philosophy, history; compel apprehension but not its articulate expression. Make them face cliffs, billows, animals, finding their own formula of conquest.

Thrust Truth on them tirelessly, careful only to make its range all-comprehensive; trust them to use it.

V

Let children educate themselves to be themselves. Those who train them to standards cripple and deform them. Alien ideals impose parasitic perversions.

Every child is a Sphinx; none knoweth its secret but itself; presumeth Ignorance to initiate Isis?

Let the Sphinx brood on its secret, until its hour; one can assist only by leaving it to contemplate existence. Let it behold all things in Earth and Heaven.

Guard it inviolably; strengthen it by successive struggles. Be it omniscient, omnipotent, perfected by its own Virtue to serve its own purpose—individual, independent, initiated—Itself!

VI

Procrustes-teachers,[1] assuming Themselves the "Measure of Mankind," deform children deliberately by Ideals.

Gardeners never assimilate poppies to potatoes; they nourish each plant by its own norm, towards excellence in its particular properties.

Even elementary education should be adapted to individuals; each mind has its own peculiarities. Why not put boys' bodies into plaster moulds of "Perfection"?

All pressure on plastic material is pernicious, thwarting its true tendencies, and perverting its proportions. Monstrous growths compensate constrictions.

Education must accustom the mind to meet all eventualities, interpreting, judging, and reacting as its individual necessity demands.

VII

Most people mislead children purposely, alleging necessity to shield them. One falsehood confuses correct conceptions; the brain, bewildered, soon finds conflicting evidence. The contradiction between observed facts and teaching revolts its righteousness.

Children distrust the Universe; intelligence revolts; years of aching uncertainty avenge the original deception. Children are also trained to falsify, sophisticate, deny or forget facts; forbidden to face them.

Wielding wrong weapons, they encounter unknown or misguided enemies.

Nature turns traitor; they distrust themselves; like Gilbert's billiard-sharper, they play "on a cloth untrue with a twisted cue and elliptical billiard balls."[2]

VIII

At Cefalù's Abbey of Thelema children are as adults. Realities are their right; they observe dispassionately and act responsibly. They are made

---

[1] [Procrustes was a mythical Greek figure who made travellers fit his bed, either by stretching or by amputating their limbs.]

[2] [Gilbert and Sullivan, *The Mikado, or The Town of Titipu* (1885); see Works Cited.]

to extricate themselves from graduated emergencies. They drill, swim, climb, play games, explore town or country alone; they listen to time-tested words. They use their minds accordingly, never in forced forms.

They learn truth-seeing, courage, courtesy and independence; to mind their own business, respecting the rights of others, while resenting interference.

Apprehending actualities accurately and acting adequately thereon, instead of crying, clinging, cringing, and "making believe," they master self and surroundings.

IX

Young brains store sense-impressions without necessarily judging them. Higher mental faculties develop gradually.

It is criminal to force growth, especially in dogmatic directions. Reflection, classification, coordination are devices of the growing mind for dealing with accumulations of detail. Education should simply furnish facts, intelligible or not, of every order. Avoid comment, explanation, moral judgment; the child-mind must manage its material.

Truth must be taught as the condition of right relation, courage as that of right reaction.

The individual equal to his environment, evolves in perfection. Children so educated are absolutely themselves, adjusted to apprehend and act by autonomous evolution.

X

Evolution demands exceptional individuals, fitter to their environment than their fellows. Species prosper by imitating efficient eccentrics.

Mediocrity, self-styled morality, protects the unfit, but prevents progress, discourages adaptability, and assures ultimate ruin to the race.

Standards of education, ideals of Right-and-Wrong, conventions, creeds, codes, stagnate Mankind. Encourage original individuals.

Beware of squaring the Keystone, or heaving it over among the rubbish!

Mediocrity wanted Keats druggist, Gaugin banker, Clive clerk, Mohammed camel-man![1]

---

[1] [John Keats (1795-1821) was one of Crowley's favorites poets. The painter Paul Gaugin (1848-1903) was made a Gnostic saint by Crowley. Baron Robert Clive of Plassey (1725-1774) established British colonial rule in India. Mohammed (570-632), the prophet and founder of Islām, was originally a camel-driver.]

Nature needs nobility
Vitality vindicates variety.
Preeminence purchases progress.
Superiority safeguards survival.
Abnormality averts atrophy.
Breed for Behemoth!

XI

Every child is absolute.
Dare not bias it or bind!
Give the seed fair play to shoot!
At maturity its mind
Shall perfect its proper fruit,
Self-determined, self-designed!

Durst thou twist that tenderness
To thy whims or theories?
Who adjured thee to assess
Marvels hidden from thine eyes?
Meddler, muddler! Is thy guess
Guaranteed most wondrous wise?

Let it meet and measure things,
Match itself against them, span
Safely the abyss—Earth sings:
"If you know and will, you can!"

On Sexual Freedom

I

Bodily secretions, suppressed, infiltrate the tissues, poisoning them. Semen unnaturally accumulated clogs the brain as bile does; morbid mental and moral symptoms result.

Sex is a physiological process; interference perverts it. Sex has no moral implications, except the welfare of the race. Sexual superstitions have made sex paramount. Toothache tyrannizes thought; the nerve seems All-Reality. Disease destroys proportion and precision of perception. Obstructed organs disturb and disorder the whole system; the poisoned blood infects the brain, mind utters body, sense misinstructing spirit, reason misreading the report, will misapplying power, and muscle mistranslating motive.

II

In the Abbey of Thelema at Cefalù sex is studied scientifically without shame or subterfuge. Passions are physiologically assayed; all acts are allowed, if they injure not others; approved, if they injure not self. This liberty, far from fomenting lust, destroys sex-obsession. Sex-fever abates; the inflamed imagination recovers its proper proportion; the function, freed from friction, acts automatically. We forget about it as a half-drowned man forgets about breathing as soon as his lungs are clear again. "The word of Sin is Restriction." "Do what thou wilt shall be the whole of the Law."[1]

III

Healthy human beings who innocently obey instinct are no more liable to cause trouble than other animals; sex-calamities are artificial creations

---

[1] [*Liber Al vel Legis* I:41, I:40.]

of a savage superstition. Chained mastiffs become dangerous; repressive laws breed revolutionaries.

Bedlam made murderous maniacs of harmless imbeciles; kindness and recognition of their rights disarms the madman's desperation.

Sex is the sacred song of the soul; sex is the sanctuary of Self.

Scoff; the priest shrinks or snarls. Protest; he grows fanatical or cunning. Persecute; he abjures his faith, is martyred for it, or, sceptre changed for sword, asserts it against the aggressor.

In every case, his intimate absorption suffers, his individuality is invaded; his Absolute is profaned by his reaction to the Relative. Sex is the supreme sacrament, wherein the body and blood are offered up to the soul. The elements thereof must be worthy, their consecration absolute. They must be utterly consumed, the God in Matter and Motion slain for the sustenance of the God in Spirit and Soul. This Eucharist is every man's, inalienably, uniquely his; let no man dare approach another's altar! Who should presume to legislate for the inscrutable, or arrogate authority over an alien Absolute? Who criticizes sex, condoning this, condemning that, not only usurps for himself the Universe, and proclaims his prejudices omnivalent, but abdicates his own autonomy by manifesting his own Mysteries, and praying the profane to pollute his priesthood by mimicry of his Mass, that can be naught for them but mockery, and now no more to him than formal fiction, seeing he valued his own Isis less than his own vanity, thinking men flattered him by fouling her!

He who censures and constrains the sexual character of another not only makes himself the measure of the Universe, but sets himself up against inexorable Necessity, denying the Order of Existence, and resisting the rights of Reality; but condemns also himself, for he is one of the causes of the Cosmos, and constricts himself, for to change the course of another would cause a reaction, a counterpoise falling on him.

All souls exist, eternally; identical in essence, individual in expression. Each is equally ineffable, impenetrable, inaccessible. The nature of each is necessary, therefore all Destiny is also Design, and its Way no more than the name of Will. None can be aught but what it is; did it will to be anything else, that will would be the norm of its nature; self-contradiction may be its proper quality, just as the idea of a square number contains that of two equal roots of opposite sign whose self-multiplication generates it with impartial propriety. Each soul is thus absolute and independent, not less but more for its inherent identity with itself, is implicitly involved in its consubstantial co-existence with an infinity of coordinate companions. Each seeks to interpret itself, and to increase itself (without impairing its integrity) by imagining itself in a medium of illusion—matter, motion, and mind. This enables it to gain indirect experience of other souls, just as we convey thought (more or less exactly) by creating conventional symbols to represent our ideas.

Why then should certain illusions conflict with others, and cause their creators to suffer? One would suppose that these phantom shapes would mingle like shadows in a room with several sources of light. But we have expressly designed our phantoms so that they may make definite contacts; thus, though A and B are arbitrary and unsubstantial glyphs for meaningless sounds, we cannot use them indiscriminatingly, as if one could write *Blight* for *Alight*.

We suffer when our illusions make inharmonious contacts with other illusions, because we sometimes (too often!) forget their nature and our own. We think ourselves involved in the conflict, although we know that the resolution of the struggle is the very device by which we become aware of ourselves and our relation with others, the apparent antagonism being no more than an opportunity to increase our comprehension of the cosmos and our capacity to contain it. The "patriot" protests against the word "*amour*," and suffers the penalty of his delusion that the word "love" is the reality of love, the sole expression of the idea; the philosopher accepts "*amour*" as synonymous, is glad that the strife of the symbols is a sham, and delights to find "love" on his Oxonian lips melt into "*amour*" on the lips of his leman[1] as they kiss in the shadow of the Sorbonne and realize the sublimity of their Selfhood, and the ecstasy of surrendering Self to each other, both the Two as One—rejoicing in Self-Knowledge attained by the Mystery of separation in spirit and manifestation in matter.

But one soul may be so absorbed in its error as to think real incompatibility is possible. They are thus led to assail a set of illusions, and seek to prevent their projection.

The sexual nature of a man is his most intense expression of himself; his subconsciousness endeavours thereby to inform his consciousness of his Will. Sex is thus rarely intelligible to its possessor, save in very partial

---

[1] [An archaic word for a mistress, sweetheart or lover.]

and ambiguous terms. It is supremely sacred to him, and to interfere with its expression, or try to edit it, is an abominable crime. But it is this sacredness which makes some people think that their personal peculiarities are universal truths. This error has caused more disasters than all others combined; for the warfare is an unmitigated mistake, and is conducted with insane cruelty on account of the atrocious suffering inflicted by even trifling wounds, which almost always cripple, and hardly ever kill. The curse of moral deformation is hereditary, and the whole organism is infected by the disease of this one part, which is the generating idea whereby the character of the whole is determined.

It requires elaborate investigation and indefatigable efforts to eliminate the error. The wound must be probed and cleaned thoroughly before it can heal. Anæsthetics and salves aggravate the case.

We cannot in this place enter into details of curative treatment, which differs with each patient.

But the underlying principle in all is to establish understanding of the nature of sex, to make all its forms familiar, and all equally proper to the person who prefers them. The patient is accustomed to analyze "shock," and so to become immune to it. He is taught to observe his own reactions to various practices, so as to perfect his technique.

As the cure proceeds it constantly occurs that various aberrations of the instinct, supposed ineradicable, disappear, or at least lose their importance.

It ends in serene self-confidence and in total destruction of the power of perverse irritation to interrupt the functions of the mind.

Duty

"Do what thou wilt shall be the whole of the Law." [1]   I:40

"There is no law beyond Do what thou wilt."   III:60

"...thou hast no right but to do thy will. Do that, and no other
shall say nay. For pure will, unassuaged of purpose, delivered
from the lust of result, is every way perfect."   I:42–44

"Love is the law, love under will."   I:57

"Every man and every woman is a star."   I:3

A. Your duty to yourself.

1. Find yourself to be
   the centre of your
   own Universe.

   "I am the flame that burns in every heart of man, and in the   II:6
   core of every star."

2. Explore the Nature
   and Powers of your
   own Being.

   This includes everything which is, or can
   be, for you; and you must accept everything exactly as it is in itself, as one of the
   factors which go to make up your True
   Self. This True Self thus ultimately
   includes all things soever; its discovery is
   Initiation (the travelling inwards) and as its
   Nature is to move continually, it must be
   understood not as static, but as dynamic,
   not as a Noun but as a Verb.

---

[1] [Quotations from *Liber Legis* are cited in marginal notes.]

3. Develop in due har-
    mony and propor-
    tion every faculty
    which you possess.

II:70 "Wisdom says: be strong! Then canst thou bear more joy. Be not animal; refine thy rapture! If thou drink, drink by the eight and ninety rules of art: if thou love, exceed by delicacy; and if thou do aught joyous, let there be subtlety therein!"

II:71 "But exceed! exceed!"

II:22 "Be strong, o man! lust, enjoy all things of sense and rapture: fear not that any God shall deny thee for this."

4. Contemplate your own Nature.

Consider every element thereof both separately and in relation to all the rest, so as to judge accurately the true purpose of the totality of your Being.

5. Find the formula of this purpose, or "True Will," in an expression as simple as possible.

Learn to understand clearly how best to manipulate the energies which you control to obtain the results most favourable to it from its relations with the part of the Universe which you do not yet control.

6. Extend the dominion of your consciousness, and its control of all forces alien to it, to the utmost.

Do this by the ever stronger and more skilful application of your faculties to the finer, clearer, fuller, and more accurate perception, the better understanding, and the more wisely ordered government, of that external Universe.

7. Never permit the thought or will of any other Being to interfere with your own.

Be constantly vigilant to resent, and on the alert to resist, with unvanquishable ardour and vehemence of passion unquenchable, every attempt of any other Being to influence you otherwise than by contributing new facts to your experience of the Universe, or by assisting you to reach an higher synthesis of Truth by the mode of passionate fusion.

8. Do not repress or
   restrict any true
   instinct of your
   Nature; but devote
   all in perfection to
   the sole service of
   your one True Will.

> "Be goodly therefore: dress ye all in fine apparel; eat rich   I:51
> foods and drink sweet wines and wines that foam! Also, take
> your fill and will of love as ye will, when, where and with
> whom ye will! But always unto me."

> "The word of Sin is Restriction. O man! refuse not thy wife, if   I:41
> she will. O lover, if thou wilt, depart! There is no bond that
> can unite the divided but love: all else is a curse. Accursèd!
> Accursèd be it to the aeons! Hell."

> "So with thy all; thou hast no right but to do thy will. Do that, I:42–44
> and no other shall say nay. For pure will, unassuaged of pur-
> pose, delivered from the lust of result, is every way perfect."

> "Ye shall gather goods and store of women and spices; ye   I:61
> shall wear rich jewels; ye shall exceed the nations of the earth
> in splendour & pride; but always in the love of me, and so
> shall ye come to my joy."

9. Rejoice!

> "Remember all ye that existence is pure joy; that all the sor-   II:9
> rows are but as shadows; they pass & are done; but there is
> that which remains."

> "But ye, o my people, rise up & awake! Let the rituals be   II:34–35,
> rightly performed with joy & beauty!" ... "A feast for fire and   41–44
> a feast for water; a feast for life and a greater feast for death! A
> feast every day in your hearts in the joy of my rapture! A feast
> every night unto Nu, and the pleasure of uttermost delight!
> Aye! feast! rejoice! there is no dread hereafter. There is the
> dissolution, and eternal ecstasy in the kisses of Nu."

II:64   "Now rejoice! now come in our splendour & rapture! Come in our passionate peace, & write sweet words for the Kings!"

II:66   "Thrill with the joy of life & death! Ah! thy death shall be lovely: whoso seeth it shall be glad. Thy death shall be the seal of the promise of our agelong love. Come! lift up thy heart & rejoice!"

II:19–20   "Is a God to live in a dog? No! but the highest are of us. They shall rejoice, our chosen: who sorroweth is not of us. Beauty and strength, leaping laughter and delicious languor, force and fire, are of us."

B. Your duty to other individual men and women.

I:57   1. "Love is the law, love under will."

I:12   "Come forth, o children, under the stars, & take your fill of love!"

Unite yourself passionately with every other form of consciousness, thus destroying the sense of separateness from the Whole, and creating a new base-line in the Universe from which to measure it.

III:59   2. "As brothers fight ye!"

II:59   "If he be a King, thou canst not hurt him."

To bring out saliently the differences between two points-of-view is useful to both in measuring the position of each in the whole. Combat stimulates the virile or creative energy; and, like love, of which it is one form, excites the mind to an orgasm which enables it to transcend its rational dullness.

3. Abstain from all interference with other wills.

II:24   "Beware lest any force another, King against King!"

(The love and war in the previous injunctions are of the nature of sport, where one respects, and learns from, the opponent, but never interferes with him, outside the actual game.) To seek to dominate or to influence another is to seek to deform or to destroy him; and he is a necessary part of one's own Universe, that is, of one's self.

4. Seek, if you so will, to enlighten another when need arises.

This may be done, always with strict respect for the attitude of the good sportsman, when he is in distress through failure to understand himself clearly, especially when he specifically demands help; for his darkness may hinder one's perception of his perfection. (Yet also his darkness may serve as a warning, or excite one's interest.) It is also lawful when his ignorance has led him to interfere with one's will. All interference is in any case dangerous, and demands the exercise of extreme skill and good judgment, fortified by experience. To influence another is to leave one's own citadel unguarded; and the attempt commonly ends in losing one's own self-supremacy.

5. Worship all!

"Every man and every woman is a star." I:3

"Mercy let be off: damn them who pity." III:18

"We have nothing with the outcast and the unfit: let them die II:21 in their misery. For they feel not. Compassion is the vice of kings: stamp down the wretched & the weak: this is the law of the strong: this is our law and the joy of the world. Think not, o king, upon that lie: That Thou Must Die: verily thou shalt not die, but live. Now let it be understood: If the body of the King dissolve, he shall remain in pure ecstasy for ever. Nuit! Hadit! Ra-Hoor-Khuit! The Sun, Strength & Sight, Light; these are for the servants of the Star & the Snake."

Each Being is, exactly as you are, the sole centre of an Universe in no wise identical with, or even assimilable to, your own. The impersonal Universe of "Nature" is only an abstraction, approximately true, of the factors which it is convenient to regard as common to all. The Universe of another is therefore necessarily unknown to, and unknowable by, you; but it induces currents of energy in yours by determining in part your selection of facts for contemplation and by exciting your reactions. Use men and women, therefore, with the absolute respect due to inviolable standards of measurement; verify your own observations by comparison with similar judgments made by them; and, studying the methods which determine their failure or success, acquire for yourself the wit and skill required to cope with your own problems.

Pity, sympathy and like emotions are fundamentally insults to the Godhead of the person exciting them, and therefore also to your own. The distress of another may be relieved; but always with the positive and noble idea of making manifest the perfection of the Universe. Pity is the source of every mean, ignoble, cowardly vice; and the essential blasphemy against Truth.

III:62   "To Me do ye reverence! to me come ye through tribulation of ordeal, which is bliss."

C. Your duty to mankind.

1. Establish the Law of Thelema as the sole basis of conduct.

The general welfare of the race being necessary in many respects to your own, and that well-being, like your own, principally a function of the intelligent and wise observance of the Law of Thelema, it is of the very first importance to you that every individual should accept frankly that Law, and strictly govern himself in full accordance therewith.

You may thus regard the establishment of the Law of Thelema as an essential element in your True Will, since, whatever the ultimate nature of that Will, the evident condition of putting it into execution is freedom from external interference.

Governments too often exhibit the most deplorable stupidity, however enlightened and intelligent may be the men who compose and constitute them, or the people whose destinies they direct. It is therefore incumbent on every man and woman to take the proper steps to cause the revision of all existing statutes on the basis of the Law of Thelema. This Law being the Law of Liberty, the aim of the legislature must be to secure the amplest freedom for each individual in the state, eschewing the presumptuous assumption that any given positive ideal is worthy to be attained.

"The word of Sin is Restriction."   I:41

The essence of crime is that it restricts the freedom of the individual outraged. (Thus, murder restricts his right to live; robbery, his right to enjoy the fruits of his labour; coining, his right to the guarantee of the State that he shall barter in security; etc.) It is then the common duty to prevent crime by segregating the criminal, and by the threat of reprisals; also, to teach the criminal that his acts, being analyzed, are contrary to his own True Will. (This may often be best accomplished by taking from him the right which he has denied to others; as by outlawing the thief, so that he feels constant anxiety for the safety of his own possessions, removed from the ward of the State.) The rule is quite simple. He who violates any right declares magically that it does not exist; therefore it no longer does so, *for him.*

Crime being a direct spiritual violation of the Law of Thelema, it should not be tolerated in the community. Those who possess the instinct should be segregated in a settlement to build up a state of their own, so to learn the necessity of themselves imposing and maintaining rules of justice.

All laws against artificial crimes should be abolished. When fantastic restrictions disappear, the greater freedom of the individual will itself teach him to avoid acts which really restrict natural rights. Thus real crime will diminish dramatically.

The administration of Law should be simplified by training men of uprightness and discretion whose will is to fulfill this function in the community to decide all complaints by the abstract principle of the Law of Thelema, and to award judgment on the basis of the actual restriction caused by the offense.

The ultimate aim is thus to reintegrate Conscience, on true scientific principles, as the warden of conduct, the monitor of the people, and the guarantee of their governors.

D. Your duty to all other beings and things.

1. Apply the Law of Thelema to all problems of fitness, use, and development.

It is a violation of the Law of Thelema to abuse the natural qualities of any animal or object by diverting it from its proper function, as determined by consideration of its history and structure. Thus, to train children to perform mental operations, or to practice tasks, for which they are unfitted, is a crime against nature. Similarly, to build houses of rotten material, to adulterate food, to destroy forests, etc., etc., is to offend.

The Law of Thelema is to be applied unflinchingly to decide every question of conduct. The inherent fitness of any thing for any proposed use should be the sole criterion.

Apparent, and sometimes even real, conflict between interests will frequently arise. Such cases are to be decided by the general value of the contending parties in the scale of Nature. Thus, a tree has a right to its life; but a man being more than a tree, he may cut it down for fuel or shelter when need arises. Even so, let him remember that the Law never fails to avenge infractions: as when wanton deforestation has ruined a climate or a soil, or as when the importation of rabbits for a cheap supply of food has created a plague.

Observe that the violation of the Law of Thelema produces cumulative ills. The drain of the agricultural population to big cities, due chiefly to persuading them to abandon their natural ideals, has not only made the country less tolerable to the peasant, but debauched the town. And the error tends to increase in geometrical progression, until a remedy has become almost inconceivable, and the whole structure of society is threatened with ruin.[1]

The wise application based on observation and experience of the Law of Thelema is to work in conscious harmony with Evolution. Experiments in creation, involving variation from existing types, are lawful and necessary. Their value is to be judged by their fertility, as bearing Witness to their harmony with the course of Nature towards *perfection*.

---

[1] [The typescript has the deleted passage: "To turn one hemp-seed from its proper use is to disturb the balance of Nature."]

An Open Letter to
Rabbi Joel Blau

Reverend Sir and Brother:[1]

Do what thou wilt shall be the whole of the Law.

Your article on "The Cry of the Modern Pharisee" in *The Atlantic Monthly* of January 1922, has left a deep impression upon my mind. On the one hand, the sublimity of courage, pride and sadness which informs it, demands consummate respect; not less so, on the other, does the masterly intellectual grasp of the situation.

But while finding myself in substantial agreement with the psychological position set forth, I must submit that the correct conclusion from these premises is not repatriation. To take refuge in a physical Zion seems to me an anticlimax, a confession of defeat, and an acquiescence in that materialism which you deplore as the mark of your own Sadducees.

Permit me to introduce myself as the one who has found the Word (which you have lost) by means of your own Chokmah Nesethrah,[2] the secret Wisdom which you despise as superstitious folly. By the right use of your Qabalah, we have discovered the Lost Word. We have pronounced the Ineffable Name, we have reopened the Gates of Eden and we offer you the fruit of the Tree of Life. The division between Jew and Gentile dates only from Abraham. We, no less than you, are of the seed of Adam, of mankind.

---

[1] [Rabbi Joel Blau (1878–1927) was connected with Temple Peni-El in New York City, and was the author of *The Wonder of Life* (1925); see Works Cited. Crowley's address suggests that he may have been a Freemason. His son was Joseph Blau, author of the seminal study *The Christian Interpretation of the Cabala in the Renaissance* (1944). Crowley records in his diary for March 20, 1922 ("Liber Tzaba vel Nike sub figura 28"): "Heard from Rabbi Blau, who much appreciates my letter." Crowley discusses this article, and his distress at its abridgment in the *The English Review*, in his *Confessions*, abridged ed., p. 893.]

[2] [Hebrew חכמה נסתרה, "the secret wisdom," a name for the Holy Qabalah.]

It was by your own Secret Tradition that I obtained the Knowledge and Conversation of my Holy Guardian Angel: the Word of that Angel is written in our *Book of the Law*.[1] This Law contains the solution of all the problems of the Æon of whatever kind. I address myself particularly to you because you show a profound comprehension of this Law. You express this Law in various phrases. What seems to me the one failure of your article is due to the interference of your intellectual perceptions of the conditions of your environment with the essential truth of your soul. You must hold fast this Truth if it is to make you free.[2] You must pass through the ordeal of being attacked by phenomena which threaten or allure, seeking to turn you from your spiritual integrity. Ignore these seeming facts, you will soon realize that they are vapours of the Void. Your salvation lies in spiritual self-realization.

I venture to quote a few passages from your essay which seem to me to witness that the truth of our Law has been revealed to you.

> It is depressing to see the Jewish problem discussed, even by Jews, from without and not from within; as if its inner aspect did not matter; at all events, as if this were something in which the world at large need take no interest, it being the concern of a few Jewish zealots only. Over against this mistaken position, these very Jewish zealots, who are far from obsolete, claim that the only way to solve the Jewish problem is from within. Find the right solution for the internal problem of the Jew, and the external problem, created by the persistence of anti-Semitism, will solve itself.
>
> ... he [the Modern Pharisee] would rather lose the whole world than lose aught of the riches of his soul.
>
> ... as for pride, he admits it, yet holds himself guiltless. For pride is no sin, except when one will not live up to it. ... It is compounded of a clear knowledge of one's place, a consciousness of both powers and limitations, and a desire to participate wholeheartedly in the passionate business of living. This pride is the child of reverence: the last summing-up of the sanctities of Individuality. ... Its presence is the distinguishing sign of divinely stubborn men, "terribly meek," who inherit the earth—and heaven, too. [3]

---

[1] This Book has been published in *The Equinox* I(7,10); also separately.
[2] [An allusion to John 8:32.]
[3] [An allusion to Psalm 37:11.]

Of peoples, too, even as of persons, the same holds true: modesty is a sin in any people. The chief duty that a people owes both itself and the world is reverence for its own soul, the mystic centre of its being. ... Personality spells the mystery of mysteries—the last word of life for which all the worlds and all the ages are in ceaseless travail. ...

The Jew must be led back to the Discovery of the Jewish Soul.[1]

---

[1] Despite these utterances, we find elsewhere in the essay that the only practical solution in view is repatriation. A physical Zion is contemplated, and this proposal implies the very materialism which the learned Rabbi deplores as the mark of the modern Sadducee. Now the division between Jew and Gentile dates only from Abraham. The children of uncircumcision no less than those of the Covenant are of the seed of Adam, of mankind. It was by means of the secret tradition of the Hebrews that the leader of the hosts of the new Law obtained "the knowledge and conversation of his Holy Guardian Angel," whose words constitute the whole Law. This Law is the master-key to the Future of Mankind, and the learned Rabbi, being a master in Israel, is able to interpret the *Zeitgeist* intuitively. Accordingly, he exhibits a profound comprehension of this Law; indeed, he actually expresses some of its corollaries in various phrases. What then is the one weakness of his admirable essay? What is it that compels him to a sceptical conclusion, despite the sublimity of courage, pride, and sadness which informs his thought, and the magistral grasp of the situation? These qualities demand consummate respect; and yet their owner hesitates to articulate an "Everlasting Yea." The difficulty arises from the interference of the learned Rabbi's intellectual perception of the conditions of his environment with the truth of his soul. He must hold fast to this truth if it is to make him free. The Relative must not be applied as a measure of the Absolute, of which it is but one of the infinitely numerous symbolic representations. It is, then, here that Rabbi Joel Blau is tempted to lose touch with the essential truth. He has still to pass through the ordeal of being attacked by phenomena which threaten or allure, seeking to turn him from his spiritual integrity. It is the task of the initiate to learn to ignore these seeming facts, to recognize that these are vapours of the void.

The historical aspect of this doctrine may be elucidated briefly as follows:—In the dawn of history we have the Pagan period, when the central object of worship is Isis (or similar idea) the Mother. Matriarchy abounds; the function of Man in reproduction is not understood. Then comes a period in which the Father is the main object of worship. We have Solar-Phallic religions, in which the Sun, and Man, must die to live again. Science has now shown that the Sun, and is showing that Man, does not "die"; darkness is due to our being in the shadow of the earth; death to our being veiled from our Reality by our gross bodies. The New Law proclaims the Crowned and Conquering Child as the central idea which represents That Which Is.

This subject is discussed at great length in *The Equinox* I(1–10) and III(1), in *The Book of Lies*, in *The Star in the West*, by Capt. (now Col.) J. F. C. Fuller, and elsewhere.

Our Law contains these words: "Every man and every woman is a star." [1] A reasonable corollary would be the proposition that every race is a group of stars distinguished by possessing certain elements in common. But it should be evident that the salvation of any such group cannot lie in its segregation, or even in its solidarity. The economy of space demands that each star should satisfy its own conditions, move in its proper orbit. No artificial arrangement will secure harmony. It is not for an astronomer to propose a plan by which one group of stars may be kept from colliding with others; the fact of such catastrophes in the past proves that the stars concerned have lost their way in Heaven. Each star is equally inviolable, eternal, individual. The Jewish Spirit cannot be destroyed any more than a grain of sand or an ohm of electrical resistance. The problem is perennial. If every Jew were instantaneously abolished, the Jewish question would be unaltered.

You have yourself [2] demonstrated, with admirable clearness, that the "extraversion" of your Sadducees has merely defiled their honour, and that reliance upon outworn formalism has failed to protect the integrity of your Pharisees.

When Moses gave His new Law, His was the Word which expressed the spiritual truth fit for that age and that folk. Other Masters have appeared from time to time with other words. Thus the Buddha, proclaiming the absence of *ātman*, [3] emancipated the East from its time-rotted conditions. Mohammed, with His Word Allāh, proclaimed a new Æon in which the diversity of phenomena should be referred to a single ultimate source. In the same way, the Word of our Law which I now proclaim, formulates an ethical principle by the acceptance of which every man and every woman, of whatever race, may become sole arbiter of his or her own destiny, and achieve the automatically demonstrated certainty that every Star is supreme in its own sphere, all collision and confusion being due to that very mistake of moral misalliance which you indicate as the root of most of the monstrous growths in the Lord's vineyard.

"Do what thou wilt shall be the whole of the Law." "There is no law beyond Do what thou wilt." "thou hast no right but to do thy will. Do that,

---

[1] [*Liber AL vel Legis* I:3.]

[2] [I.e., Rabbi Blau.]

[3] [Sanskrit, "self" or "substance"; in Advaita it is identical with *brahman*. The Buddha's Word was the Pali *anatta*, equivalent to the Sanskrit *anātman*, meaning "without substance" or "not-self."]

and no other shall say nay." "Love is the law, love under will."[1] Such are some of the fundamental principles of our new Law, the Law of Thelema.

The solution of the Jewish Question has baffled society completely since the earliest records. It is quite evident that before the Exodus Pharaoh was confronted by precisely the same dilemma as the Tsar of yesterday in Russia and the President of today in America. It is the problem of an endothermic chemical compound. The instability of chloride of nitrogen does not lead us to blame either the nitrogen or the chlorine; the elements tend to fly apart with destructive violence because neither of them is satisfying its own true nature to the full. Each has joined the other without enthusiasm because it could find no more suitable element union with which would fulfil to the uttermost its need of a complement. Nitrogen chloride is not formed if the chlorine passes over moist sodium before reaching the ammonia, or if that ammonia is mixed with nitric acid.

Jew and Gentile have been forced into contact under innumerable varieties of social condition. Friction has been at a minimum when the Jew has been in contact either with Arabic civilization or English jurisprudence. These two environments have a common factor: non-interference. English indifference and Moslem self-respect are agreed on the ethical principle: "Mind your own business." This is one of the moral postulates of our own Law.

The incompatibility between Jew and Gentile has been based, superficially indeed, upon prejudice, ignorance, and instinctive antipathy, but this seems to me hardly more than a disguise for the real motive, which I take to be the fear of alien aggression. The Jews are charged with many crimes, from ritual murder and usury to lack of patriotism. But all these charges are merely diverse expressions of the feeling that there is an irreconcilable antagonism between two spirits whose juxtaposition is an offense to nature.

I feel sure that so far I may count upon your assent to this analysis. I will be bold enough to proceed to synthesis. Let us pursue the chemical analogy. In a mixture of sodium chloride and sodium nitrate, the atoms of nitrogen and chlorine are intimately mingled; but there is no tendency to explosion. The reason is that both elements have already fulfilled their own natures. Neither is unsatisfied; neither is under stress.

Is there here no hint to guide us to a practical proposal? It is useless to tinker with the environment of chloride of nitrogen; the more we meddle with the explosive, the more likely we are to provoke a crisis. We

---

[1] [*Liber AL* I:40, III:60, I:42–43, I:57.]

must prevent the formation of the substance altogether; and so long as either element is unsatisfied, so long is there a risk of conditions occurring in which they will combine disastrously with each other. Just as most human beings contract unsuitable marriages, or experiment with unconsecrated unions, rather than suffer the physiological agony of abstention; just as the only secure social system rests on a basis of sexually satisfied individuals; so countries inhabited by heterogeneous races invite civil collision if the inherited instincts of any race are starved or suppressed.

This letter not being addressed to Gentiles, I make no allusion to their part in my proposal. I simply appeal to you to face the fact that from the time of Abraham's discontented departure from his father's pastures, and the dream-drawn journey of Joseph, to the desperate adventure of Moses in search of a "promised land," and the continual craving for a Messiah, the Spirit of the Jew, behind all its expressions, is stamped with the stigma of soul-starvation. The patriotic passion of the Chroniclers, the plaintive cries of the Psalmists, the relentless rage of the Prophets, the acrid agony of Ecclesiastes, each in its own way expresses the fact that the Jew has always wanted Something desperately, has never known precisely what it was, has never fooled himself for very long into fancying that he has found it. When national degradation and religious mummification had reduced the ragged remnant of repatriated refugees to despair, Paul proclaimed his Freudian Phantasm as the Messiah. But in vain did he try to conciliate his people, in vain did he prove that Christ fulfilled the prophecies, in vain did he seek to reconcile circumcision and crucifixion. Israel preferred to die in the dark rather than stumble by the light of corpse-candles into the ditch of self-deception.

The same spirit stamps the Jew to this day. He has endured every possible persecution; without faith, hope, or love, to help him.[1] He has not found himself in wealth, power, or anything else. Neither Spinoza in philosophy, Heine in poetry, nor Einstein in science, have found any way of escape from the fiend appointed to scourge Israel.[2] From the most sublime complaints of the musician to the grossest grumblings of the *Schnorrer*,[3] the same phrase recurs: it is the cry from the Abyss, the cry of the lost soul. The glories of Solomon did not prevent him from seeing

---

[1] [The three theological virtues proclaimed by Paul in I Cor. 13:13.]

[2] [Baruch Spinoza (1632–1677) was a Dutch rationalist philosopher, and the primary exponent of philosophical pantheism. Heinrich Heine (1797–1856) was a German poet. Albert Einstein (1879–1955) was a German-American physicist.]

[3] [A slang term for a beggar (Yiddish *shnorer*), especially a musician.]

the vanity of all things; nor would repatriation in Palestine delude one single Jew into supposing that his soul could be satisfied by so romantically narcotic a remedy.

"Do what thou wilt shall be the whole of the Law." The solution of the Jewish problem is simply this: "Shiloh shall come."[1] The Messiah must arise, and His name shall be called Anti-Christ, even as I who am already arisen, am called The Beast and my number is the number of a man, six hundred and three score and six.[2] And this shall be the sign of the Messiah, Anti-Christ, He who shall lead at last His people Israel into the Holy Mountain, the True Zion: He shall come to understand the Magical Formula of Israel; He shall interpret the history of Israel; He shall declare unto Israel the nature of the spirit of the people; He shall express the true purpose of His people; He shall demonstrate to them the direction of their destiny; He shall formulate their function in the physiology of mankind.

It may indeed be that this function is such that even its free fulfillment does not satisfy it. He, the Messiah, Anti-Christ, shall know, as I do not, whether it be so. In our own bodies there are principles which never cease to urge us. The secret of the Soul of Israel may be that it is a ferment; the history of humanity shows us this spirit constantly consuming every civilization with which it has been in contact. Israel has corrupted the world, whether by conquest, by conversion, or by conspiracy. The Jew has eaten his way into everything. The caricature of Semitic thought, Christianity, rotted Roman virtue through introducing the moral subterfuge of vicarious atonement. The Eagles of Cæsar degenerated to the draggled buzzards of Constantine. Soon they were no more than hens, dispersed and devoured by the fierce hawks of Mohammed and the savage ravens of the North. Jewish commercial cleverness has created cosmopolitanism. Jewish sympathy with suffering has made the cliffs of caste to crumble. Jewish ethical exclusiveness has created a tyranny of conventional formalities to replace the righteousness of self-respect. The Jew, living so long on sufferance, by subterfuge, servility, and self-effacement, has taught his tricks to the whole world. Civilization is an organized system of craft, concealment, cunning, camouflage, of cringing cowardice and craven callousness. The world is one great Ghetto. The Jew has failed to realize himself; and, as you so brilliantly break out at the end of the third paragraph of your article, it is in infamy that Gentile and

---

[1] [Gen. 49:10. The Hebrew is שילה יבא = 358 = "Messiah" and "Serpent."]
[2] [Rev. 13:18.]

Jew are reconciled at last. Gentile and Jew bend on the same bench of the galley; the same whip drips with blood from the bare backs of the two brothers in bondage. We share the same suffering and shame; we eat the same bitter bread of exile. Neither of us has known who he is, dared to be himself, or willed to do his Will. Neither has kept the silence which alone preserved his soul from profanation. It was far better when ignorance and prejudice prevailed; we had at least faith in our own fetishes. It is better to have something that one is willing to die for, though it be but a lie; to have something to live for, though it be but a dream. Today, Jew and Gentile alike are pursuing despicable objects by dishonourable devices; and, having attained them, there is disillusion, disgust, and despair. We have swept away the superstitions which sustained our self-respect. We have discovered that the sun is only one star of many, and, perceiving our infinitesimal importance, we have lost our self-esteem.

We have still to complete analysis by synthesis. Instead of interpreting Democracy as confusion in a common degradation, we must understand that, although each individual is equally an element of existence with every other, each is sublimely itself. Mankind is a republic of aristocrats; our equality is that of the essential organs of the body. The honour of each is to secure the harmony of all. It is the most fatal error of modern thought to interpret the dependence of each of us upon the rest as confounding us all in a common vileness.

I appeal to you then, out of your own mouth, to accept the Law of Thelema as the foundation of the future of Israel.[1] I ask you to agree that

---

[1] This Law may be summarized: Do what thou wilt shall be the whole of the Law. The theory underlying this injunction is that "Every man and every woman is a star." Each star is equally inviolable, eternal, individual. It has its own proper course through space. This physical fact has its moral parallel in, "There is no law beyond Do what thou wilt"; that is to say, every individual has his own necessary and proper direction, which is called his "True Will." Similarly, just as there are certain groups of stars, there are groups of human beings which, while preserving the individual integrity of each unit, have a certain common direction. It is thus legitimate to calculate the destiny of a race, as the astronomer calculates the course of a galaxy. It is the first business of every individual to discover what his True Will is, and then to occupy himself to doing that and nothing else. But he must also reckon with the drift of his race and of humanity as a whole. As soon as this Law is properly understood, its truth becomes self-evident. To fail to do one's true will is to stultify oneself, to create a conflict in oneself, to become morally insane. The school of Freud and Jung has rediscovered a part of this thesis by showing that self-suppression leads to neurosis. The task of every man is to express himself fully, but he must take into consideration his relationship with the community,

your salvation depends upon understanding the spirit of your people in the light of history, ethnology, and psychology. Having understood your function, and formulated your will in a fixed phrase, it is only necessary to keep your unswerving course, each Jew as his own soul shows him for himself, and for the race, as the soul of the race is shown him, by the spirit of Anti-Christ, your Messiah, who shall arise in Israel for this purpose.

One word in reconciliation of an apparent antinomy. Do not think of Anti-Christ as opposed to Christ, any more than you think of the pleura as opposed to the lungs which it bounds. Woman is not the opposite of man—the difference between them is necessary to their cooperation. Without it, neither could reproduce their common elements in either component. Every star is necessarily different from every other star. The annihilation of one would disturb the equilibrium of all, and destroy the Universe. The Jewish spirit is an essential element of humanity. The pitiable tragedies of the past have been the result of failing to understand, to insist upon, to execute, the eternal office of each existing individual idea. The arising of Anti-Christ will make possible the coming of Christ. If Christ came, he was baulked, as He himself is supposed to have said, because no one was ready to receive Him.

As your first paragraph points out, non-resistance defies power. Mechanics presumes opposition. Structuralization depends upon the cooperation of diverse unities, each of which is stubbornly itself. Evolution is aristocratic. To aim at homogeneity is to revert to nullity. Fear not then that Anti-Christ, in establishing Israel, will injure Christianity. He will, on the contrary, assist the Christian spirit to cleanse itself from the confused acquiescence in anarchical amiability which it calls "charity," and is really cowardice, really the slave's shame of his own condition, the sense of guilt which he soothes by minimizing all misdemeanours.

"Do what thou wilt shall be the whole of the Law." Let Anti-Christ arise, let Him announce to Israel its integrity. Let Him make clear the past, purged of all tribal jargon; let Him prove plainly how inevitably event came after event. Let Him gather the past to a point; let Him assign its proper position to the present by showing its relation with the axes of

---

since it is a part of his True Will to be a member thereof; and any act of his which conflicts with the True Will of the community, conflicts to that extent with his own True Will. This Law of Thelema is therefore the complete solution of all ethical problems. What is required is a technical apparatus for calculating its practical application in any particular case. Many persons are already at work to perfect this psychological instrument.

Space and Time. Let Him then calculate what forces are focussed at that point so that its proper course may be thereby determined. Then let Him speak the Word of the Will of his People, so that all Israel with united energy, disciplined and directed, move as one man irresistibly to fulfil Destiny.

Such action will induce a complementary current in every other racial and religious section of humanity. The Chinaman who has given up politeness, filial reverence, and philosophy for European ideas; the Russian who has bartered mystic melancholy for Marxism; the Mohammedan who has been taught to despise the faith, virtue, virility, and valour of his forebears, and to appreciate cocktails, cocottes, pork, and profanity; all these are hybrids, all these are self-mutilated cowards, garbage of self-surrender.[1] They are monsters bred of the shame of being different to other people. The modern Italian has discarded the noble and beautiful toga for shoddy city clothes. The Mongol's sweeping silken robes are gone; dignified in them, he prefers to look ridiculous in the frock-coat and stove-pipe hat of a Bermondsey bank clerk. The Hindu, once clean and comfortable in cotton cloths, sweats and stinks in starched shirts and shabby suits in the hope of looking like a *sahib*. Mongrels and monsters, all these! Diverse as they are, they are bastards of one mother, Conventionality, by one father, Shame.

Let the Jew lead the way! Let the Jew find himself and be sure of himself; let him assert himself without fear of others, or reference to their ideals and standards. They will be forced to respect him. In self-defense, each one will find for himself the formula of his own function. From that moment, the friction between the various parts of the human machine will begin to diminish.

"The earth is the Lord's and the fulness thereof."[2] The social and economical crises of today are not due to over-population, to lack of supplies, or to inefficiency. They are due to the suppression of individuality. Instead of each person and each race doing its own will, the whole of humanity is being thrown into a melting-pot; the only ambition is to get to the top. The earth affords infinite scope for each soul, as the sky affords space for each star. But instead of each soul seeking the satisfaction proper to itself, it is persuaded by the popular press, by the pressure

---

[1] [This reading is from *The English Review*; the typescripts have "all these are self-surrender."]

[2] [Psalm 24:1.]

of public opinion, and by the contagious delusion of Democracy, that nothing is worth having save wealth in its grossest interpretation, "modern conveniences" in the crudest sense of the term, and social success in its silliest and shallowest shape. Pleasure itself is prescribed, like the diet of a diabetic. Respect is inseparable from envy, since the superiority of one is incompatible with the equivalent superiority of others. Formerly, Virgil and Horace could admire each other's qualities.[1] Today, they must be measured by the balances at their banks. There are not enough automobiles and diamonds to go around, any more than there were in the time of Buddha or Villon.[2] But the ascetic Prince and the starving scholar could each be unique and supreme without struggling for shekels.

The Jew has no claim to consideration on account of his alleged success in money-getting. Every race in the world can produce rivals in that art. The True Spirit of Israel shines in the splendour of his literature, and in such moral qualities as that rigorous sense of Reality which made him the torchbearer of Science through the Dark Ages, that persistent patience which preserved his racial peculiarities through proscription and persecution, in the fidelity to tradition which kept him true to himself until he was assimilated in the American ant-heap, where no animal can live except the aimlessly active insects that swarm in its mould.

Hail, Master in Israel! You have indeed divined the need of your people. By your insight and your eloquence, you are worthy to be their prophet in these times. Let not your eyes grow dim by seeking in the dark. Lift up your eyes unto the light! The Sun of Righteousness has risen, and he hath healing in his wings.[3] Hear thou the Word of the Lord! "Do what thou wilt shall be the whole of the Law." For in this Word shalt thou be sealed, and thou shalt save thy people from their sin, for "The word of Sin is Restriction,"[4] and the sin of Israel is this: that it has never known itself, or done its Will.

Love is the law, love under will.

---

[1] [Horace (Quintus Horatius Flaccus, 65 BCE–8 CE) was a Roman poet and satirist. For Virgil see p. 80, note 4.]

[2] [The French poet François Villon (1431–?) is generally considered the finest poet of the late Middle Ages; he became a popular fictional outlaw figure in the 19th century.]

[3] [Malachi 4:2.]

[4] [*Liber AL vel Legis* I:41.]

A Memorandum Regarding The Book of the Law

Almost every verse of *The Book of the Law* contains profuse mathematical and philosophical truths concealed in apparently standard English, which English has none the less its regular meaning. You will have noticed that the style of the Book is for the most part astoundingly sublime, and the ineffable wonder about the whole thing is that I should have written it down from the dictation of a voice whose owner I could not see, one hour exactly for each chapter, on three consecutive days. It is thus quite certain that the author is somebody possessed of knowledge and ingenuity utterly beyond my capacity. Indeed, I feel confident in saying, beyond the capacity of any human being imaginable. Incidentally there are passages in the Book which baffled exegesis until certain events took place, years after writing it, which were entirely beyond my control, yet which furnished fresh proof that the Author of the Book knew what was going to happen or was able to bring events to pass.

May I give you one very strange example?[1] I have studied the Book all these eighteen years. Verse 19 of Chapter III utterly baffled me. How could I "count well" the name of the Stèle; it never had a name! But I played about with the figures and it suddenly dawned on me that 718 was the value of the name "Stèle 666." "That's it," I said to myself. "In a sense the Stèle is my Stèle." But I wasn't quite satisfied, and then it came upon me like an earthquake, that after all, the Stèle did possess a name—its description in the catalog of the Museum at Būlāq—that name, the only name it ever had, was actually Stèle 666.

As to controlling external events, let me tell you one extraordinary incident. In November, 1917, appeared the end of my article in *The International*, "The Revival of Magick."[2] It challenged the readers to

---

[1] [This was written to the American novelist James Branch Cabell (1879–1958), the author of *Jurgen: A Comedy of Justice* (1919). Chap. 22 of *Jurgen* was loosely based on Crowley's "Liber 15," the O.T.O. Gnostic Mass.]

[2] [See "The Revival of Magick," p. 13 above.]

find who was meant by 666 (my Magical Motto ΤΟ ΜΕΓΑ ΘΗΡΙΟΝ[1] adds to 666). One night in January, I asked an Intelligence[2] with whom I was in touch, if I could spell my motto in Hebrew so as to get new numbers which might throw some light on something. He replied, "Yes." I asked, "All three words of the name or the last only?" He said, "The last only." I then tried all sorts of ways of spelling Therion and got no results. That was on a Saturday night. I went to the office on a "Workless Monday" for my mail. Nothing there. But on Tuesday Viereck[3] sent round a letter addressed to him which had arrived on Monday, having been written on Saturday night at about the time when I had made my enquiry. The writer was a perfect stranger to all of us. He asked Viereck to tell me that he had solved the riddle in my article of November and gave the spelling of Therion in Hebrew making the value 666. This was astonishing enough; but much more was to come. The stranger signed himself as Samuel bar Aiwaz bie Yackou de Sherabad, from which I deduced that his father's name was Aiwaz.[4] This name had been given me as the Author of *The Book of the Law*; see Chapter I, Verse 7. I had only *heard* the name, which I supposed to be a made-up name like Tzadquiel or Taphthartharath;[5] I had no idea that it was a regular human name. I had tried to spell it and made it 78. Now, however, I wrote to Friend Samuel for the correct spelling, which he gave. I was astonished to find that the value was 93 like that of Θελημα,[6] the word of the Law, and Αγαπη,[7]

---

[1] [Greek, "the Great Beast," Crowley's motto as a Magus 9°=2□ A∴A∴.]

[2] [Amalantrah; the interview in question was actually February 24. See "Liber 729, The Amalantrah Working," *The Equinox* IV(3). Crowley gives another account of this episode in *Book 4*, Part III, Appendix 3.]

[3] [George Sylvester Viereck (1884–1962), Crowley's employer as the editor of *The International*.]

[4] [Samuel Aiwaz Jacobs (c. 1891–1971) was a typographer and book designer who founded the Golden Eagle Press. An essay from Jacobs (that—like *Jurgen*—paraphrases the Gnostic Mass) is republished as the Afterword to this collection of essays. The holograph letter from Jacobs survives in the Yorke Collection, Warburg Institute, University of London, and is appended to "Liber 729," loc. cit.]

[5] [Tzadkiel is from the Hebrew *tzaddiq* ("righteous, just") and *El*, God. Hence, he is the angel of justice. The name Taphthartharath comes from Paracelsus' work on talismans, wherein the spirit of the planet Mercury is identified as Tophtharthareth. With no known etymology, it qualifies as a "made-up name."]

[6] [Greek, *thelema*, will.]

[7] [Greek, *agape*, love.]

the method of carrying out that Law. The Author of the Book had therefore, so to speak, signed it, infallibly identifying himself by means of this
number with the essence of the message which he had come to impart.

These two incidents are mere samples chosen from an immense number. I hope to be joined this month by a mathematical Professor[1] so that
we may collect, classify, and make clear the innumerable evidences that
this book is of præterhuman origin. You will at least understand how it is
that I regard it as incomparably the most important human document
existent. You will excuse me, in fact, if I seem a little mad on the subject;
but really, hardly a moment passes without the discovery of some new
and important secret in its secret pages. The very mistakes in the Book,
as they seem, conceal strange secrets. For example: Chapter III, Verse
47—"this circle squared in its failure". The Hebrews concealed the
value of π in the Name of God $ALHIM$,[2] which is incorrect in the fourth
place.[3] But by putting our secret key ShT to sanctify this name we get
3.141593, π correct to six places (note 31 and 93).[4]

But this note must not be as endless as the decimal of π! You must
forgive a sick and lonely man for inflicting upon you the subject nearest
his heart. I am really very eager that you should bring the Law of
Thelema into your work as a solution of the dreadful hopelessness, futility, and fatuity of this riddle-life. "Do what thou wilt" explains and justi-
fies existence. We do what we do because it is our nature; the Geis[5]
which we lay upon ourselves to make a figure of our Secret Idea. "Lust of

---

[1] [Norman Mudd (c. 1890–1934) was educated at Cambridge and was professor of
mathematics at the Grey University College, Bloemfontein, South Africa, before
joining Crowley at the Abbey of Thelema in Cefalù. He made a determined study
of the mathematical intrepretation of *The Book of the Law*, but took it to such
extremes that Crowley came to reject his results.]

[2] [Usually transliterated as *Elohim*, "the gods," אלהים = 86.]

[3] [Crowley's teacher Allan Bennett explained this in his essay "A Note on Genesis,"
The Equinox I(2) (1909), p. 183. "Write the letters of this Name in any Invoking
Pentagram; and the Banishing Pentagram thereof will read 3.1415 (by Qabalah of
nine Chambers)." That is, by arranging these five letters as a pentagram, one can
then read them backwards while dropping the zeroes in their Hebrew numerical
values. This yields ל (3) א (1) מ (4) ' (1) ה (5), i.e., 31415.]

[4] [*ShT* is שט, whose Hebrew numerical values 9 and 300 become 9 and 3 by the
Qabalah of nine Chambers, i.e., 93. See *Book 4, Part IV (The Equinox of the
Gods)*, ch. 7, §3.]

[5] [Literally "tabu," from Gælic *geas*, "prohibition, tabu," and *geasa*, "obligation,"
either magical or one of honor.]

result" ruins our work and makes it ridiculous. There can be no result. We are bounded by our own illusion—Self-devised. The life of Manuel[1] was Success, being wholly the symbolic self-realization of a creative boy—a series of illusions which came to nothing, yet allowed him to see, externalized, the reaction of the Universe upon various facets of the diamond Soul. Jurgen's excursion was a failure, because he worked with "lust of result" to obtain something outside himself, not knowing what (and still less that nothing of the kind exists), because he could not face the fact that he had sold the poet to the pawnbroker.[2] Have I read you aright? I was a little sad about chapter 22 of *Jurgen*,[3] feeling that you had to some degree misunderstood my message. For none of us, not even the least spiritually developed, may fulfil himself wholly by self-gratification. Each of us has a Will of eternal import, necessarily related to everything that exists, and all our conscious desires are so many masks—one fixed expression concealing our infinite variety. We are all Ideal Triangles, and every triangle we draw is but a single case—true, yet concealing and even denying all the other possibilities of the real Truth, inexpressible in form, and so mocked as illusion by sense-bound spirits.

Verily and Amen! My silent solitude in this Abbey,[4] with its windows open upon the Eternal, and its gates closed to the Conditioned,[5] constantly strengthens my conviction that so great a Master of Thought and Language as yourself dare not leave the world without Hope. Your deepest, so far, has been to proclaim an irrational Faith that selfless Heroism somehow avails a man against the abject aimless inanity of life. You cannot rest there. It must be shewn that energy is indestructible, that nothing is wasted, that all True Work is worthwhile. And I hope that my Masters may be using you to put Their Key into your hands, that you may fling open the doors of the Secret Palace of the King, and shew the people what inexhaustible riches are theirs—just when it seemed that Famine was universal. You have shewn that nothing in the world, however great

---

[1] [Count Manuel is the hero of Cabell's *Figures of Earth* and the ruler of the land of Poictesme.]

[2] [In *Jurgen*, the title character is a middle-aged pawnbroker who, when given a year of youth, leaves his wife, Dame Lisa, for erotic adventures in the land of Poictesme.]

[3] [The chapter that drew on Crowley's "Liber 15, Ecclesiæ Gnosticæ Catholicæ Canon Missæ," the O.T.O. Gnostic Mass.]

[4] [Crowley was writing from the Abbey of Thelema at Cefalù, Sicily.]

[5] [The typescripts have "close to the Conditioned," probably in error.]

and glorious, is worth stretching forth an hand to take; shew now that everything in the world, however small and contemptible, is worth a life's danger and hardships to attain. (You have done this, in a way, in *Domnei*.)[1] I want a book to complete the Jurgen-Manuel group in a Trilogy, and behold the Great Fool, knowing nothing because identified with All (which, not being divided against itself cannot be known), doing nothing because doing his True Will, fulfilling the Universal Will by opposing no resistance to it in an attempt to grab some illusion, and suffering nothing because realizing that all that happens to him is a mirror-description of himself. He goes laughing and dancing through the world, and destroys all evil and sorrow as he goes, by the simple method of showing everybody he meets that their vices and their discontent arise from ignorance, that they are each one perfect in his way, each a necessary illusion through which the All becomes conscious of itself (just as the Fool interprets himself to himself through his own set of illusions) and each only a nuisance to himself and others by following false Ideals, interfering with others for various mistaken reasons, and so on, thereby causing all sorts of collisions, losing his way and so despairing of Direction, fearing the Future, regretting the Past, and misapplying — the Present. The Fool shows each one his proper path and puts him on it; it soon appears that there is room in the world for all alike, that all are equally worthy of wonder and worship, that Perfection is inherent in the Whole, and that the object of Life (which is motion) is to display an every-changing pageant, thus enabling each to become conscious of the All, which otherwise would remain homogenous, devoid of quantity and quality, Unknown and Unknowable.

I do hope you see this point of view. It has saved me from spiritual despair, made all things intelligible and adorable for me, set me radiantly revelling in my Work, which I had almost abandoned as fatuous; I am in love with life, and ready to ride with Death towards a new Adventure.

The world is dying with disgust with its own dread vanity; the treadmill its one task, the Sodom-apple its one food,[2] oblivion its only joy, and "Hope not" its final word of wisdom. You have declared this doom more

---

[1] [James Branch Cabell, *Domnei: A Comedy of Woman-Worship* (1920); see Works Cited. This was Cabell's book after *Jurgen*.]

[2] [*The Book of Lies*, chap. 67 is entitled "Sodom-apples." In his commentary, Crowley remarks that "it is useless to try to abandon the Great Work."]

dreadfully than any man since Gautama;[1] for you have left no loophole, either in time, or space, or condition of existence, for any being, from Koshchei to Dame Lisa.[2] The world is waiting for you to utter the wizard-word Thelema, which changes every curse into Blessing, gives meaning to the most incoherent gibberish, and bows down the most barren tree with sun-ripe fruit.

Forgive this spate of speech! My words are of little worth; but if you will read *The Book of the Law* often enough, the Spirit of the Lord which is in you will shew you the splendour of this Freedom, and inspire you to send forth its sunlight through the prism of your Art, that men may behold your "Bow in the Cloud"[3] and know that the floods are diminished upon the face of the Earth.

---

[1] [Gautama Buddha (c. 563–483 BCE), founder of Buddhism.]

[2] [Koshchei is a figure in the Russian fairy-tale "The Death of Koschei the Deathless" in Andrew Lang's *Red Fairy Book*. In Cabell's *Jurgen*, Dame Lisa is the wife whom Jurgen abandons; they are reunited in the end.]

[3] [Gen. 9:13.]

The Antecedents
of Thelema

I

It has been remarked by some critics of the Law of Thelema that the words "Do what thou wilt" are not original with the Master Therion; or, rather, with Aiwass, who uttered to the scribe Ankh-f-n-khonsu, the priest of the princes, *The Book of the Law*.[1]

II

This is true enough, in its own way; we have, firstly, the word of St. Augustine: "Love, and do what thou wilt."[2]

This is however, as the context shows, by no means what is meant by *The Book of the Law*. St. Augustine's thesis is that if the heart be full of love, one cannot go wrong. It is, so to say, a rider upon the theorem of St. Paul's 13th chapter of the 1st Epistle to the Corinthians.[3]

---

[1] [The Master Therion is Crowley. Ankh-f-n-khonsu (or Ankhefenkhons I) was an Egyptian priest (c. 725 BCE) whose funerary stèle (the Stèle of Revealing) is paraphrased in *Liber AL vel Legis*, *The Book of the Law*; Crowley identified with him. Aiwass is the præterhuman intelligence who dictated *Liber AL* to Crowley.]

[2] [*Homilies on the First Epistle of John*, VII, 8: "The deeds of men are only discerned by the root of charity. For many things may be done that have a good appearance, and yet proceed not from the root of charity. For thorns also have flowers: some actions truly seem rough, seem savage; howbeit they are done for discipline at the bidding of charity. Once for all, then, a short precept is given thee: Love, and do what thou wilt: whether thou hold thy peace, through love hold thy peace; whether thou cry out, through love cry out; whether thou correct, through love correct; whether thou spare, through love do thou spare: let the root of love be within, of this root can nothing spring but what is good." The American philosopher and psychologist William James (1842–1910) commented that "Saint Augustine's maxim, *Dilige et quod vis fac*—if you but love (God), you may do as you incline—is morally one of the profoundest of observations, yet it is pregnant, for such persons, with passports beyond the bounds of conventional morality." *The Varieties of Religious Experience* (1902), §4; see Works Cited.]

[3] [I Cor. 13:13 reads "And now abideth faith, hope, charity, these three; but the greatest of these is charity." Some translations give love instead of charity.]

III

Far more important is the Word of Rabelais,[1] *Fais ce que veulx*.[2] The sublime Doctor does indeed intend, so far as he goes, to set forth in essence the Law of Thelema, very much as it is understood by the Master Therion himself.

The implications of the context are significant.

Our Master makes the foundation of the Abbey of Thelema the quite definite climax of his history of Gargantua; he describes his ideal of society.[3] Thus he was certainly occupied with the idea of a new Æon, and he saw, albeit perhaps dimly, that *Fais ce que veulx* was the required Magical Formula.

The Cardinal Jean du Bellay, indeed, reported to Francis I that *Gargantua* was a "new Gospel."[4] It was, in fact, the Book that the Renaissance lacked; and had it been taken as it should have been, the world might have been spared the ignominy of Protestantism.

As the character of his parable demanded, he confines himself to painting a picture of pure Beauty; he does not enter into the questions of political economy (and like subjects) which must be solved in order to realize the ideal of the Law of Liberty. But he says distinctly that the

---

[1] [François Rabelais (1494?–1553) was a French humanist, physician and satirist whose principal works are *The Terrible Deeds and Acts of Prowess of Pantagruel, King of the Dipsodes* (1532) and *The Very Frightful Life of the Grand Gargantua* (1534), later collected as *Gargantua and Pantagruel*; see Works Cited.]

[2] [French, "Do what thou wilt." In Rabelais' original this is *"Faictz ce que vouldras,"* from *Gargantua* (1534); see chap. 54 of the first edition (chap. 57 of book I of *Gargantua and Pantagruel*).]

[3] [*Gargantua and Pantagruel*, book I, chaps. 52–57, has a description of the Abbey and its monastic rule:

"LII: How Gargantua Caused to be built for the Monk the Abbey of Theleme."

"LIII: How the Abbey of the Thelemites was built and endowed."

"LIV: The Inscription set upon the Great Gate of Theleme."

"LV: What Manner of Dwelling the Thelemites Had."

"LVI: How the men and women of the religious Order of Theleme were appareled."

"LVII: How the Thelemites were governed, and of their manner of living." This chapter reads "All their life was spent not in laws, statutes, or rules, but according to their own freewill and pleasure … In all their rule and strictest tie of their order, there was but this one clause to be observed: DO WHAT THOU WILT."]

[4] [Cardinal Jean du Bellay (1492–1560) was Rabelais' principal patron, and Francis I (1494–1547) was the King of France.]

religion of Thelema is to be contrary to all others. True, for Thelema is Magick, and Magick is science, the antithesis of the religious hypothesis.[1]

There are to be no walls to the Abbey. To him, as to us, "The word of Sin is Restriction."[2] He says plainly that constriction merely gives rise to murders and conspiracies. It is impossible to quench the flame of the Holy Spirit of Man; and the attempt to smother it leads infallibly to con-flagration of explosive fury.

Even in the matter of the petty restrictions of Time, the conventions with which we all unthinkingly comply, Rabelais sees the peril to the freedom of the Soul. In his Abbey of Thelema there are to be no clocks, no fixed routine; what must be done should be done when need actually arises. The test is fitness.

We should not take this passage too literally. Our time-conventions are devised by experience to secure to us the greatest possible margin of freedom.

Rabelais insists on the members of his Abbey being physically fit; so too *The Book of the Law*: "Wisdom says: be strong!"[3] and similar passages.

There is to be no separation of the sexes, and no artificial restrictions upon Love. *The Book of the Law* is even more explicit upon this most fundamental social principle.[4]

With all this we find no suggestion of any communistic theories; they are in fact specifically disowned. The ethics of the Æon of Horus are equally individualistic. "Ye shall gather goods and store of women and spices; ye shall wear rich jewels", etc.[5] "Ye shall see them at rule, at vic-torious armies, at all the joy".[6]

Members of superstitious religions are not to be allowed to enter the Abbey of Thelema. In *The Book of the Law* the attitude is not merely defensive; the implication is that superstition is to be stamped out, or at least that its victims are to be definitely relegated to the slave-class. The Freeman is to war down the serf: "on the low men trample in the fierce lust of your pride, in the day of your wrath."[7] There is no place in the

---

[1] Also see [*Liber AL vel Legis,*] *The Book of the Law* III:49–54.
[2] *Liber AL* I:41.
[3] *Liber AL* II:70.
[4] See *Liber AL* I:12, 13; I:41; I:51–53; II:52.
[5] *Liber AL* I:61.
[6] *Liber AL* II:24. See also II:18; II:21, II:58, etc.
[7] *Liber AL* II:24.

Abbey imagined by Rabelais, and to be realized by the Master Therion, for those parasites of society who feed upon the troubles caused by Restriction: officials, lawyers, financiers, and the like. Ill-disposed people—that is, those whose failure to understand their own true will of Freedom leads them to interfere with others—are not to be tolerated.

In *The Book of the Law* this is implied throughout. The true will of every Free Man is essentially noble.[1]

Thus ends Rabelais his account of the qualifications of admission to his Abbey: that the Postulant should be filled with the spirit of Nobility, of Truth, and of Beauty. With this idea *The Book of the Law* is so penetrated that quotation would overwhelm.

We may then conclude that the masterpiece of Rabelais contains in singular perfection a clear forecast of the Book which was to be revealed by Aiwass to Ankh-f-n-khonsu 370 years later.

IV

Was the mighty spirit of Alcofribas Nasier[2] aware of the prophetic fire of his immortal book?

He has fortunately left us in no doubt upon this point; for he did not content himself with having created in parable that Abbey of Thelema which his eager gaze foresaw from the black abyss of those Ages not yet thrilled by the morning Star of the Renaissance, and dimly heralded by the Wolf's Tail of the Reformation.

He proceeded to envelop himself in the mist of oracular speech, to fulminate his light through dark sayings, to clothe the naked beauty of his Time-piercing thought in the pontifical vestments of prophecy.

The reader of today, plunged from the limpid waters of his allegory into the glooming gulfs of sibylline and subterranean song, is startled indeed when, after repeated efforts to penetrate the mystery of his versicles, he perceives the adumbration of dim forms—and recognizes them, with something of terror, for the images of the events of this very generation of mankind!

Writing at a period when the Divine Right of Kings under the Supreme Governance of Almighty God was yet unchallenged, Rabelais

---

[1] It might well be that a man's True Will were to see Justice established; but this is not the normal conception of a lawyer. And so for other cases.

[2] [An anagram of François Rabelais, and a pseudonym under which he issued *Pantagruel* (1532).]

describes the rise of Democracy. Idle people, he writes, will stir up social strife, so as eventually to destroy all proper relations between classes and individuals. The ignorant will have as much political power as the instructed. The dullest and the most stupid people will be entrusted with government.

Just as we see it today! For genuine knaves are rare enough in governments; real capacity, even for dishonesty, is baffled by our political machinery. A clever man must at least pretend to be stupid to attain, and act with consistently dense imbecility to maintain, his place among the rulers of the world. No sooner is he suspected of possessing even one spark of intelligence that the herd distrust him, butt him from his pedestal, and trample him to death beneath their hooves.

The style of the oracle at this point becomes unfathomably obscure; it is hard to discover what exact process Rabelais describes as the means of terrestrial catastrophe which culminates in universal revolution. But, the horror at its height, the Master becomes admirably lucid in his description of the avenging lightning which Destiny has prepared for the salvation of the race.

A great flame will spring up, he says, and put an end to this flood.

What clearer reference could be desired to the Æon of Horus? Is not Horus "force and fire,"[1] the victorious foe of the dark waters of the Nile? Is not To $M\epsilon\gamma a$ $\Theta\eta\rho\iota o\nu$, the Great Wild Beast, the Lion of the Sun, the destined conqueror of Iesous, the Fish?[2]

And so at last the elect, the sons self-chosen of Freedom, come into their own, and the false slaves of Restriction stripped of their knavish

---

[1] [*Liber Legis* II:20.]

[2] [In the magical theory of dispensationalism, the dominant force of an era is determined by the astronomical precession of the equinoxes; every 2,156 years, the sun rises at the spring equinox in a different astrological sign. During the Christian era it rose in the sign of Pisces, the fish, and fish symbolism pervaded Christianity (e.g., the identification of the Greek word for fish, $\iota\chi\theta\upsilon\varsigma$, as the acronym for Christ's title "Jesus Christ, Son of God, Savior" [$I\eta\sigma o\upsilon\varsigma$ $X\rho\iota\sigma\tau o\varsigma$ $\Theta\epsilon o\upsilon$ $\Upsilon\iota o\varsigma$ $\Sigma\omega\tau\eta\rho$]. Other aspects of Christianity were represented by Pisces' opposing sign, Virgo the Virgin. In the New Æon of Horus the sun rises in Aquarius, and this energy has replaced (or "conquered") the Piscean current as the dominant energy in this age. Crowley, however, felt that Aquarius' opposing sign, Leo the Lion (ruled by the Sun), better characterized the present Æon. See his letter to W.B. Crow, November 11, 1944, quoted in the editor's introduction to *Liber CXI vel Aleph*, 2nd ed. (1991), p. xvii; see Works Cited.]

spoils, their hoarded dross of stupidity, and put in their proper place as slaves of the true Men of the Race. Nor does the great Magician of Touraine stop with any mere symbolic identification; he indicates the Master Therion by name! The very last verse of his oracle runs thus:

O que est à reverer
Cil qui pourra en fin perseverer.[1]

He who is able to *endure unto the end*, he insists, is to be blessed with worship. And what is this "I will endure unto the end" but PERDURABO, the magical motto at his first initiation of the Master Therion?[2]

V

Superb as is this adumbration of the Law of Thelema by Rabelais with his Word *Fais ce que veulx*, *The Book of the Law* gives us more—it gives us "all in the clear light".[3]

Through "Do what thou wilt shall be the whole of the Law",[4] we have a deeper truth for the strong student, a more detailed and accurate technique for the Aspirant to practice: "The word of the Law is Θελ-ημα."[5] In the analysis of this word is to be found the master-key to every theorem and to every problem of the day. There lies concealed from the profane, yet open to the consecrated, the proof of the nature of Aiwass Himself, of his superiority in intelligence to any mere human being. The whole doctrine of the Universe, the solution of every question of Ontology, is given thereby. So also it reveals fully many a mystery of Science. I suppose that my research has yet revealed not one tithe of its marvels; but the time has come to disclose what truths I have discovered therein. They shall serve both as the warrant of my Work, and as the earnest (to the stern seeker after Wisdom) of further rewards—that shall surpass my holiest imagination!

---

[1] ["How praiseworthy he / Who shall have persevered even unto the end!" is the ending of the "prophetic riddle" at the end of *Gargantua* (1534), chap. 56, "*Enigme trouve es fondemens de l'abbaye des Thelemites*" (book I of *Gargantua and Pantagruel*). See also Matt. 10:22, 24:13, and Mark 13:13.]

[2] [When Crowley was initiated as a Neophyte in the Golden Dawn in November of 1898 he took his first motto, *Perdurabo*, "I will endure unto the end."]

[3] [*Liber AL* I:56.]

[4] [*Liber Legis* I:40.]

[5] [*Liber AL* I:39. Θελημα is *thelema*, the Greek for "will."]

VI[1]

The Universe = 0 (or it would not be complete). But $0 = 1 + (-1)$.

(0 = 2) = Magick = the Will to Live.

(2 = 0) = Mysticism = the Will to Die.

"Every man and every woman is a star."[2] (A star is an individual identity; it radiates energy, it goes, it is a point of view. Its object is to become the whole by establishing relations with other stars. Each such relation is an Event: it is an act of Love under Will.

Love = $1 + (-1) = (a)$ 0 and (b) 2.

This is expressed by Mother (*hé*), Father (*yod*), then Son (*vau*) (= 2), then Daughter (*hé* final) (= 0).

This process repeats itself perpetually. An Event is the ultimate *thing* in the Universe; it is the conjunction of an Individual with a Possibility. Each (I + P) is unique and infinite; so is each Event.[3] The Individual is measured by the number and importance of the Events belonging to his growth; i.e., to the number of Possibilities he has fulfilled.

I + P always = 0, such being a term in a series a^0. They are indistinguishable, Ia from Ib, etc., as the series is homogenous; there are no coordinate axes. But Events are theoretically distinguishable: Ea = IaPb, Eb = IbPa, etc., so that as soon as we can define an Individual of the Second Order [as] I to the power of I, one to whom belongs Events Ea, Eb, etc., we can have a practical distinction between Events; this gives us the idea of "Events of the Second Order" E'. Thus E'a is not E'b, though both [are] composed of identical elements—at least of indistinguishable ones. All relations are meaningless in themselves; but one relation may be contrasted with another. The Ego grows by establishing relations with other points of view and absorbing them. Hence the bigger the Ego, the less the sense of Egoity. The Universe is a set of Events; they do not *exist*, they occur.[4] It is a dynamic, not a static, phenomenon. Any stasis is a mere temporary resolution. Logic describes the process of Thought, which is the essence of Action. Mathematics is the language of Logic. A man must think of himself as a LOGOS, as going, not as a fixed idea. "Do

---

[1] [Crowley noted that this section was in draft in the form of rough notes.]

[2] [*Liber AL* I:3.]

[3] Cf. *Berashith* on value of 0 to the power of 0. [Abhavānanda (pseud. of Crowley), *Berashith, an Essay in Ontology* (1903); see Works Cited.]

[4] Cf. the electron, which has no mass, but is an electric charge.

what thou wilt" is thus necessarily his formula. He only becomes Himself when he attains to the loss of Egoity, of the sense of separateness. He becomes All, PAN,[1] when he becomes Zero. Note that Events may be considered for convenience in any or all of three modes of projection: (*a*) as extended in space; (*b*) ditto in time; (*c*) as causally connected. These are forms of (*a*) sensation; (*b*) consciousness of going; (*c*) reason.

The Universe is an Act of Faith.

Its Reality is an Act of Love.

Men resent Happiness, "knowing that it cannot last"; but other animals—and Wise Men—accept things as they are.

Marriage is the strait-waistcoat of Love.

Art and Science consist in selecting, arranging and presenting facts so as to illustrate some aspect of Truth.

Law is the corpse of Justice.

Morality is the corpse of Conduct.

Religion is the carcass of Fear.

Happiness is the state of mind resulting from the free fulfillment of a function.

A holy man is one who is not bound by normal desires.

A prostitute is one who is obliged to treat individuals as a member of a class, *ob pecuniam*.[2]

All proofs turn out on examination to be definitions. All definitions are circular. (For $a = bc$, $b = de \ldots w = xy$, and $y = za$.)

Consider the proposition: Thought is possible.

Realism = Romanticism to one strong enough to worship things as they are.

The true Artist loves all his characters equally.

Punishment: increase of sensibility at the expense of control.

Reduce the A logical proposition to 2: thus A and E are extreme cases of 1 and 0, as the circle is of the ellipse.

---

[1] [The Greek Παν (*pan*) means "all."]

[2] [*Lat.*, "in exchange for money."]

The Beginning of the New World

Unrest is the sign of this moment.

No man, however rich or safely placed, feels sure of next week.

No man knows where he is going.

This is because no man knows where he ought to go.

The bases of society have been so shaken that it has become impossible for anyone to make a plan, just as a banker or a surveyor could not work if he were no longer sure of the multiplication table.

Now, this state of things is not wholly due to the actual conditions of material existence, to political unrest, or to economic confusion.

Circumstances have not the power to wreck the soul of man as long as he has in himself adequate driving-power and wit and skill to steer.

When men have a definite aim to pursue, they instinctively find means of overriding mutual interference, and may even work together (unselfishly, as it is polishedly called) to obtain their separate ends with the minimum of friction.

But when they are aimless they become distracted and witless; they push each other aside in their desperation; even the simplest tasks become impossible.

Today the mass of mankind has no longer any law by which to live, any unchallenged principles of right action.

The one deep cause of the present universal anarchy is the loss of all man's moral sanction.

The many religions of the world have all lost their power to guide chiefly because the development of means of transport and of international commerce have convinced the educated that any one religion is about as good or as bad as another for the purposes of social discipline, and that none has any validity from the standpoint of actual fact, or historical or philosophical truth.

The remedy is evidently to be found only in one way. There must be found a formula based upon absolute common sense, without one trammel of theological theory or dogma, a formula to which no man of intelligence can refuse assent, and which at the same time affords an absolute sanction for all laws of conduct, social and political no less than individual, so that the right or wrong of any isolated or concerted action can be determined with mathematical accuracy by any trained observer, entirely irrespective of his personal idiosyncrasies.

This formula must be scientific, not religious.

This formula is:

"Do what thou wilt shall be the whole of the Law."[1]

This formula does not, as ignorant or malicious people pretend, mean "Do anything you like." On the contrary, it is a most severe self-control of every individual or social unit to concentrate its whole energy performing his true proper function; and this function is to be determined by a profound, accurate calculation of the potentialities inherent in its constitution.

The first practical step towards this end is the formation of a strong central organization to direct coherently the activities of the numerous adherents already established in many countries.

It will then be necessary to convene conferences of experts in all the sciences, which treat of mankind in his social and individual character, in order to draw up a comprehensive international programme.

---

[1] [*Liber AL* I:40.]

On Thelema

Do what thou wilt shall be the whole of the Law.

The Universe is the fulfillment and the sum total of all possibilities. Indeed one may almost say that this is so by definition.

A conscious being—i.e., an individual centre of consciousness, a Monad—can possess in itself no qualities. Its idea of the existence of not only the Universe but itself is evidently dependent upon and conterminous with those sets of possibilities which it has itself experienced. That part of the Universe which has as yet not entered within the sphere of its experience has no existence for it. It is as a new world—a universe awaiting discovery. Each conscious being, therefore, must differ from every other by virtue of its position in the universe; one not of latitude and longitude, nor of time and space, but rather a position of degree or state of consciousness, of point of view. Its identity, likewise, must of necessity be one of pure negation. The value of any being is determined by the quantity and quality of those parts of the universe which it has discovered, and which therefore compose its sphere of experience. It grows by extending this experience, by enlarging, as it were, this sphere. In the case of two beings possessing little or no experience in common, mutual understanding is clearly impossible. Sympathy is thus seen to be more a question of experience being approximately conterminous, or at least coincident with respect to a large proportion of the experiences to which special value is attached by both. The real value of any new experience is determined by its aptitude for increasing the sum total of knowledge, or the degree of understanding and illumination it sheds on previous experiences.

As a general rule, then, the greater the sum of coincident experiences of any two beings, the greater the likelihood of their general agreement. Thus, at a certain point in development a being is very likely to consider any disagreement with him as definite error, and it is an extremely important stage in progress to reach an habitual attitude of mind which realizes that any divergent view of a given question is due not to moral obliquity, but to a greater variety of assimilable experiences. Such individuals grow in a very special manner when they learn to welcome divergent points of view and contrary experiences, and seek to assimilate them, as understanding that this is the best possible way to acquire at a single stroke an immensity of new experiences instead of having to go through them in detail.

It should be clear from the foregoing that the Law of Thelema "Do what thou wilt" must be a logical rule of conduct to anyone who accepts the above premises, for the ultimate Will of every conscious being must be to so increase his general experience as to understand and know himself, which he can only do by studying and understanding the whole universe. That the task is endless is no detriment to this process, but makes it all the more interesting. It is the way of the *tao*. Finality would cloy.

Now then, with regard to the explanation of the Law given elsewhere in *The Book of the Law*, "Love is the law, love under will",[1] while will as above shown is of absolute logical and ethical validity, it can only be executed by the process of assimilation of all foreign elements; that is, by love. To refuse to unite oneself with any phenomenon soever is to deprive oneself of its value—even of life itself, as in the case of the Black Brothers, shut up in the Abyss, and doomed to conscious disintegration in the realm of disconnected ideas and experiences, to "perish with the dogs of Reason."[2] This refusal is only enacted when one is convinced that the new phenomenon is hostile to the set of experiences already acquired and made part of onself. But it is a serious mark of imperfection, of grave failure to realize the facts in the matter, to take this attitude. Even supposing, for one brief moment and for argument's sake alone, that the new idea under consideration is so incompatible with the experiences already acquired and assimilated that their destruction is necessitated if it is to be accepted, then one fact stands out vividly, showing clearly that the old set of experiences is so imperfect as to be actually unfitted to continue its erstwhile existence; its destruction would be an

---

[1] [*Liber AL* I:57.]

[2] [*Liber AL* II:27. The A∴A∴ teaches that those Adepts who cannot or will not surrender their egos in the Ordeal of the Abyss remain there to become Black Brothers, misguided seekers who mistake their own egos for the Godhead. See *Liber 418* and "One Star in Sight"; see Works Cited.]

advantage to that being, enabling a reconstruction along totally different lines—a reconstruction which would lend itself more readily to the acquisition of new experiences and apparently contradictory ideas.

Needless to say, of course, it is necessary in actual practice to use one's judgment in choosing the phenomenon which one next proposes to assimilate. One should not necessarily shoot oneself or another out of mere curiosity. The right of choice is with the individual. At the same time it should be remembered that "The word of Sin is Restriction."[1] No other individual has any right to determine or restrict the choice of another except in such cases as the experience of one includes for all practical purposes the experience of the other; as in the case of parents and young children. There are also various other cases where the free choice of the individual must be restricted insofar as that unhampered choice might interfere with the equal rights of others. But this is in no way a question of abstract right and wrong, but a matter of practical politics.

The phrase "pitiless love," thrown scornfully at times in the faces of Thelemites, although not itself occurring in *The Book of the Law*, has nevertheless a certain justification. Pity implies two very grave errors— errors which are utterly incompatible with the views of the universe above briefly indicated.

The first error therein is an implicit assumption that something is wrong with the Universe, and that moreover one is so insidiously obsessed by the Trance of Sorrow as to have completely failed in the task of solving the riddle of Sorrow, and gone through life with the groan of a hurt animal—"All is Sorrow."[2] The second error is still greater since it involves the complex of the Ego. To pity another person implies that you are superior to him, and you fail to recognize his absolute right to exist as he is. You assert yourself superior to him, a concept utterly opposed to the ethics of Thelema—"Every man and every woman is a star"[3] and each being is a Sovereign Soul. A moment's thought therefore will suffice to show how completely absurd any such attitude is, in reference to the underlying metaphysical facts.

---

[1] [*Liber AL* I:41.]
[2] [*Dukkhā* is the realization that everything connected to the physical world leads to pain and suffering. It is the "First Noble Truth" of the Buddha.]
[3] [*Liber AL* I:3.]

"… for there are love and love. There is the dove, and there is the serpent."[1] Sympathy, obviously, is the more correct frame of mind, for it is a pitiless love involving in reality an identification of oneself with the other; it is therefore an act of true love. "There is no bond that can unite the divided but love".[2]

If we translate the Greek word into Latin and say "compassion" instead of "sympathy," the process of degeneration of language gives it a false connotation. It must be remembered that the Greek word *pathein*[3] does not necessarily mean to suffer in the same etymological sense of *sub fero*,[4] which implies inferiority and therefore pity. Of compassion, is it not written "Compassion is the vice of kings"?[5]

Love is the law, love under will.

---

[1] [*Liber AL* I:57.]

[2] [*Liber AL* I:41.]

[3] [A word signifying "to suffer, to be affected."]

[4] [Latin, *sub* ("under") and *fero* ("to bear"), i.e., to endure or undergo, and the etymology of the English word "suffer."]

[5] [*Liber AL* II:21.]

The Method of Thelema

At the moment when the doors of human progress are creaking on their hinges, when mankind seems almost resigned to the cynical contemplation of its own agony in the hope of delaying its inevitable decay; when Europe has the aspect of a vast and insecure hospital for sick nations; when the Far East is drinking itself into madness on the arrack of Western democratic shibboleths, and when America is foundering in ceaselessly renewed and insoluble problems; — when, in a word, the whole earth seems weary and out of joint, at its critical angle, it is interesting to glance attentively at the efforts of certain men whose researches have led them to the intimacy of the most secret laws of Nature.

From the beginning of history, wise men have tried to overcome error, and to help their fellow-men to find and recognize the truth. To them must we attribute the real, the deep-lying causes of all social and political revolutions. It has always been their pride to nail to the mast the standard of liberty.

Mankind owes much to men of this stamp, for it is they who guide and guard it. By the development of certain faculties as superior to those of normal human intelligence as that is to the mentality of the insect, they have attained a certain comprehension and made a certain synthesis of the facts of life which enable them from time to time to announce a new fundamental principle, by the application of which humanity may take a clear-cut step in the right direction. It is only necessary to recall the names of Plato, Aristotle, Kepler, Newton, Bacon and Descartes.[1] In

---

[1] [Plato (c. 427–347 BCE) and Aristotle (384–322 BCE) were Greek philosophers. Johannes Kepler (1571–1630) was a German astronomer. Sir Isaac Newton (1642–1727) was an English mathematician. The chronology suggests that the English philosopher Francis Bacon is intended (see p. 122, note 7), not the 13th c. scientist Roger Bacon. René Descartes (1596–1650) was a French philosopher, mathematician and scientist.]

each case we find an absolute challenge to all accepted principles and a complete sceptical destruction of them; followed by the formulation of a new principle which resumes in itself, while transcending, the old.

At the exact moment when the futility of the formalized faiths of the world has been recognized, despite the stoutest denials; when the first principles of religion and ethics have been subconsciously rejected, so that a kind of spiritual neurasthenia broke loose in the hysteria of the world-war, there appeared a mysterious figure who is generally known as the Master Therion. Instructed by chiefs who have hitherto preferred to remain in the background, he brings to free and enlightened men a law by virtue of which mankind may arrive at a new and higher stage of advancement on every plane, from the biological to the spiritual. It is a law of liberty and of love, but also of discipline and of force. This law is already in operation under the name of the Law of Thelema.

The formula of this law is: Do what thou wilt.[1] Its moral aspect is simple enough in theory. Do what thou wilt does not mean Do as you please, although it implies this degree of emancipation, that it is no longer possible to say *à priori* that a given action is "wrong." Each man has the right—and an absolute right—to accomplish his True Will.[2]

The more one examines the deepest implications of the Law of Thelema, the more one understands that it constitutes a sublime synthesis, and the only one possible, of the teachings of every science, from embryology to history.

It is the key of every problem which can confront the human mind; for it does not imply exactly a new religion, but rather a new philosophy, a new ethic. For the first time in history, we are able to conceive of moral science as truly a science; for our conclusions are derived from dynamic measurements without reference to absurd axioms and impudent postulates. It coordinates the several discoveries of Science in a perfectly consistent and coherent framework.

The Law of Thelema is thus capable of accomplishing a profound revolution of the thought and action of mankind. The Master Therion furnishes (in a series of essays, which only few have hitherto been privileged to read) proofs historical, philosophical, physical and mathemati-

---

[1] [*Liber AL* I:40, III:60.]

[2] [*Liber AL* I:42–43 reads "… thou hast no right but to do thy will. Do that, and no other shall say nay." See also *Liber Oz sub figura 77*.]

cal, of the justice and the accuracy of his claim that *The Book of the Law* contains the complete formulæ of the next great step in human progress, which is to set every man to the task precisely suited to his individual nature, and furnish him with the means of discovering the nature of his true Will.[1]

It seems not unreasonable to suppose that the new generation, directing itself consciously or subconsciously by this indication, will develop human personality to its full stature. The whole of our present civilization, with its cohorts of hereditary possibilities, which until now have never been utilized to full advantage, will form itself on this new law of spiritual perfection.

Nor let it be forgotten that the full blossoming of this new era is perceptible on every hand. Governments, it is true, have not yet taken official notice of the subtle evolution which is taking place under their eyes. They are bewildered and alarmed; they either break down in chaos or react savagely against the manipulations which disturb their stupidity. But they will not prevent the prodigious dawn which is taking place in the essence of man.

We have given some idea of the nature of the Law of Thelema and the general meaning of its formula, Do what thou wilt. A theory of indestructible solidity and perfection has been presented to the world. The question then arises, How is it to be put into practice?

It is here that [there] appears the necessity of creating an immense and universal technique which shall permit its application in the immediate future. The first step is to constitute a sort of General Council, composed of the most intelligent men of science in the world. Their first business will be to interpret, each in the light of his own knowledge, fortified by the cross-rays of the knowledge of his colleagues, the deepest and widest sense of the Law of Thelema. Existing sciences must be closely knitted into a harmonious pattern, of which the Law of Thelema supplies the *artistic* motive.

The work of formulating the plans for the administration of the Law will fall within the province of subcommittees, directed by the central

---

[1] [A probable reference to the New Commentary to *The Book of the Law*; cf. Crowley, *The Law is for All*, ed. Louis Wilkinson and Hymenæus Beta; see Works Cited.]

Council, composed of men of the less abstract sciences, and of the professions, trades, arts and crafts, which afford constant experience of practical problems.

Apart from this general constructive scheme, the Council and the committees, in regular interplay, will tackle, *seriatim*,[1] the various crises which at present threaten the planet, understanding how each in its own way represents some breach or other of the Law of Thelema, which is the law of fitness. They will be able to remedy the evil at its source.

These problems are, in their ultimation, of infinite diversity. Many have hitherto appeared impossible to resolve.

There is no need to insist on the interior crises of mankind, his crises of conscience. These may conceivably be resolved by a definite education; on one side, the practices of all oriental sages, so ill-understood owing to the confusion of their science with the religions of their country; on the other, by the rituals vulgarly called magical, equally fallen into contempt, although of a very real efficacy, on account of the gross misunderstanding of their real nature which has always obscured them. By such means it may prove possible to create (rather, to develop), in man, a faculty superior to reason; immune from intellectual criticism. Such a faculty would permit man—does, indeed, already permit certain men—to contemplate the problem of the suffering and sorrow of life with a complete detachment and serenity, because it would no longer be protected by the superficiality and incompleteness of its data.

But it is not of such internal crises, of such spiritual sickness, that one need speak at present. It is of more immediate and practical importance to discuss external crises, those which devastate political and social conditions.

In order to apply the Law of Thelema, to investigate the solutions indicated by *The Book of the Law*, and to utilize them to remedy existing difficulties, the appeal is only to technicians. Bankers, architects, engineers, biologists, chemists, doctors, must combine their knowledge and apply it to the discovery of the general practical formulæ of the Law of Thelema.

The ploughman deserts his furrow to lose himself, and with himself the essence of his race, in the maw of the city. He has been tempted, by false education and visions of a phantom happiness, to violate the true

---

[1] [Latin, "in order," "in series" or "in sequence."]

law of his being. ... More subtle error is to be seen in the class struggle. The Sisyphus-stone of the labour question has been poised by those radical misinterpretations of the problem of well-being, which consist in supposing that the possession of an automobile is the *summum bonum*.[1] Craftsmanship is dead. The technical perfection, combined with the inventive genius, of the artisan, is no longer the pride and happiness of every village. The modern workman hides, beneath the rags of socialism and democracy, incurable indolent ulcers. Colonization once more is everywhere in a critical condition. In some cases, both the ruling and the subject nation are staggering beneath the weight of veritable crosses, because neither understands how to arrange their interrelation in such a way as to secure, for both equally, the maximum possibilities of their natural growth.

Commerce itself again——. But here we must break off. The reader will find it only too easy to think of a hundred cases where the error of unfitness, the violation of what we may call biological law in its widest philosophic sense, threatens the well-being and even the very existence of the individual; whether that individual be a crop, an idea, a person, or an institution.

In their actual state of mental evolution, men have not yet been able to free their minds from the absolutely false idea that each of the troubles indicated above has its particular malignant bacillus. Opinion is still in the stage of chemistry before the discovery of the Periodic Law—we may even say of the Law of Combining Weights. In those days each chemical reaction appeared more or less an isolated, and even an arbitrary, phenomenon. It was the discovery of the uniformity of chemical action which made possible the organic branch of the science, with its synthesis of compounds whose properties were predicted, before they were ever prepared, on purely theoretical general principles. And it is to organic chemistry that mankind owes a good half of modern conveniences, dyes, medicines, high explosives, and what not. By the adoption of a similar principle of uniformity in ethics, we may not unreasonably expect a parallel development of constructive social and political science. It is sheer folly to continue to lose oneself in details; during the analysis of a problem, to neglect to keep in mind the subtle currents which connect the diverse manifestations of our complex nature.

---

[1] [*Lat.*, "greatest good."]

By reconciling the most opposite points of view, the Law of Thelema has supplied a Master Key to every strong room in the Safe Deposit of the human soul. The evils which afflict humanity have not an independent cause for each; the only possible form of error is the violation of the law of one's own nature. This is no more and no less true of a cripple who wants to be a wrestler, or a miser who wants to be loved for himself alone, as of a cranberry bush that should want to live in the Sahara, or an atom of gold whose dream was to combine with argon.

The application of the Law of Thelema, which implies the development of the individual within its own proper limits, following a moral law determined by the real conditions of his deepest nature, demonstrates on the first examination how each of the vast mass of human errors is due to this one original mistake.

The Book of the Law says: "Every man and every woman is a star."[1] The image is nobly suggestive: no other could show more clearly the essence of the application of the Thelemite formula. Each human being should consider himself the centre of an infinite circle; his universe is, in fact, for him different from that of every other person, and he simply leaves reality for phantasm when he tries to calculate in terms of what he has been stupidly taught to consider as the "real" universe—that objective universe, which consists merely of phenomena apparently common to all observers.

The reality of that universe, which is the universe of science, is only an abstraction; it is, no doubt, *nearly* true for everybody, roughly speaking; but it is *quite* true for nobody. A thousand men looking at a clock see a thousand different clocks, although we assume the unity of the object. But the man who sees the front of the clock is a great pedant if he refuses to tell the time by it, on the ground that somebody else can only see the back. Yet this stupidity is the foundation of the old morality in general, and altruism in particular.

Each man is therefore absolutely justified in regarding himself as the centre of the universe, and acting accordingly. To displace this centre, to break the harmony of a human system (which corresponds with strange precision, on the one hand, to the Sidereal Universe, and, on the other, to that of electrons) is to break the Law of Thelema, to blaspheme oneself. And, so far as anyone can tell, there is no other self. His fellow-

---

[1] [*Liber AL* I:3.]

percipients, whether God or his neighbour, are—so far as he knows them—only ideas created by the chemical and mechanical changes in his brain; and he does not really know that!

But assuming he knows anything at all, he knows himself. Therefore to sin against himself is his only possible sin. If I commit this crime (whatever external form it may assume) it is not against the law of man, against an alien law that I blaspheme; it is against my own law, the cornerstone of my life, the complete development of my personality.

Consider a star, its gravitational relations with the universe! On every other mass in space it exercises a pull in accordance with the well-known law, a law unique. Every moment, as it passes on its course, the amount of that pull changes; but the Law is always the same. The parallel with human life is so accurate, so complex, and so intense, that it is rather a subject for meditation than for exposition. But the practical conclusion for each man will be the same. He must arrange his life in conformity with the universal Law, which is also his peculiar law, and which will assure him freedom from disturbance in his own well-ordered function and that of the system which immediately concerns him.

The extent of the advance which the strict application of the formula, Do what thou wilt, is able to secure for humanity, surpasses the imagination to conceive. Our wretched generation, bleeding from a thousand wounds, its nerves in rags from its blind excesses and misapprehensions, cannot escape from the Law. Whether we like it or not, the Law of Thelema is manifestly everywhere at work.

It is a blind Sphinx which will devour us, unless we can read its riddle, harness it to our chariot, and drive it triumphant into Thebes. Let those who constitute the intellectual and executive corps of pioneers of humanity be the first to enroll themselves in the army of the colleagues of the Master Therion, a master designated by no alien authority but by a power against which no revolt has ever been successful: the power of logic.

The paramount question is: how to teach man to act in accordance with the facts of Nature? He must cease to try to ignore or deny them in the interest of prejudice, to transcend them by fantastic idealism based on falsehood or fatuity; just as an architect must never misunderstand, miscalculate, or misapply, the law of strains and stresses.

The Law has been proclaimed. It is for us to interpret and to establish it.

Those who understand the importance of this appeal, those (to speak the language of the Law itself) whose true Will it is to direct the destinies of the race, will begin by organizing themselves into a body whose function will be to study and realize the Law, under the ægis of the Master Therion, and to proceed to the elaboration of the method of directing the course of events intelligently and naturally, for the first time in history.

This essay is primarily addressed to bankers, captains of industry, and, generally speaking, to all those whose natural office it is to manipulate social forces. It is the first condition of their existence, to say nothing of their security and prosperity, that they should direct the stream of commerce, the life-blood of the world. They are bound to understand the Law of Thelema, at least subconsciously, for they do not ship Brazil nuts to Brazil, or try to import corn from the Baltoro Glacier. Their only failure has been to see that the same principles of common sense which prevent them from perpetrating such absurdities can be applied, with the assistance of trained experts, to every possible problem which confronts them in their daily work. No men know better the frightful waste of "overhead" caused by unfitness in the staff, and similar errors. (I will not risk angering them by reminding them of idealistic legislation.)

Such men are ready for the message of the Master Therion, for they rule the mainspring of the economic clock. They should be the first to devote themselves to the cause, to accept the idea of the Law of Thelema, and to come forward to organize the scientific investigation which must be undertaken in order to bring the great branches of modern science, from political economy to biology and psychology, to contribute their force to swell the irresistible river of human attainment.

A Letter to Henry Ford

Sir:

Most men are sensible of, and occupied with, the welfare and progress of themselves, their families, their cities, or their countries; and they devote their energies to the advancement of these interests at the expense of those which they regard as alien.

But in every age and clime there have been a very few who have had at heart the sorrows of mankind as a whole, without distinction of persons or classes; and to the greatest among such men have been due all, without exception, of the real gains which the race has won from Nature.

We may balance the advantages against the losses which accrue from the activities of an ambitious man, like Napoleon, a civic hero, like Pericles, or a patriot, like Washington; but the real benefactors of mankind are men like Aristotle and Newton, Gautama Buddha and Pasteur, the inventors of the printing press and the automobile, the scope of whose work is as universal as their motives are, in the best cases, impersonal.[1]

For many centuries men capable of this degree of greatness, that they are able to consider the problems of human suffering and attainment with the benevolent detachment of a deity, have been secretly organized to watch over the well-being of their fellows, and to lend mutual aid in the Great Work of directing and assisting Mankind to achieve its sacred Destiny. Quietly and informally, yet strongly with the strength of their noble passion, they have fought against tyranny and obscurantism, they have

---

[1] [Pericles (495?–429 BCE) was an Athenian statesman. George Washington (1732–1799) was a revolutionary general and the first president of the United States. Aristotle (384–322 BCE) was a Greek philosopher. For Newton see p. 44, note 5. The French bacteriologist Louis Pasteur (1822–1895) proved the germ theory of disease transmission. Henry Ford (1863–1947) founded the Ford Motor Company; he did not invent the automobile, but introduced standardized parts and the mass production process.]

brought light into the dark places of the earth, they have made sure the way of genius, and they have maintained that silence which is at once their safeguard against oppression and the first condition of their vigilance.

These men, possessors of a moral energy which endows them with powers that to the ordinary mind often appear miraculous, employ their faculties independently and without ostentation whenever this course is possible. But there occur from time to time certain crises in the affairs of men which compel them to act in concert, and to select and send forth one of their number to put publicly forward such portions of their secret doctrine as will enable men to solve the current problem which baffles them, and to triumph over the dangers which beset them round.

Two and twenty years ago, such a situation reached its climax. It was already evident to the Watchers that all the sanctions which had served humanity for guidance had lost their compelling force. The fear of hell no longer restrained any but the most ignorant serfs; the attempt to replace religious threats and promises by moral obligations had taken hold of a few minds of the highest class, and, even so, its assumptions had been shown to be arbitrary and absurd by Ibsen and Nietzsche.[1] Souls weary of the search for Truth were falling back exhausted either upon the categorical assertions of fixed faiths like Romanism, or were abandoning themselves to the cynical materialism of the irreligious Jew.

Mankind was faced with the choice, often subconscious but none the less critical, between abject mental and moral submission to a system of despotic falsehoods, and an anarchy deprived alike of purpose and of principle, swayed only by the motive of immediate and superficial advantage. The inmost truth of the soul is Nobility; its deepest instincts revolt against the dishonour of surrender either to superstition or to scepticism. The best minds of every country were united in the bonds of despair.

The Watchers in the Silence understood that the time had come for them to take action. They foresaw that men, left guideless and incapable of wisdom, would plunge into the madness of the World War, and all its consequence of aimless unrest. They saw that the one way to save the

---

[1] [Crowley discusses the works of the Norwegian poet and playwright Henrik Ibsen (1828–1906) in "Good Hunting!," p. 111 infra. The works of the German philosopher Friedrich Wilhelm Nietzsche (1844–1900) were a major influence on Crowley's thought.]

race from such red ruin as has overwhelmed the civilizations of the past
was to send forth a Man with a Message. He must proclaim a positive
Law by which to measure human conduct; and this Law must not
depend for its authority on abstract theories, on doubtful legends, or on
any external foundation whatever: it must prove its own claim to compel
obedience by its own inherent righteousness and inevitability, and it
must be equally cogent for every individual man and woman in the
world.

Such a Law must evidently be most simple and universal, yet capable
of being applied in detail to all possible problems by the normal canon of
reason.

It would seem to have been desirable that this Law should be proclaimed by a man free from the imperfections of mankind; but the Watchers thought not so. To them it appeared wiser that their Messenger
should, however great his qualifications in some respects, be in others
the most ordinary of human beings, a partaker of every defect of his fellows. It was then a Man unfitted in almost every possible way to be a
leader whom they chose to bear the Message. That the Master Therion,[1]
as he is called, should be nothing in himself is no criticism of the perfection of his Law, but rather the guarantee of its virtue, that it is the Law for
all, and not for rare superior intelligence.

And of the perfection of this Law, of its supreme efficacy to form an
unshakable foundation for all future morality, those only can doubt who
have failed to examine it with that patient and impartial thoroughness
which Nature demands of every man that would explore her secrets, and
wrest from her treasuries the pearl of Truth.

For this Law is, in essence:

Do what thou wilt.[2]

There are upon this earth ignoble hearts, slaves who demand to be
driven, and tyrants who desire to dominate; such fear this Law, and
oppose it with malignant falsehoods. Their readiest weapon is to pretend to misunderstand it: to misquote it as "Do what you please."

No lie could be more stupid or more sinister. For the Law

Do what thou wilt

---

[1] [Crowley's magical motto as a Magus 9°=2□ of A∴ A∴..]
[2] [*Liber AL* I:40, III:60.]

is a Law austere beyond any yet given to Man. It leaves no room for idle or wanton conduct; it has no lenience for laxity or whim.

We read in *The Book of the Law*, given to the Master Therion to instruct him:

> There is no law beyond Do what thou wilt. [...] thou hast no
> right but to do thy will. Do that, and no other shall say nay.[1]

There is a class of sincere and intelligent critics, men who accept the Law

Do what thou wilt

as being self-evidently righteous, as being just to all, and binding upon all. It is, they rightly say, the Law of Fitness. For the True Will of a Man is the Resultant of all the Forces that compose his Nature; and it is clear as any other simple theorem of Dynamics that for a man to seek to deviate from his true Path is to neglect certain elements in his Equation, to leave unsatisfied some of the Energies which impinge upon him, and so to induce Error in his Ways; for what he has sought to ignore will press upon him secretly, will force him to waver, will redress the balance by unsuspected violences.

This Law

Do what thou wilt

is thus, they say to the Master Therion, in theory perfect; to contradict it is to be absurd. But its very axiomatic truth, its very universality and cogency, are just the grounds of our distrust of its value in practice. For men must always have subconsciously assumed this Law; how then should it serve them in this crisis?

To this caveat the answer leaps from History. The Errors of Mankind have almost uniformly sprung from the pursuit of false Ideals, born of irrational beliefs, and fathered by the Ignorance of Self-distrust. Aware of their own sorry state, men have grasped wildly at every straw of philosophy, have swallowed every glittering bait of falsehood. They have sought to be not what they are, but what they have been persuaded they ought to be, or what they think it would be fine to be; as, in the fable, the Frog, on hearing of the Ox, blew himself out in emulation until he burst.

---

[1] [*Liber AL* III:60, I:42–43.]

Ay! cries the critic, there is truth in that, so far as it goes; but that is not so far. Granted that man should seek perfection in his own true Nature, that "Know Thyself" is indeed the first of his duties, that his True Will is the expression in action of the Word of the purpose which God, or Nature, constructed him just as he is, and not in any other way, in order to fulfill—granted all this—your Law

Do what thou wilt

frankly accepted as the canon of the highest Wisdom and as the Rule of Life, there still remains the urgent practical question "How shall he know his Will? And, even did he know it, how fulfill it?"

The Master Therion understands this difficulty—alas, too well! What are more common to the race of Man than Ignorance and Impotence? He, knowing his True Will, knows also with what shock of struggle through how many years of research he won that knowledge. And, furthermore, he knows with bitterness intense how powerless he has been even to carry on the Work, much less to bring it to success.

So, for this final question of these friendly critics, he ventures to address himself to you, sir, in the hope that you may find it your True Will to help him to the answer—for the sake of that immanent Spirit of Man, most holy, most concealed, which awaits the Saviour to strike off the fetters from its limbs, the Sun-ray to disperse the clouds which brood, black, charged with thunder, over his mind.

The Master Therion, as a man, is but a poet, a dreamer; he can devise, but he cannot execute. He makes his appeal to you, as to a captain of men, an organizer forceful and precise, an employer capable and humane, an expert in efficiency, and a genius for translating Idea into the language of Reality.

You, sir, whether you are aware of it or not, possess most notably the faculty of true imagination in the scientific sense of the word. You saw the possibilities of social development which must follow those of the rapid travel of individuals, and of the transport of their merchandise, independent of established routine. You saw the conditions which would make this dream economically possible, and you set to work to realize them.

Sir, you succeeded; I offer you a greater dream.

Behold, you have made men free to travel swiftly and surely where they will. You have done this by abating the conflict between unnecessarily contending wills. You have brought peace to many millions by making each man independent of time and space, in a small sphere of his many activities, and in the degree of the present possibilities of science.

I ask you now to do for his spirit what you have done for his body.

The greatest curse of your great country is the obsession of the lust of riches. Wealth is too commonly regarded as a goal, not as a means; or if as a means, then only to pander pleasure, vanity, or unjust power. It is as if a man should spend his strength, wear out his life, to buy a motor-car; and having it, do nothing more than gloat on its possession, insist on the whole world admiring him for it, use it to crush pedestrians, and the like, instead of using it for spiritual ends, to take delight in the beauty of Nature, to joy in keen fresh air, to travel to fresh fields of knowledge, to scale new heights of Wisdom.

What is the cause of the deep spiritual discontent that mars the marvellous material welfare of your people of the great United States? What but this, that having attained the means of enjoyment and advancement, they know no purpose worthy of their endeavour?

They know not their True Wills.

Look back upon the Middle Ages! Ignorance, poverty, dirt, disease; oppression, superstition and disorder. Yet, in their myriad ills, what beauty, what attainment! Each worker a proud craftsman; in his leisure, rapt in music; his faith a living light, his love an eternal romance. His mind was not debauched by newspapers, with their incessant glorification of riches, crime and fashion, their ghoulish clamour for war, their scandal-mongering as of barren hags, and their muck-raking as of unwholesome schoolboys. What was the secret of their essential happiness? This, that each man respected himself, believed in himself, sought to discover and develop in himself the deepest and the highest qualities of his own nature. He did not wish to be as rich as this duke, or richer than that bishop; but only, to be rich enough to carry out the purpose in life for which he believed himself ordained.

Today such souls are rare indeed; men chase foul phantoms decked in glittering gauds by the spellbinders of popular hallucination. How sordid the scramble of even the honest worker! Yet, hateful consequence, his prosperity breeds parasites. We have two classes whose existence threatens the very structure of society: the crook whose sole gospel is "Get rich quick," and the robber and murderer whose morbid mind finds Romance, elsewhere denied him, in criminal violence. So powerful have these vermin become in the last few years, so bold has impunity made them, that they dare openly defy the laws of the republic, corrupt the Legislature itself, and prey upon society by force of arms in open daylight. Another step, and they will threaten civil war.

Economic pressure is destroying the ideal of the family; and the craze for pleasure is both eating away the health of the individual and mortgaging the future of the state.

What other remedy than this, the Law of Thelema?

Do what thou wilt

is the sole possible answer to these suicidal aberrations of the moral sense, the one constructive policy that can unite self-interest with righteousness. The world-weariness of this generation is principally due to the standardization of just those things whose use and delight lies in variety: building, cooking, clothing, custom, opinion, and the like; so that the wealth-burdened mules of the so-called prosperous classes, their glazed eyes starting from their bedighted[1] harness, travel frantically to the ends of the earth in search of the more picturesque, which flees before them as it is pulled down to make more room for the conventional Pullman, the mechanical monotony of the Jazz-band, and the soul-stupefying banality of the Cosmopolitan Hotel; while the indigent seek excitement in the phantasmagoria of the Sunday Newspaper and the Cinema, or risk the penitentiary or the gallows in the maniacal attempt to stimulate the nervous system that has been dulled by the poor-house routine of respectability.

Deprived, incapable, or ignorant of the very nature of true aspiration, the starved soul turns to things forbidden; foul books and plays, poisonous drinks, vaudeville cults, brutalizing drugs—come death, come madness, come disgrace, but let us get away from daily life, and the enforced pursuit of aims which are not ours!

Then, oh the spirits too dull, too prudent, or too cowardly to know what they lack, or to seek to escape from their invisible prisons! The ribbon-clerk who would be happy as a cowboy, the slaughterer whose qualities fit him to be a tailor, the stenographer who could only find herself as a milliner, the athlete penned in a counting-house, or the born

---

[1] [An archaic word for "arrayed, accoutred, bedecked."]

Engineer strangling in a waiter's livery of mock gentility—how deeply all these suffer in silence from their often unsuspected malady, in silence broken only by the stifled moan, the moan that, multiplied by countless millions, is dully heard as the deep discontent of the republic!

All these, no less than their more articulate fellows, await the word of deliverance, the word of the Law

Do what thou wilt.

Will you bring freedom to their souls, restore to them the meaning of the Life they have lost?

Let every man and woman learn to see life as a sacred trust, a well-designed machine for a particular purpose independent of all praise and blame, one whose fulfilment is the only, as the most admirable, reward, with abundance of joy!

For the mode whereby this noble revolution may be brought to pass? The details I must leave to your experience, your genius. But the main plan is evident enough. We must apply our modern science to the problem. We need first of all to summon a council of the acutest minds of the world, of biologists, historians, psychologists, economists...

They must devise a scheme for measuring a man, for penetrating his inmost nature no less than for estimating the effect of his environment.

They must be able to help him to discover the work for which he is really best fitted, the work which will satisfy his spiritual as well as material needs.

They must be able to advise him how to develop his powers in this direction, how to discipline himself and to steel himself against hostile forces so as to defend his Will from internal and external hindrances.

They must train experts to be able to judge men rapidly and surely, so as to assign them their place in the social organization.

They must help every man to discover in himself that insatiable Spirit, independent of Space, Time, and the prejudices of other men, which is the mark of genius; so that his purpose is a deathless flame to consume in him all perishable ambitions.

They must show him that true freedom which neither tolerates the domination of alien ideals, nor seeks to impose the arbitrary predilections of the individual upon the community.

Little by little, as they acquire experience, they will be able to establish experimental districts where the Law

Do what thou wilt

shall be the sole and sufficient guarantee of the righteousness and prosperity—spiritual, moral, and physical—of the inhabitants. The success of such experiments will create a worldwide demand for the establishment of the Law.

The final form of the work will be a system of Education in which each child will receive the individual attention necessary to the full development of its peculiar genius, instead of consisting, as now, of an attempt to crush out every spark of personality, and to produce a standardized product on a pattern as impossible as it is ultimately undesirable.

But it is useless to adumbrate even the outlines of a plan so fertile in amazing possibilities. I have written enough—in my enthusiasm, perhaps too much—to show alike the desperate need of taking resolutely in hand the sickness of society, and the superb prospects of achievement latent in studying and applying the Law

Do what thou wilt.

Will you be the man to give true freedom to every spirit that breathes, to create in every human heart the heaven of its inmost Will, and to declare to every mind the one way to attain it?

THE BANNED LECTURE

Gilles de Rais

to have been delivered before the
Oxford University Poetry Society by
ALEISTER CROWLEY
on the Evening of Monday, February 3rd, 1930

FIRST FRIEND.   Dost surmise
    What struck me at first blush?   Our Beghards, Waldenses,
        Jeronimites, Hussites—does one show his head,
    Spout Heresy now?   Not a priest in his senses
        Deigns answer mere speech, but piles faggots instead,
    Refines as by fire, and, him silenced, all 's said.

    Whereas if in future I pen an opuscule
        Defying retort, as of old when rash tongues
    Were easy to tame,—straight some knave of the Huss-School
        Prints answer forsooth!   Stop invisible lungs?
    The barrel of blasphemy broached once, who bungs?

SECOND FRIEND.   Does my sermon, next Easter, meet fitting
        acceptance?
    Each captious disputative boy has his quirk
    "An cuique credendum sit?" [1] Well, the Church kept *"ans"*
    In order till Fust set his engine at work!
    What trash will come flying from Jew, Moor and Turk

    When, goosequill, thy reign o'er the world is abolished!
        Goose—ominous name!   With a goose woe began:
    Quoth Huss[2]—which means "goose" in his idiom
        unpolished—

---

[1] [Latin, meaning loosely "I wonder if everybody has to believe it?"]
[2] [John Huss (c. 1371–1415), Czech preacher, religious reformer and university professor whose followers (the Hussites) fought a military campaign against the papal armies in Bohemia; he was burnt at the stake.]

> "Ye burn now a Goose: there succeeds me a Swan
> Ye shall find quench your fire!"

FUST.   I foresee such a man.

BROWNING[1]

Long ago, when King Brahmadatta reigned in Benares, a gentleman whose Christian names were Thomas Henry—you may possibly have heard of him—he was no less a personage than the grandfather of the great Aldous Huxley—once found himself threatened by a predicament similar to that in which I stand tonight.[2] He had been asked to lecture to a distinguished group of people.

What bothered him was this: what assumption was he to make about the existing knowledge of the audience? He adopted the sensible course of asking the advice of an old hand at the game; and was told "You must do one of two things. You may assume that they know everything, or that they know nothing." Thomas Henry thought it over, and decided that he would assume that they knew nothing.

I think that merely shows how badly brought up he must have been; and explains how it was that he became a dirty little atheist, and repented on his death-bed, and died blaspheming.

No! No! that would be quite impossibly bad manners. I shall assume that you know everything about Gilles de Rais; and that being the case, it would evidently be impertinent for me to tell you anything about him.[3] So that we can consider the lecture at an end, and (after the usual vote of thanks) pass on immediately to the discussion, which I think ought to be more amusing, if scarcely as informative.

---

[1] ["Fust and his Friends: An Epilogue." *The Complete Poetic and Dramatic Works of Robert Browning*; see Works Cited.]

[2] [For the elder Huxley see p. 41, note 2. The English novelist and essayist Aldous Huxley (1894-1963) was, like Crowley, an early investigator of entheogenic drugs. Accounts of Crowley having given Huxley mescaline are unfounded; they may have met and discussed the subject, but no record of a meeting survives.]

[3] [The military marshal of France, Gilles de Rais (or Retz or Rays, 1404-1440), was a wealthy baron whose court rivalled that of the King in opulence. Financial pressures led him to alchemy, in the hope of making gold. He was charged at his trial with having abducted, tortured and murdered over 140 children; he maintained his innocence at trial, but eventually confessed under torture and was executed. Critics of the trial have raised doubts about its impartiality, as the Duke of Brittany had a financial interest in the outcome; there was also a lack of evidence. Rais is the basis for the legend of Bluebeard.]

It is rather an hard saying—however worthy of all acceptation in a university like Oxford, where, I understand, the besetting sin of the inmates is lecturing and being lectured, but discussions are always apt to turn out to be amusing, especially if conducted with blackthorns or shotguns, whereas lecturing is merely an attempt, foredoomed to failure, to communicate knowledge which usually the lecturer does not possess.

I am sure that we all recognize that an attempt of this kind is impossible in nature. No! I am not proposing to inflict upon you my celebrated discourse on Scepticism of the Instrument of Mind. I am not even going to refer to the first and last lecture which I suffered at a dud university somewhere near Newmarket, in which the specimen of old red sandstone in the rostrum began by remarking that political economy was a very difficult subject to theorize upon because there were no reliable data. Never would I tell so sad a story on a Monday evening, with the idea of Tuesday already looming darkly in every melancholic mind. I should like to be just friendly and sensible, though it is perhaps too much to expect me to be cheerful.

The fact is that I am in a very depressed state. My attention was attracted by that little word "knowledge," of which we hear so much and see so little. I don't propose to inflict upon you the M.C.H., and demonstrate that the life and opinions of Gilles de Rais were inevitably determined by the price of onions in Hyderabad. But I do think that in approaching a historic question, we should be very careful to define what we mean—in our particular universe of discourse—by the word "knowledge."

May I ask a question?

Does anyone here know the date of the battle of Waterloo?

Pause. (Someone—I bet—tells me "1815.")

Thank you very much. To be frank with you, I knew it myself. I did not require information on that particular point. What I asked was, whether anyone knew the date. I felt that, if so, it would have created a sympathetic atmosphere.

But since we are talking about Waterloo, we may ask ourselves what, roughly speaking, is the extent of our knowledge?

I have heard plenty of theories about why Napoleon lost the battle. I have been told that he was already suffering from the disease which killed him. I have been told that he was outgeneralled by Wellington.[1] I have

---

[1] [The Battle of Waterloo was the final defeat of Napoleon Bonaparte. The Duke of Wellington (Arthur Wesley, 1769–1852) commanded of the British Army during the Napoleonic Wars; he later became Prime Minister of England.]

been told that his army of conscripts was underfed and not properly drilled. I have also been told that the battle was won by the Belgians.

Now, all these things are merely matters of opinion. There may be a little truth in some of them. But we have practically no means of finding out exactly how much, even if our documentary support is valid to establish any of these theories. It is, also, almost impossible to estimate the causes of any given event, if only because those causes are infinite, and each one of them is to a certain extent an efficient determining cause.

Take a quite simple matter like the time of year. If it had been winter instead of summer, the hens would not have been laying and Hougoumont and La Haye-Sainte would not have been able to nourish the contending forces.[1] But though it is profitable for the soul to contemplate the extent of what we don't know, it is in some ways more satisfying to our baser natures to consider what we do know in a reasonable sense of the word.

It is not disputable that the battle of Waterloo was fought and won. It is not disputable that it was the climax, or rather the *dénouement*, of campaigns lasting over a number of years. And there is no reason for doubting that Napoleon was born in Corsica, that he entered the French army, and rose rapidly to power by a combination of military genius and political intrigue.

There is a vast body of indirect evidence which confirms these statements at every point. Taken as a whole, they would be totally inexplicable on any other hypothesis. But when we consider the character of Napoleon, we are at once involved in a mass of contradictions. Probably no one in history has been more discussed, and every writer gives a totally different account. Each seeks to buttress his opinion by incidents which we have no reason to suppose other than authentic, but seem incongruous. So far as we can get any truth out of the matter at all, it is that the character of Napoleon, like that of everybody who ever lived, was extremely complex. And the writers are more or less in the position of the Six Wise Men of Hindustan who were born blind and had to describe an elephant.

Spiritually fortified by these simple meditations, we may apply their fruits to the problem of Gilles de Rais, and ask ourselves what we really *know* about him as opposed to what we have *heard* about him.

---

[1] [These are Belgian villages near the site of the Battle of Waterloo.]

was a brave soldier, and a comrade of Joan of Arc.[1] We know that he had a passion for science, for the basis of his reputation was that he frequented the society of learned men. We know finally that he was accused of the same crimes as Joan of Arc by the same people who accused her, and that he was condemned by them to the same penalty.

I do not think that I have left out any verifiable fact. I think that all the rest amounts to speculation. The real problem of Gilles de Rais amounts, accordingly, to this. Here we have a person who, in almost every respect, was the male equivalent of Joan of Arc. Both of them have gone down in history. But history is somewhat curious. I am still inclined to think that "there aint no such animile." In the time of Shakespeare, Joan of Arc was accepted in England as a symbol for everything vile. He makes her out not only as a sorceress, but a charlatan and hypocrite; and on top of that a coward, a liar, and a common slut.[2] I suspect that they began to whitewash her when they decided that she was a virgin, that is a sexually deranged, or at least incomplete, animal, but the idea has always got people going, as any student of religion knows. Anyway, her stock went up to the point of canonization.[3] Gilles de Rais, on the other hand, is equally a household word for monstrous vices and crimes. So much so, that he is even confused with the fabulous figure of Bluebeard,[4] of whom, even were he real, we know nothing much beyond that he reacted in the most manly way to the problem of domestic infelicity.

A moment's digression; in fact, the main point. What is the most precise and most atrocious charge that is made against him? That he sacrificed, in the course of alchemical and magical experiments, a matter of 800 children! I submit that, *à priori*, this sounds a little improbable. Gilles de Rais was the lord of a district whose population could not have been very extensive, and even in that age of slavery, dirt, disease, debauchery, poverty and ignorance, which seems to Mr. G. K. Chesterton the one ideal state of society, it must have been a little difficult to carry out abductions and murders on such wholesale principles.[5]

---

[1] [For Jeanne d'Arc see Crowley's "Eulogium on Jeanne d'Arc," p. 113.]

[2] [Joan had a vision that she was to deliver France from the English.]

[3] [She was canonized by the Roman Catholic Church in 1920.]

[4] [In Charles Perrault's collection of fairy tales, Bluebeard is a bloody ogre.]

[5] [The English essayist and writer Gilbert Keith Chesterton (1874–1936) criticized Crowley's *The Soul of Osiris* (1901). Crowley replied with "The Creed of Mr. Chesterton" in *Why Jesus Wept* (1904).]

Whenever questions arise with regard to black Magic or black masses, invocations of the Devil, etc., etc., it must never be forgotten that these practices are strictly functions of Christianity. Where ignorant savages perform propitiatory rites, there and there only Christianity takes hold. But under the great systems of the civilized parts of the world, there is no trace of any such perversion in religious feeling. It is only the blood-thirsty and futile Jehovah who has achieved such monstrous births. Such *upas*-trees can only grow in the poisonous mire of fear and shame where thought has putrefied to Christianity.

There is thus no antecedent improbability that Gilles de Rais (or any other person of that place and period) was addicted to black magical practices, for they were all Catholics. The power of the Church was, at that time, absolute, and even research was limited by the arbitrary theology imposed upon the mind of everyone. The abomination was at its height. But its decline has been rapid. True, one hundred years later it was still possible for Queens to be bulldozed by Presbyterian pulpiteers, but the time was already predictable when their best was for undergraduates to be bluffed by homosexual ecclesiastics. I suppose it is all in the family.

While these profound thoughts were producing a hypochondriac obnubilation of my mental faculties, it suddenly occurred to me that after all, I had heard this story before. And I saw the connection.

In the pitch-dark ages, when Christianity held unchallenged sway over those portions of this globe which it had sufficiently corrupted, the pursuit of knowledge—knowledge of any kind—was justly estimated by the people in power as the one and only dangerous pursuit. Even so, as late as 300 years ago, it was not considered very gentlemanly to be able to read and write. I am not sure that it is.

In any case, it is a great error in education to teach these things. Grammar, we must never forget, appears in the word "Gramarye," beloved of Sir Walter Scott,[1] and "grimoire," a black magical ritual—that is to say, any written document.

Precious little knowledge filtered through Christianity. It was against the interests of the Church, and in those times it was much easier to suppress people and ideas than it is now, though even today we find priests—at least in Oxford—who appear not to have heard of a certain recent invention by a notorious Magician inspired by the Devil—the Printing Press.

---

[1] [See p. 13, note 1.]

But they feared. So those who pursued knowledge were at the best under strong suspicion of heresy. I need not quote the obvious names. But there were certain *bodies* of people who did carry on the old knowledge, mostly by oral tradition, and who were perforce tolerated to a certain extent, because even the little knowledge that they did possess was so exceedingly useful. The best way to make armour, or to build Cathedrals, or to heal sickness, would enable the Christian to get ahead of his friends. Therefore, although conscience evidently demanded the maximum amount of persecution compatible with the existence of the villains, the Jews and the Arabs were at least allowed to live. Besides, the Arabs saw to that themselves.

But no one was better aware than the Pope that knowledge was power. For all he knew, and he probably knew that he did not know much, the Jews and the Arabs might get together and overturn the whole construction of society. Had he not in his own records the very best example of such a catastrophe?

There is a large number of excellent people, possessed of even less that the minimum amount of brains required to grease a gimlet, who are always boring us with the bogey of the Jew-Bolshevist peril. But as most of them are Roman Catholic laymen, unaware that Rome is laughing in its sleeve at them, they conveniently ignore what should be—if they realized it—their best argument. What was the ultimate cause of the destruction of the great civilization of Rome? What corrupted the spirit of a people unconquerable in arms? What but the spread of the slave morality of the Jewish communists of the period? If you will take your New Testaments from your pockets, you will find in the fourth chapter of the Acts of the Apostles and the thirty-second verse: "And the multitude of them that believed were of one heart and soul; and not one of them said that aught of the things that he possessed was his own, but that they had all things in common." Of course one of them, and he too was a Jew, tried to hold out on the kitty, and was struck miraculously dead for his pains. Lenin and Trotsky never did as well! [1]

So, as Roman Catholics are always telling us, the Church has a monopoly of logic, and the Pope argued that all Jews were communists.

---

[1] [See Acts 5:1-11. Vladimir Ilyich Lenin (born V. I. Ulyanov, 1870-1924), founder of the Comintern and dictator of the USSR 1917-1924. Leon Trotsky (born L. D. Bronstein, 1877-1940), Russian revolutionary leader and historian, expelled from the Comintern in 1927, exiled from the Soviet Union in 1929, and assassinated in Mexico in 1940.]

Anyone who had or wanted knowledge must be a Jew, and therefore a communist, and therefore—well, the Pope too believed in preparedness, though he probably called it a programme of disarmament. When people scrap battleships in the name of peace on earth and goodwill to men, it means that they have found battleships useless and too expensive, and that they have found something cheaper and more deadly. So the Curia[1] kept a weapon in reserve, in order to be sure of having a nice jolly pogrom whenever they gave the word. And what was the word to be?

Nice quiet peasant folk, or genial hard-working hunters and fighters, are not easy to arouse to indiscriminate slaughter without reason. In order to get them going, there are only two things which you can play on—greed and fear. The motive behind the Crusades was the story of the fabulous wealth of the East. We find, in fact, that well-organized armies of buccaneers, such as the Templars, did bring back incalculable spoils, while the honest pious mugs ruined themselves in the process.

Now, in this particular sport of suppressing earnest enquirers, it was not much good trying to play on people's greed. For everyone knew that even if the Jews had wealth, they managed to hide it very successfully, and that they had a nasty way of arranging for protection with people who were too powerful to be bullied, and too good business men to be fooled into killing the goose that laid the golden eggs. So the only motive available was fear, and in those ages where ignorance was fostered with infinite devotion, it was even easier to create a scare about bogies than our propaganda in the recent scrap found it.

I was in Venice just before the war, when Halley's comet was around, and although the Pope himself sprinkled holy water over the comet, and sent it his special benediction, and told the people it would do no harm, in his most *ex cathedrâ*[2] manner, the Venetians gathered themselves in panic-stricken crowds in the Square of St. Mark and waited, howling, for the end of the world.

It was accordingly easy enough to associate the pursuit of knowledge with the most abominable crimes, real or imaginary or both. For this reason, we hear—not as a demonstrated thesis, but as a commonplace of inherited knowledge—that Jews were sorcerers and wizards. In other words, they knew something about grammar. We hear that they trans-

---

[1] [A collective term for officials of the papal government.]

[2] [Latin, "from the chair," i.e., with high authority; typically the Vatican, seat of the Roman Catholic church.]

formed themselves into cats or bats, and sucked people's big toes. I have never, personally, investigated the question as to whether this form of nutrition is palatable. But, alas! even in those idyllic Chestertonian times there was a *little* shrewd common sense knocking about; the instinct—sometimes very splendidly described as horse sense—which comes from intimate wordless unintellectual communing with Nature (please do not take that word "communing" in any bad sense; if it were not for Baldwin, I would be a Conservative myself)—the instinct of some people, who at the bottom of their hearts, did not so much believe in these phantasms. It was not so easy to get them to go out and murder a lot of inoffensive people at the word jump. They had to be supplied with something a little more tangible.

You will notice how all this sort of argument is invariably of the *ad captandum*[1] variety. It is produced out of nowhere for a definite purpose; and, as the French say, does not rime with anything. If it did, of course, it would immediately be exposed as nonsense. It is satisfied that nobody can disprove it any more than they can prove it.

Take a concrete example. A nice young gentleman the other day wanted (very properly) to earn his living, and not being peculiarly endowed by Nature in the matter of original invention, he thought he might make a story out of the idea of a Suicide Club. In this he was evidently correct. Robert Louis Stevenson[2] had in fact proved the point. So he took Stevenson's story and transferred it to Germany, and drivelled on about the ace of spades, and quoted statistics of suicides, and said that I was the president of the Club and that the Berlin police were after me.

Now, I am afraid it would be a little difficult for anyone to prove that I am responsible for any suicides that may take place in Germany. But, on the other hand, it is quite impossible for me to disprove it. So now, if you want to attack anybody without the slightest fear of contradiction, you know how to set to work.

I omitted to mention that all these suicides were excessively beautiful and even voluptuous young women of high social position, and that the wicked president had blackmailed them out of vast sums. You see, the people for whom this dear young gentleman was writing all get sexually excited by pictures of young women, and also by any statement about

---

[1] [Latin, "for the sake of pleasing."]

[2] [Robert Louis Balfour Stevenson (1850–1894), Scottish novelist, essayist and poet.]

large sums of money. For they immediately have a wish phantasm—if they had large sums themselves, what terrible fellows they could be.

In the Middle Ages, the art of exciting the people was not very different. The Jew had always an immense hoard of ill-gotten wealth, and of course every penny that was exacted by Reginald Front-de-Bœuf [1] was laid to the Jews' account. But there was another treasure that the peasant was afraid to lose, the dearest treasure of all, his children. As little boys, thank God, have a habit of straying in search of adventure and getting lost in the process, which is good for their souls, the peasant naturally has moments of serious disquietude as to whether something terrible can have happened to little Tommy. Very Good. All we have to do is to play on that alarm.

We put into his mind that little Tommy (who turns up all right, if rather muddy, half an hour later) has almost certainly been kidnapped by the Jews for purposes of ritual murder.

The main accusation against Gilles de Rais is therefore just this general accusation against anyone in Christendom who exhibited any desire for knowledge. Only, in his case, it was concentrated and exaggerated to fantastic lengths by some factor or other on which I feel it useless to speculate. The one thing of which I feel certain is that 800 children is a lot. I don't know over how many years these practices were supposed to have spread. As I think you must all feel sure by now, I know nothing whatever of my subject.

But scientific experiment in those days was always a very prolonged operation. They thought nothing of exposing some unknown substance to the rays of the sun and moon for periods of three months at a time, in the hope that in some mysterious way the first stage of some dimly-visaged operation might be satisfactorily accomplished. And even if they sacrificed a child every day, it would have taken a matter of two and a half years to dispose of 800 children. Besides, it must have taken more than a few minutes to kidnap a child with the secrecy obviously required. Did the disappearance of the first four hundred, say, put no parents on their guard?

I think, at the best, it is a case of little Johnny who told his mother that there were millions of cats on the wall of the back garden, but under

---

[1] [Reginald Front-de-Bœuf is an exploitative Anglo-Norman feudal lord in Sir Walter Scott's *Ivanhoe*.]

cross-examination, in the style made popular by the dialogue of Lot with Almighty God, admitted that it was "Tom and another."

Of course, it will be obvious to you by this time that I have been seduced by Jewish gold, and the only way that I can think of to disarm your suspicions is to bring forward another case of the same kind, little more than a century old, with which Jews had nothing to do.

There was a poet laureate—I am not quite sure what this species of animal is—but his name was Robert Southey, and he lived, if you can call it living, about the time of William Blake.[1] He wrote a number of words arranged in some scheme connected with rime and rhythm; apparently, like golf clubs, "a set of instruments very ill-adapted to the purpose." But, anyway, he called it a poem, and the title was something to do with the old woman of Berkeley and who rode behind her. The person who rode behind her was Mr. Montague Summers' friend, the Devil.[2] What she actually did to merit this favour is to me rather obscure, because I have forgotten the whole beastly thing. But I do remember two lines, because I am in the same line of business myself.

> "I have candles made of infants' fat,
> I have feasted on rifled graves."[3]

Southey was an ambitious man. He was not content with the brilliant success of this masterpiece of the poetic art. He immediately sat down and wrote *another* alleged poem all about infants' fat and rifled graves and the Devil coming for the villain at the proper moment. This poem has nothing to do with witchcraft. It is called "The Surgeon's Warning."[4]

---

[1] [Robert Southey (1774–1843), English writer and poet, made British Poet Laureate in 1813. See Crowley's essay on William Blake, p. 115.]

[2] [Alphonsus Joseph-Mary Augustus Montague Summers (1880–1948) was a British scholar of witchcraft and black magic; he was an acquaintance of Crowley's.]

[3] [Southey, "The Old Woman of Berkeley, A Ballad, Shewing How an Old Woman Rode Double, and Who Rode Before Her," in *The Poetical Works of Robert Southey* (1838); see Works Cited. The poem actually reads: "'I have 'nointed myself with infant's fat, / The fiends have been my slaves, / From sleeping babes I have suck'd the breath, / And breaking by charms the sleep of death, / I have call'd the dead from their graves.'"]

[4] [Southey, "The Surgeon's Warning," ibid. This poem gives: "I have made candles of dead men's fat, / The Sextons have been my slaves, / I have bottled babes unborn, and dried / Hearts and livers from rifled graves."]

I think this is the best evidence in support of my thesis—whatever that is, I am not quite sure—that it is possible to adduce.

In the minds of the kind of people who believe in their neighbours making candles of infants' fat and digging up corpses to economize on the butcher's bill, the surgeon—that is to say, the man in pursuit of knowledge which it is hoped may alleviate human pain—is the same kind of animal as the witch and the ritual-murdering Jew.[1]

It is, no doubt, because it is a part of the old taboo complex about the corpses of one's relatives, that the clerical attack on surgeons concentrated itself on one fact—the fact that to learn to be a surgeon you must have corpses to dissect. For at that time, it will be remembered, hospitals were not as flourishing as they are today, and it was very difficult to find living people whom you could cut up to see what came of it. The surgeon was, in fact, not understood at all, except in the one way which such people were capable of understanding; i.e., as the body-snatcher. The rest of his proceedings were perfectly mysterious to them.

You notice that even Charles Dickens—who may yet go down to history for having wished to prosecute Holman Hunt, of all people in the world, for painting indecent pictures—takes very much this popular view of medicine and pharmacy in *Pickwick*.[2]

I think, then, it is not altogether unfair to assume that Gilles de Rais was to a large extent the victim of Catholic logic. Catholic logic: and the foul wish-phantasms generated of its repressions, and of its fear and ignorance. He wanted to confer a boon on humanity; therefore he consorted with the learned; therefore he murdered little children.

I think it is about time that somebody got after J. B. S. Haldane.[3] It is too late to do anything more to Ridley and Latimer, but I am quite sure

---

[1] [Witches and Jews have historically been falsely accused of these atrocities, and persecuted by the Catholic and Protestant churches.]

[2] [Charles Dickens (1812–1870), English novelist; Crowley probably refers to the *Pickwick Papers* (1836–37). The English painter William Holman Hunt (1827–1910) was a cofounder of the Pre-Raphaelite Brotherhood with Rosetti.]

[3] [John Burdon Sanderson Haldane (1892–1964) was a British biologist. The son of the Oxford physiologist J. S. Haldane, he studied Crowley's works, worked in psychical research, and became an acquaintance of Crowley's in the mid-1940s.]

that the candle they lit was made of infants' fat.[1] It is no use your starting to rifle Graves, because his publishers might resent your interference.[2]

Those in favor of the motion will now please signify the same in the usual manner. And may the Lord have mercy on your souls!

---

[1] [Hugh Latimer (1485?-1555) and Nicholas Ridley (c. 1500-1555) were both English Catholic bishops and reformers who became Protestant martyrs when they were tried at Oxford and burnt at the stake by the Roman Catholic church. Latimer's last words to Ridley were "We shall this day light such a candle by God's grace in England as I trust shall never be put out."]

[2] [Probably a reference to the Oxford-educated poet Robert Graves (1895-1985), later W. H. Auden's successor as professor of poetry at Oxford (1961-66).]

A Lecture on the Philosophy of Magick

I am sorry if I am not as frivolous as might be required by the exigencies of the occasion, but Magick is a very serious subject, and I have a very serious message to bring to you. It is very little understood what Magick is. It is connected in the minds of some people with conjuring. In the minds of others it is connected with charlatanism. I want to tell you that Magick has been since the very earliest ages of humanity the tradition of the wise men. I want to tell you what the essential doctrine of the magician is with regard to man's place in the universe and that it is given in *The Book of the Law* that "Every man and every woman is a star."[1] What is a star? Philosophers have always agreed about one thing—that is that the Universe to be intelligible at all must be considered as one and homogeneous. Therefore you can understand the position of the mystic who says that each of us is a member of the body of God.[2] You can understand what is written in the Bible, "Your bodies are the temples of the Holy Ghost."[3] It is upon these postulates that the general theory of Magick is founded.

Why should this be so? We are all agreed, no doubt, that everything that happens is in some philosophical sense a necessary happening. Let us consider the adventures of an atom of oxygen. That atom of oxygen is not different from any other atom of oxygen in itself. First, it is identical in the same sense that we are all of us identical. The question is—why alter that state? Why descend from the absolute to the material? And the answer is that we will suppose the atom of oxygen is self-conscious and became aware of this possibility only by entering into combination with all the other atoms. Nothing in making that combination can destroy the oxygen. The oxygen will remain oxygen and can be extracted as oxygen,

---

[1] [*Liber AL* I:3.]
[2] [See I Cor. 12:27.]
[3] [1 Cor. 6:19, paraphrase.]

but in the process of combination it has got experience, and the magical theory of the Universe is that we have all come to the particular star or planet we happen to be living on in order to get experience. We all go through stages in that experience. Some of those stages are pleasant and some rather unpleasant, but they are all necessary in order that we may obtain the full comprehension of ourselves.

This is the reconciliation in the magical theory between freewill and destiny. It is true, as the determinist has told us, that our actions are all automatic—that we are no more capable of thinking original thoughts or performing original and willed actions than any other piece of machinery. That is the doctrine of the materialist. And we say, "Yes, very good, but who invented this machinery?" And the answer is, "We ourselves. Each one of us."

We are in the middle of a world crisis. It is a very good world crisis— better than any crisis we have had before, and there is no man alive with an intellect big enough to grasp the threads of the problems which confront the world today. There are two ways out of that. Either to consult a superior intelligence, which Magick shows you the way of doing, or you can develop your own mind, for it has a faculty which is as superior to the intellect as the intellect is superior to the emotions.

All magical operations require a very elaborate training of one kind or another, but I think the only way out is that we have got to put men in charge of this planet who are really more than men. We must get back to the times of the prophets or we must make ourselves prophets. And we must look at world problems from a standpoint which is entirely alien to that existing at present.

The Scientific Solution of the Problem of Government

THEOREM.

The scientific solution of the problem of Government is given in *AL (Liber Legis)*. This Law supersedes all the empirical theories hitherto current.

QUOTATION.

CHAPTER 1.

3. Every man and every woman is a star.
10. Let my servants be few & secret: they shall rule the many & the known.
40. Do what thou wilt shall be the whole of the Law.
41. The word of Sin is Restriction.
42. thou hast no right but to do thy will.
43. Do that, and no other shall say nay.
44. For pure will, unassuaged of purpose, delivered from the lust of result, is every way perfect.
57. Love is the law, love under will.

CHAPTER II.

19. Is a God to live in a dog? No! but the highest are of us. They shall rejoice, our chosen; who sorroweth is not of us.
20. Beauty and strength, leaping laughter and delicious languor, force and fire, are of us.
58. Yea! deem not of change: ye shall be as ye are, & not other. Therefore the kings of the earth shall be Kings for ever: the slaves shall serve.

CHAPTER III.

4. Choose ye an island!
5. Fortify it!
6. Dung it about with enginery of war!
7. I will give you a war-engine.
8. With it ye shall smite the peoples; and none shall stand before you.
58. But the keen and the proud, the royal and the lofty; ye are brothers!
59. As brothers fight ye!
60. There is no law beyond Do what thou wilt.

DEMONSTRATION.

1. *The average voter is a moron.* He believes what he reads in newspapers, feeds his imagination and lulls his repressions on the cinema, and hopes to break away from his slavery by football pools, crossword prizes, or spotting the winner of the 3:30.

    He is ignorant as no illiterate peasant is ignorant: he has no power of Independent thought. He is the prey of panic.

    But he has the vote.

2. The men in power can only govern by stampeding him into wars, playing on his fears and prejudices until he acquiesces in repressive legislation against his obvious interests, playing on his vanity until he is totally blind to his own misery and serfdom.

    The alternative method is undisguised dragooning. In brief, *we govern by a mixture of lying and bullying.*

3. This desperate resort to archaic weapons is the heritage of hypocrisy. *The theories of Divine Right, aristocratic superiority, the moral order of Nature, are all today exploded bluffs.* Even those of us who believe in supernatural sanctions for our privileges to browbeat and rob the people no longer delude ourselves with the thought that our victims share our superstitions.

4. Even dictators understand this. Mussolini has tried to induce the ghost of Ancient Rome to strut the stage in the image of Julius Cæsar; Hitler has invented a farrago of nonsense about Nordics and Aryans; nobody even pretends to believe either, except through the "will-to-believe."

    And the pretence is visibly breaking down everywhere. They cannot even be galvanized with spasms of pseudo-activity, as still occasionally happens with the dead toads of superstition.

5. *There is only one hope of uniting the people under intelligent leadership; because there is only one thing in which everyone really believes.* That is, believes in such a way that he automatically bases every action of his daily life on its principles.

   (This is true of practically all men, whatever their race, caste, or creed.) *This universally accepted basis of conduct is Science.*

6. *Science has attained this position because it makes no assertion that it is not prepared to demonstrate to all comers.* (This part is so well understood that all the "false prophets"—Spiritualism, Christian Science, ethnological cranks, Great Pyramid puzzle-mongers, and the rest of the humbugs—all pretend to appeal to evidence, not to authority, as did the Kings and the Churches.)

   The problem of Government is therefore to find a scientific formula with an ethical implication. This formula must be rigidly applicable to all sane men soever without reference to the individual qualities of any one of them.

7. *The formula is given by the Law of Thelema. "Do what thou wilt shall be the whole of the Law."*[1]

   This injunction, in one sense infinitely elastic, since it does not specify any particular goal of will as desirable, is yet infinitely rigid, in that it binds every man to follow out exactly the purpose for which he is fitted by heredity, environment, experience, and self-development.

   The formula is thus also biologically indefeasible, as well as adequate, ethically to every individual, and politically to the State.

8. *Let this formula be accepted by every government.* Experts will immediately be appointed to work out, when need arises, the details of the True Will of every individual, and even that of every corporate body whether social or commercial, while a judiciary will arise to determine the equity in the case of apparently conflicting claims. (Such cases will become progressively more rare as adjustment is attained.) All appeal to precedent and authority, the deadwood of the Tree of Life,[2] will be abolished, and strictly scientific standards will be the sole measure by which the executive power shall order the people. *The absolute rule of the state shall be a function of the absolute liberty of each individual will.*

---

[1] [*Liber AL* I:40.]

[2] [The symbolic representation of the universe in the Qabalah; its "deadwood" is termed the Qliphoth—"shells," or "excreta."]

SAMUEL AIWAZ JACOBS

Fragments

Every man, woman, and child, no matter how illiterate, is an artist in one way or another, if he or she has an urge to make things. Every maker is a creator of one thing or another. Every creator is a specialist of one sort or another. This urge to make things is felt by the artist and translated into an æsthetic emotion which is felt or appreciated by those who have the awareness to respond to it and understand it, even though they may have no desire to produce it themselves. It is produced for them by the artist as an æsthetic echo, not through his or their intellect, but by his and their feeling. It is communicated by the artist and shared by the people. It is the vision of the artist conveyed in his work. This vision of the artist is reflected in his work as the record of his experience. This experience is a work of art. It cannot be explained in words. It has a language of its own, peculiar to itself and not found in the lexicon of the logicians. This language is rather an idiom of the heart, spoken and understood by every man, woman, and child, no matter how illiterate, if he or she has an urge to make things or an awareness in response to that which is made, be it drama, painting, sculpture, poetry, writing, music, or architecture.

Art springs not from rules and regulations but from feeling. If there is no feeling, logic is a blind alley and reason a dead end. Logic is a poor guide without the light of feeling. Logic at best is the crossword puzzle of the mind, and reason its solution. We can readily see how unreasonable a solution can be when it is reached by the logic of an erroneous mind. Not so with feeling: a man is not in the clouds but on safe ground when he strives to acquire a concept of the world of things which contains all the symbols of the world of ideas. From time immemorial ideas have been born—to flower, to grow, to become old and die, to be born again. This recurring rebirth evokes a certain new experience; but there is nothing original in our awareness of, or even our response to, old ideas come to life again. Only our experience with the old ideas, our awareness of and our response to them, is new. Nobody has a monopoly on ideas, especially the borrowed ones. And there is nothing original about the ideas borrowed from the ancients—ideas borrowed, put through modern washing machines, ironed by new methods, and sold as contemporary products. Knowledge is essential to understanding relation. All knowledge is relation of fragments. Fragments are the very sum and substance of creation: without the fragments, broken from the Whole, there could not have been anything but Darkness, before Whom time is ashamed, imagination dark, and the mind bewildered.[1]

To those of you who will begin, as I did, at an early age to be interested in creative effort, I have a word or two to say: Follow no one. Only you can lead yourself. Be open-minded and ready to reject every extraneous influence. Use your own. Talk is cheap; let others talk. Pay no attention to them or to me. Shun them and me with your self-discipline. Value your freedom from the shackles of the strait jacket. A rose is a rose regardless of its position on the bush. Approach your line of activity as an individual. Be independent. There is but one law to obey, the law of freedom; and obedience to that law is liberty.

---

[1] [A direct paraphrase of Crowley's "Liber 15, Ecclesiæ Gnosticæ Catholicæ Canon Missæ," the O.T.O. Gnostic Mass.]

Editorial Notes

Humanity First. This article was published in *The International* XI(11), November, 1917.

The Revival of Magick. This article ran serially in *The International* XI(8–11), August–November 1917. Of his editorship at *The International*, Crowley wrote: "I devoted every energy to proclaiming the Law of Thelema in its pages both directly and indirectly. My first important step in this direction, the thin end of the wedge, was an article 'The Revival of Magick' which ran serially, ending in November." The *Confessions of Aleister Crowley*, abridged ed., ed. John Symonds and Kenneth Grant (cited hereafter as *Confessions*), p. 827; see Works Cited.

The Camel. This essay was probably written in 1909–1910, and was first published in *The Occult Review* XIII(4), April, 1911. Like "The Soul of the Desert," written some five years later, it drew its inspiration from the Sahara. Crowley explains the inspiration of these essays: "In the desert each impression is beaten into one's brain with what at first seems maddening monotony. One feels starved; there are so few facts to feed on. One has to pass through an abyss of boredom. At last there comes a crisis. Suddenly the shroud is snatched away from one's soul and one enters upon an entirely new kind of life, in which one no longer regrets the titillation of the thoughts which tumble over each other in civilized surroundings, each preventing one undergoing the ordeal involved when it becomes necessary to penetrate beneath the shadow-show to the secret sanctuary of the soul." *Confessions*, abridged ed., pp. 627–628.

The Soul of the Desert. This essay, entitled "At Tozeur" in MS, was written at Tozeur, Tunisia, on March 17, 1914, during a trip to North Africa that is unusual in that it is undocumented in Crowley's diaries or his *Confessions*. It was first published in *The Occult Review* XX(1), July 1914. This version is taken from a copy of the first printing with holograph revisions—probably made much later—as well as the original holograph manuscript, both at the Yorke Collection, Warburg Institute, University of London.

A Hindu at the Polo Grounds. This article appeared in *Vanity Fair*, New York, August, 1915.

Three Great Hoaxes of the War. This article appeared in *Vanity Fair*, New York, January, 1916.

Mystics and Their Little Ways. This article appeared in *Vanity Fair*, October 1916.

The Attainment of Happiness. This article appeared in *Vanity Fair*, November 1916. Portions of this essay were incorporated into *Liber 888, Jesus*.

An Improvement on Psychoanalysis. This article appeared in *Vanity Fair*, New York, December, 1916.

Billy Sunday. According to Gerald J. Yorke, this essay appeared in *The International*, October 1915. Crowley's set in the O.T.O. Archives lacks issues for 1915; if Yorke is correct, this would be one of Crowley's first contributions to this journal. The text for this article is from a typescript with holograph corrections, Yorke Collection, Warburg Institute, University of London.

The Ouija Board. This brief article was published in *The International* XI(10), October, 1917, and was signed "by The Master Therion." The Ouija board is an apparatus for communication with the spirit world. The name comes from the French (*oui*) and German (*ja*), both words for "yes." The board is imprinted with letters and digits, and the medium operates a planchette or tripod which (under the presumed guidance of spiritual forces) rolls across the board and spells out messages. Its use is possibly ancient; a similar device was employed by the Mandæans of Iraq and Iran.

A Letter from The Master Therion. This exchange of letters was published in *The International* XI(10), October 1917. "C. S. J." was Charles Stansfeld Jones (1886–1950), a member of A.·.A.·. and O.T.O. who lived in British Columbia. The title was provided for this publication.

How Horoscopes are Faked. This brief article was published in *The International* XI(11), November 1917, and was signed "Cor Scorpionis." This article was an attack on the methods of his former collaborator and employer, the famous New York astrologer Evangeline Adams. Crowley had written his *Liber 536, The General Principles of Astrology* in 1915, to be issued as their joint work on a partnership basis. Crowley's attack appears fully justified, as Adams later issued this work as two books under her own name; see Works Cited.

Art and Clairvoyance. This essay and review first appeared in *The International* XI(12), December 1917.

Geomancy. This article appeared in *The International* XII(1), January 1918; a note is included from Crowley's annotated set of *The International*, O.T.O. Archives.

Good Hunting! This essay first appeared in *The International* XII(3), March 1918 under the byline "Baphomet, Grand Master of the Knights of the Holy Ghost." Minor holograph corrections by Crowley from his set of *The International* (O.T.O. Archives) have been made, and a few parenthetical remarks have been moved to footnotes.

Eulogium upon Jeanne d'Arc. This previously-unpublished prose poem is taken from a typescript with holograph corrections in the Yorke Collection, Warburg Institute, University of London. The literary form, time of composition (c. 1915) and the phrase "golden rose of earth" all show that Crowley was inspired by his lover, the eponymous poet Jeanne Robert Foster, for whom he wrote a sonnet cycle entitled *The Golden Rose*. Randall Bowyer found that, using a favorite poetic device for commemorating his lovers, Crowley introduced anagrams into the text; these are noted in the text. In this period Crowley had a brief interest in *vers libre* poetry, of which this prose poem-essay is an example; outside his translations of Baudelaire, it is an unusual form for Crowley.

William Blake. William Blake (1757–1827). This previously unpublished essay is taken from an undated holograph manuscript, Yorke Collection, Warburg Institute, University of London; it probably dates from c. 1919. As discussed in the notes, Crowley subscribed to the long-discredited Ellis and Yeats theory of an Irish origin for Blake as an O'Neil. A few references to Blake as O'Neil have been changed to Blake for this first publication.

On the Education of Children. This previously unpublished essay survives in Crowley's diary for August 8, 1921, and is taken from the typed transcript in the Yorke Collection, Warburg Institute, University of London. This is the first of two essays in this collection of essays in which Crowley discusses the utopian social theories practiced at the Abbey of Thelema in Cefalù, Sicily.

On Sexual Freedom. This previously unpublished essay survives in Crowley's diary for July 6, 1921, and is taken from the typed transcript in the Yorke Collection, Warburg Institute, University of London. The diary notes "First essay obliterated"; Crowley describes this as "a second shot."

Duty. This essay is a type of commentary on *Liber AL vel Legis, The Book of the Law,* and is taken from the original typescript with holograph annotations at the George Arents Research Library at Syracuse University. This essay has been published many times in O.T.O. newsletters and journals; this is its first appearance in book form. The formatting of the article as given here follows the markup instructions in the typescript.

An Open Letter to Rabbi Joel Blau. An abridged form of this article was published as *The Jewish Problem Restated* under the byline "by a Gentile" in *The English Review* 35, July 1922. The version published here (titled in typescript "An Open Letter to Rev. Joel Blau") is considerably longer, with more theological content concerning Thelema. The sources are a typescript with holograph corrections at the Harry Ransom Humanities Research Center, University of Texas at Austin; this typescript is missing its first few pages, recovered from a second typescript with holograph corrections in the Yorke Collection, Warburg Institute, University of London. The text generally follows the typescripts, which have minor differences. "Reverend" has been changed to "Rabbi" in keeping with modern usage. Three additions have been made: two long footnotes, and a long paragraph appeared in *The English Review* version, but not the typescripts, and are given as a footnote to the quotation from Rabbi Blau's article, omitting a passage repeated in the text.

A Memorandum Regarding *The Book of the Law*. This memorandum is taken from a typescript in the Yorke Collection, Warburg Institute, University of London. It was written at the Abbey of Thelema in Cefalù, Sicily in 1923 to James Branch Cabell, who based chap. 22 of his romantic novel *Jurgen* on Crowley's "Liber 15," the O.T.O. Gnostic Mass. When Cabell was prosecuted for obscenity under the Comstock law, his defense strategy was to show that his model, the Gnostic Mass, had been published twice (in *The International* XII(3), March 1918, and *The Equinox* III(1), March 1919) without being found obscene. Crowley reviewed *Jurgen* for *The Equinox* III(2); although this issue never came to press (a reconstruction is planned), the typescript survives. A different commentary, "Another Note on Cabell," appeared in *The Reviewer* III(1–2), July 1923. This letter was simply titled "Memorandum" by Crowley; Gerald Yorke added "Re: *CCXX*." The title given in the text has been supplied for publication.

The Antecedents of Thelema. This essay is taken from a typed transcript in the Yorke Collection, Warburg Institute, University of London. Some parenthetical remarks and citations have been moved to footnotes for publication. On October 22, 1926, Crowley sent this draft to the American book collector Montgomery Evans II (1901–1954) with the following explanation: "I started an essay on Thelema with reference to Rabelais, but have not yet finished it. Our position is that Rabelais was a great adept, a sort of prophet of Thelema. Note that in the description of the Abbey is an Oracle. In this he foretells an epoch when Church and Crown shall no longer count, but the world be run by bankers. He also indicates Bolshevism and such things; and the last line is a plain reference to me personally. [See p. 167, note 1.] My first motto was Perdurabo, 'I will endure to the end.' What you have to correct is the ignorant idea that Rabelais is just a naughty writer. He was master of all the sciences no less than Dante and Leonardo, and like them he achieved an extraordinary work for intellectual freedom. … I have just dug out a copy of the Essay on Thelema and enclose it. Section VI is merely rough notes. Excuse the whole being so ragged, but I think it may be helpful."

The Beginning of the New World. This essay was written around 1925, and is taken from a typescript with holograph corrections in the Yorke Collection, Warburg Institute, University of London. Some material pertaining to Crowley's planned establishment of headquarters in Berlin has been omitted as dated.

On Thelema. This essay was written around 1926–27, and was sent to Martha Küntzel (Soror Ich Will Es) of Leipzig. It is taken from a typescript with holograph corrections in the Yorke Collection, Warburg Institute, University of London.

The Method of Thelema. This essay was written under the pseudonym Gérard Aumont around 1925, and is taken from a typescript with holograph corrections in the Yorke Collection, Warburg Institute, University of London.

A Letter to Henry Ford. This letter to the founder of the Ford Motor Company was written on April 4, 1926, when Crowley was in the coastal resort of La Marsa, Tunisia. The primary source is a typescript with Crowley's holograph corrections in the Yorke Collection, Warburg Institute, University of London.

Gilles de Rais. This essay was first published by P.R. Stephensen of the Mandrake Press—produced hastily, and sold outside the Oxford campus, after the university authorities cancelled Crowley's invitation to speak to a student group. Crowley was a loyal Cambridge man (Trinity College) so it is natural that some of his remarks are jokes at Oxford's expense, while others (like his derisory remarks on communism) reflect on the intellectual fashions of the time. For a biographical discussion of this episode see Keith Richmond's introduction to *The Forbidden Lecture. Gilles de Rais* (1990); see Works Cited.

A Lecture on the Philosophy of Magick. This brief lecture survives in the files of Christina Foyle, a member of the English bookdealing family renowned for their literary luncheon lectures; her family's London shop remaindered Crowley's *Magick in Theory and Practice*. He noted in his diary for August 17, 1932: "Saw Foyle—asked to speak at lunch Sept. 15 on 'The Philosophy of Magick' "—the occasion was Foyle's 23rd Literary Luncheon at Grosvenor House. Christina Foyle remembers that she invited Crowley despite warnings about his sinister reputation; her usual literary speakers were Auden, Eliot, et al. One guest, Rose Macaulay, remarked "I don't mind what he does, as long as he doesn't turn himself into a goat." 500 guests attended, and Crowley's diary for the day of the luncheon (Sept. 15, 1932) records "Made a good speech!!!!!!"

The Scientific Solution of the Problem of Government. This essay is a political commentary with reference to *The Book of the Law*, and opens with select quotations and partial quotations by verse number, grouped by chapter. It was first published pseudonymously as a stapled pamphlet in London by the O.T.O. around 1937. The author was given as Comte de Fénix (Crowley's secret name as Outer Head of the O.T.O. was Phœnix), and the pamphlet was marked "Strictly Private and Confidential."

Fragments. This essay first appeared in a work celebrating modern innovation in book design, *Books for Our Time*, ed. Marshall Lee (New York: Oxford University Press, 1951). Crowley was included as a book designer; the text notes: "Considering the kind of books contemporaneous with [Crowley's *The Star and the Garter* (1904)], its clean, simple asymmetry was little short of clairvoyant at the turn of the century" (p. 130). As discussed elsewhere in this book (see p. 157), Crowley had interesting dealings with Jacobs, a fascinating man whom Crowley came to consider a brother of the A∴A∴. There is nothing in this essay (probably this master's only surviving prose work) to contradict this; indeed, as an eloquent manifesto of applied Thelema, it provides ample confirmation.

Works Cited

The A∴A∴ and O.T.O. canons include books and papers that are frequently cited by Crowley or his editors by their *liber* (book) number. A convention is employed by the present editors that cites papers in quotations, and books in italics; e.g., "Liber 15" is a paper, while *Liber 777* is a book. One exception is that the titles of plays are italicized.

Part I of this reference list (*Canonical Libri*) lists the numbered A∴A∴ and O.T.O. books and papers cited in the present book, numerically crossreferenced to the bibliographic listings in Part III (*Books and Journals*) for the books or journals in which they appear. Most but not all of the papers are by Aleister Crowley; exceptions are noted; the classifications follow the revised A∴A∴ and O.T.O. curricula in Crowley's *Magick (Book 4, Parts I–IV)*, 2nd rev. ed., ed. Hymenæus Beta (1997), appendix I.

Part II of this reference list (*Miscellaneous Papers*) lists non-canonical literary works and essays cited, crossreferenced to Part III (*Books and Journals*) where possible. As the scope of the bibliography is confined to regular books and serials commonly found in libraries, no attempt has been made to cite the numerous appearances of these papers in small press booklets or O.T.O. journals.

Part III (*Books*) gives works cited by Crowley and the editors, as well as published sources for articles, poems and plays cited. Detailed publishing data is generally omitted for pre-1900 works.

I. Canonical Libri

[Liber 4, A∴A∴] *Liber ABA. Book 4.* In four parts, as (51), (61) and (78). One-volume edition as (77).

[Liber 15, O.T.O.] "Ecclesiæ Gnosticæ Catholicæ Canon Missæ." In (60.k), (60.t), (63), (77) and (78).

[Liber 27, A∴A∴] "Liber Trigrammaton sub figura XXVII." In (74), (96) and (97). Commentary in (60.u).

[Liber 49, A∴A∴] "Shih I Ch'ien." Not believed extant.

[Liber 65, A∴A∴] "Liber Cordis Cincti Serpente." In (60.k), (96) and (97). With commentary in (60.v).

[Liber 67, A∴A∴] *The Sword of Song.* As (92), and in (57).

[Liber 71, A∴A∴] "The Voice of the Silence, the Two Paths, the Seven Portals." In (60.k), (63) and (60.u).

[Liber 77, O.T.O.] "Liber Oz." As (82), with numerous reprints, and in (77).

[Liber 84, A∴ A∴] "Liber Chanokh." In (60.g) and (60.h), and (63).

[Liber 96, A∴ A∴] Liber Gaias sub figura XCVI. A Handbook of Geomancy." In (60.b).

[Liber 111, A∴ A∴] *Liber Aleph vel CXI.* As (60.p) and (76).

[Liber 157, A∴ A∴] *The Tao Te Ching.* As (93).

[Liber 216, A∴ A∴] *The I Ching.* Reconstruction as (60.q). Part-published as (88).

[Liber 220, A∴ A∴, O.T.O.] *Liber AL vel Legis sub figura CCXX.* In (60.j), (60.t), (55), (61), (63), (69), (74) and (77).

[Liber 333, A∴ A∴] *The Book of Lies.* As (52); with commentary as (53).

[Liber 335, A∴ A∴] *Adonis.* In (60.g).

[Liber 418, A∴ A∴] *Liber XXX Ærvm vel Sæculi sub figura CDXVIII. Being of the Angels of the Thirty Æthyrs the Vision and the Voice.* In (60.e), and with commentary in (98) and (60.v).

[Liber 500, A∴ A∴] "Sepher Sephiroth sub figura D." Co-authored by Allan Bennett and others. In (60.h) and (87).

[Liber 536, O.T.O.] *The General Principles of Astrology.* The majority published without attribution to Crowley in (3) and (4). Reconstructed as (64).

[Liber 729, A∴ A∴] "The Amalantrah Working." In (60.w).

[Liber 777, A∴ A∴] *DCCLXXVII Vel Prolegomena Symbolica Ad Systemam Sceptico-Mysticæ Viæ Explicandæ, Fundamentum Hieroglyphicum Sanctissimorum Scientiæ Summæ.* As (85), with additions as (86) and in (87).

[Liber 2911, A∴ A∴] "A Note on Genesis." By Allan Bennett. In (60.b).

II. Miscellaneous Papers, Poems, Plays, etc.

Baudelaire, Charles. "Intoxicate Yourself!" In (18).

Blau, Joel. "The Cry of the Modern Pharisee." *The Atlantic Monthly,* New York, January 1922.

Browning, Robert. *Fust and his Friends: An Epilogue.* In (28).

———. "Gold Hair: A Story of Pornic." In (28).

———. "Mr. Sludge, 'The Medium.'" In (28).

———. "The Ring and the Book." In (28).

Carroll, Lewis. "Poeta Fit, Non Nascitur." In (34).

Coleridge, Samuel Taylor. "The Rime of the Ancient Mariner." In (48).

———. "Kubla Khan." In (48).

Crowley, Aleister. "Art and Clairvoyance." *The International* XI(12), New York, December 1917.

———. "The Attainment of Happiness." *Vanity Fair,* New York, November 1916.

———. "At the Fork in the Roads." In (60.a).

———. "The Bartzabel Working." Text of ritual ("An Evocation of Bartzabel") in (60.i); record of working in (60.w).

———. *The Blind Prophet.* In (60.e).

——. *The Fatal Force.* In (57).

——. "The Garden of Janus." In (60.b).

——. "Geomancy." *The International* XII(1), New York, January 1918.

——. "Gilles de Rais." As (62) and (67).

——. "Good Hunting!" *The International* XII(3), New York, March 1918.

——. "How Horoscopes are Faked." *The International* XI(11), New York, November 1917.

——. "Humanity First." *The International* XI(11), New York, November 1917.

——. "An Improvement on Psychoanalysis." *Vanity Fair*, New York, December 1916.

——. "The Jewish Problem Restated." *The English Review* XXXV, July 1922.

——. "The Method of Thelema." Previously unpublished in English; German translation in (56).

——. "The Moralist." In (94).

——. "Mystics and Their Little Ways." *Vanity Fair*, New York, October 1916.

——. "One Star in Sight." In (60.u), (77) and (78).

——. "The Ouija Board." *The International* XI(10), New York, October 1917.

——. "The Revival of Magick." *The International* XI(8–11), August–November 1917.

——. "The Scientific Solution of the Problem of Government." As (84).

——. *The Scorpion.* In (60.f).

——. *Snowstorm.* In (60.g).

——. "The Soldier and the Hunchback." In (60.a).

——. "The Soul of the Desert." *The Occult Review* XX(1), July 1914, and as (90).

——. *The Temple of Solomon the King.* Coauthored with J. F. C. Fuller. Serialized in Volume I of (60), and as (95).

——. "Three Great Hoaxes of the War." In *Vanity Fair*, New York, January 1916.

Jacobs, Samuel Aiwaz. "Fragments." In (138).

Keats, John. "To Psyche," in (129).

Kipling, Rudyard. "In the Neolithic Age." In (131).

Machen, Arthur. "The Bowmen," *Evening News*, London, September 29, 1914. In (149).

Shelley, Percy Bysshe. "Epipsychidion." In (173).

——. *Prometheus Unbound.* In (173).

Southey, Robert. "The Old Woman of Berkeley." In (177).

——. "The Surgeon's Warning." In (177).

Swinburne, Algernon Charles. "Anactoria." In (178).

——. "Hertha." In (178).

III. Books

1   Abraham ben Simeon, of Worms [attrib.]. *The Book of the Sacred Magic of Abra-Melin the Mage*, trans. S.L. MacGregor-Mathers. 2nd ed., London: Watkins, 1900; rpt. New York: Dover, 1975.

2   ——. [*Abra-Melin.*] *Die egyptischen Offenbarungen*.... Cologne: Hammer, 1725 [publishing data considered spurious, probably Stuttgart, 1853].

3   Adams, Evangeline. *Astrology, Your Place among the Stars.* New York: Dodd, Mead, and London: Harrap, 1930.

4   ——. *Astrology, Your Place in the Sun.* New York: Dodd, Mead, and London: Harrap, 1927.

5   Æschylus. *The 'Agamemnon' of Aeschylus*, ed. and trans. A. W. Verrall. London and New York: Macmillan, 1889.

6   Æschylus. *The Orestes Plays: The Agamemnon, The Libation Bearers, The Eumenides*, trans. Paul Roche. New York: New American Library, 1963.

7   Agrippa von Nettesheim, Heinrich Cornelius. *De occulta philosophia libri tres.* Antwerp, 1531; 1st complete ed., [Coloniæ, 1533]; critical Latin edition, ed. Vittoria Perrone Compagni. Leiden and New York: Brill, 1992.

8   —— (spurious attribution). *Fourth Book of Occult Philosophy*, ed. and trans. Robert Turner. London, 1655; rpt. Kila, MT: Kessinger, 1992. Also rpt. as *Of Occult Philosophy, Book Four, Magical Ceremonies.* Gillette, NJ: Heptangle, 1985.

9   ——. *Three Books of Occult Philosophy, or, of Magick*, trans. J.F. London, 1651; rpt., Hastings, UK: Chthonios, c. 1986; rev. ed., ed. Donald Tyson, St. Paul, MN: Llewellyn, 1994.

10   Allen, Paul Marshall, ed. *A Christian Rosenkreutz Anthology.* Blauvelt, NY: Spiritual Science Library, 1961; rev. 3rd ed., 1981.

11   Andrea, Johann Valentin. *The Chemical Wedding of Christian Rosenkreutz*, trans. Joscelyn Godwin. Grand Rapids, MI: Phanes Press, 1991.

12   ——. *Fama Fraternitatis: oder, Entdeckung der Bruderschafft des loblichen Ordens desz RosenCreutzes: beneben der Confession, oder Bekantnusz derselben Fraternitet.* Frankfurt, 1615.

13   ——. *Fama Fraternitatis / Confessio Fraternitatis / Chymische Hochzeit: Christiani Rosencreutz*, ed. Richard van Dulmen. Stuttgart: Calwer, 1973.

14   Apuleius, Lucius (b. c. 127 CE). *The Golden Ass; being the Metamorphoses of Lucius Apuleius*, trans. W. Adlington, rev. S. Gaselee. London: Heinemann and Cambridge, MA: Harvard UP, 1965.

15   ——. *The Transformations of Lucius: otherwise known as The Golden Ass*, trans. Robert Graves. Harmondsworth, UK: Penguin, 1950, rpt. 1986.

16   Augustine of Hippo. *Homilies on the Gospel according to S. John, and his First Epistle.* London: Smith, 1884.

17   Balzac, Honoré de. *La peau de chagrin.* 1st ed. 1831; rpt. Paris: Gallimard, 1974. Translated as *The Wild Ass's Skin*, trans. Herbert J. Hunt. London; New York: Penguin, 1977.

18   Baudelaire, Charles. *Little Poems in Prose*, trans. Aleister Crowley. Paris: E. W. Titus, 1928; rev. ed., ed. Martin P. Starr, Chicago: Teitan Press, 1995.

19   Begbie, Harold. *On the Side of the Angels: A Reply to Arthur Machen.* London; New York: Hodder and Stoughton, 1915.

20   Bergson, Henri. *Creative Evolution.* New York: Holt, 1911.

21 The Bible.

22 Blake, William. *Complete Writings*, ed. Geoffrey Keynes. London and New York: Oxford UP, 1974.

23 ——. *The Marriage of Heaven and Hell*. London, c. 1790–93; facs. ed., London and New York: Oxford UP, 1975.

24 ——. *The Works of William Blake: Poetic, Symbolic, and Critical*, ed. Edwin John Ellis and William Butler Yeats. London: Quaritch, 1893.

25 Blau, Joel. *The Wonder of Life*. New York: Macmillan, 1925.

26 Blavatsky, Helena Petrovna. *The Voice of the Silence*. London, 1889; rpt. Wheaton, IL: Quest, 1992.

27 Boswell, James. *The Life of Samuel Johnson*. London, 1791; rpt. New York: Random House, n.d.

28 Browning, Robert. *The Complete Poetical and Dramatic Works of Robert Browning*. Rev. ed., Boston and New York: Houghton Mifflin, 1895.

29 Cabell, James Branch. *Domnei: A Comedy of Woman-Worship*. New York: McBride, 1920.

30 ——. *Figures of Earth: A Comedy of Appearances*. New York: McBride, 1921; rpt. London: Tandem, 1971.

31 ——. *Jurgen: A Comedy of Justice*. New York: McBride, 1919; rpt. New York: Dover, 1977.

32 ——. [*Jurgen.*] *Report of the Emergency Committee Organized to Protest Against the Suppression of James Branch Cabell's Jurgen*. New York, 1920.

33 ——. [*Jurgen.*] Holt, Guy, ed. *Jurgen and the Law*. New York: McBride, 1923.

34 Carroll, Lewis. *The Complete Works of Lewis Carroll*. New York: Modern Library, 1979.

35 Casanova, Jacques, chevalier de Seingalt [pseud. of Giacomo Casanova]. *Histoire de ma vie: suivie de textes inédits*. Paris: R. Laffont, c. 1993.

36 ——. *History of My Life*, trans. Willard R. Trask. New York: Harcourt, Brace and World, 1966.

37 ——. *Mémoires de Jacques Casanova de Seingalt*. Paris, 1833–37.; translated as *The Memoirs of Giacomo Casanova di Seingalt*, trans. Arthur Machen. London: Casanova Society, 1922.

38 Casaubon, Meric. *A True and Faithful Relation of what passed … between Dr. John Dee … and Some Spirits*. London, 1659; rpt. New York: Magickal Childe, 1992.

39 Cazotte, Jacques. *Le diable amoureux*. 1st ed. Naples [Paris], 1772; rpt. Paris, 1878.

40 ——. *The Devil in Love*, trans. Stephen Sartarelli. New York: Marsilio, 1993.

41 [*Chaldæan Oracles.*] Ruth Majercik. *The Chaldean Oracles: Text, Translation and Commentary*. Leiden; New York: Brill, 1989.

42 ——. *The Chaldean Oracles of Zoroaster as set down by Julianus*, trans. F. Patrizzi and T. Stanley. Gillette, NJ: Heptangle, 1989.

43 ——. *The Chaldean Oracles of Zoroaster*, ed. W. Wynn Westcott. London and New York, 1895; rpt. Seattle: Holmes, 1984.

44   Chalmers, George. *Caledonia; or, A Historical and Topographical Account of North Brit-ain.* Paisley, 1887–1902.

45   Chuang-tzu. In *The Texts of Taoism*, Parts I–II, trans. James Legge, *Sacred Books of the East,* vols. 39–40. Oxford: Clarendon Press, 1881; rpt. New York: Dover, c. 1990.

46   ———. *The Complete Works of Chuang Tzu,* trans. Burton Watson. New York: Columbia UP, 1968.

47   ———. Fung Yu-Lan. *A Taoist Classic: Chuang-tzu.* Beijing: Foreign Languages Press, 1989.

48   Coleridge, Samuel Taylor. *The Complete Poetical Works of Samuel Taylor Coleridge,* ed. Ernest Hartley Coleridge. Oxford: Clarendon Press, 1912; rpt. 1966.

49   Crowley, Aleister. *The Argonauts.* Foyers, UK: SPRT, and London: Chiswick Press, 1904. Reprinted in (57).

50   ———. בראשית [*Berashith*]. *An Essay in Ontology with some Remarks on Ceremonial Magic.* Paris: privately printed, 1903. In (57).

•   ———. *Bagh-i-Muattar,* see *The Scented Garden of Abdullah.*

•   ———. *The Banned Lecture.* See *Gilles de Rais.*

51   ———. *Book 4.* Frater Perdurabo and Soror Virakam [pseuds. for Crowley and Mary Desti Sturges], 2 vol. *Part 1. Mysticism.* London: Wieland, 1912. *Part 2. Magick: Preliminary Remarks.* London: Wieland, [1913]; rpt. (2 vols. in 1) Dallas: San-greal, 1969, 1972; rpt. York Beach, ME: Weiser, 1992.

•   ———. [*Book 4.*] *Magick. Book 4, Parts I–IV.* See (77).

52   ———. [*The Book of Lies.*] *Liber CCCXXXIII. The Book of Lies which is also falsely called Breaks.* Frater Perdurabo [pseud.]. London, 1913. In (53).

53   ———. *The Book of Lies … with an Additional Commentary.* Ilfracombe, 1962; rpt. York Beach: Weiser, 1993.

54   ———(editor and contributor). *The Book of the Goetia of Solomon the King,* ed. Aleister Crowley. Foyers, UK, 1904; facs. rpt. with holograph annotations, Thame, UK and Edmonds, WA: First Impressions, 1993. Rev. 2nd ed., ed. Hymenæus Beta, York Beach, ME: Weiser, 1995, 1997.

55   ———(received by). [*The Book of the Law*]. *Liber AL vel Legis sub figura CCXX.* London: O.T.O., 1938; 2nd rev. ed., Pasadena, CA: Church of Thelema [1942]; corrected rpt. of London ed., with facsimile MS, New York: Weiser, 1976, 1979; rpt. York Beach, ME: Weiser, 1993.

56   ———. *Die Botschaft der Meister Therion.* Leipzig: Thelema Verlag [c. 1927].

57   ———. *The Collected Works of Aleister Crowley.* 3 vols. Foyers, UK: SPRT, 1905–7; rpt. Des Plaines, IL: Yogi Publication Society [c. 1974].

58   ———. [*The Confessions of Aleister Crowley.*] *The Spirit of Solitude, subsequently re-anti-christened The Confessions of Aleister Crowley.* London, 1929. 2 vols. Vols. 3–6 not issued. Abridged one-volume edition *The Confessions of Aleister Crowley,* ed. John Symonds and Kenneth Grant. London, 1969; rpt. London and New York: Arkana, 1989.

59 ———. *Eight Lectures on Yoga*. Mahātma Guru Śrī Paramahaṇsa Śivaji [pseud.]. *The Equinox* III(4). London, 1939; rev. 2nd edition, ed. Hymenæus Beta, Scottsdale, AZ: New Falcon, 1991, and New York: 93 Publishing, 1992.

60 ———(editor and contributor). *The Equinox*. Aleister Crowley was series editor from 1909-1944. This series appeared semianually from spring 1909 to fall 1913. Volume II was intentionally not published. Volume III appeared between 1919 and 1986. Volume IV commenced publication in 1996.

60.a   *The Equinox* I(1), spring 1909, London; rpt. 1992, Weiser.

60.b   *The Equinox* I(2), fall 1909, London; rpt. 1992, Weiser.

60.c   *The Equinox* I(3), spring 1910, London; rpt. 1992, Weiser.

60.d   *The Equinox* I(4), fall 1910, London; rpt. 1992, Weiser.

60.e   *The Equinox* I(5), spring 1911, London; rpt. 1992, Weiser.

60.f   *The Equinox* I(6), fall 1911, London; rpt. 1992, Weiser.

60.g   *The Equinox* I(7), spring 1912, London; rpt. 1992, Weiser.

60.h   *The Equinox* I(8), fall 1912, ed. Soror Virakam [Mary Desti], London; rpt. 1992, Weiser.

60.i   *The Equinox* I(9), spring 1913, London; rpt. 1992, Weiser.

60.j   *The Equinox* I(10), fall 1913, London; rpt. 1992, Weiser.

60.k   *The Equinox* III(1), spring 1919, Detroit; rpt. 1992, Weiser.

60.l   *The Equinox* III(2), not issued. A reconstruction is in preparation.

60.m   *The Equinox* III(3), fall 1936. *The Equinox of the Gods*. See (61).

60.n   *The Equinox* III(4), spring 1939. *Eight Lectures on Yoga*.

60.o   *The Equinox* III(5), spring 1944. *The Book of Thoth*.

60.p   *The Equinox* III(6), 1961. *Liber Aleph*.

60.q   *The Equinox* III(7), 1971. *Shih Yi* [*Shih I*].

60.r   *The Equinox* III(8), 1975. *The Tao Teh King* [*Tao Te Ching*]. See (93).

60.s   *The Equinox* III(9), 1983. ΘΕΛΗΜΑ [*Thelema*]: *The Holy Books of Thelema*. See (97).

60.t   *The Equinox* III(10), 1986, New York; rpt. 1990, Weiser.

60.u   *The Equinox* IV(1), 1996. *Commentaries on the Holy Books and Other Papers*.

60.v   *The Equinox* IV(2), 1998. *The Vision and the Voice with Commentary and Other Papers*.

60.w   *The Equinox* IV(3), in preparation.

61 ———. *The Equinox of the Gods. Book 4*, Part IV. *The Equinox* III(3). London: O.T.O., 1936. Corrected facsimile edition Scottsdale, AZ: New Falcon, 1991 and New York, 93 Publishing, 1992.

62 ———. *The Forbidden Lecture. Gilles de Rais*, ed. Keith Richmond. Thame, UK: Mandrake, 1990.

63 ———. *Gems from the Equinox*, ed. I. Regardie. St. Paul: Llewellyn, 1974; rpt. Las Vegas: Falcon, 1989.

64 ———. *The General Principles of Astrology: Liber 536*, ed. Hymenæus Beta. York Beach, ME: Weiser, in press.

65 ———. *The God Eater. A Tragedy of Satire*. London: Watts, 1903.

• ———. *Goetia*. See *The Book of the Goetia*.

66 ———. *Golden Twigs*, ed. Martin P. Starr. Chicago: Teitan Press, 1988.

67 ———. [*Gilles de Rais*.] *The Banned Lecture. Gilles de Rais*. London: P. R. Stephensen, 1930.

68 ———. *The Heart of the Master*. Khaled Khan [pseud.]. London: O.T.O., 1938, and various reprints; 2nd edition, ed. K. Grant, Montréal: 93 Publishing, 1973; 3rd rev. edition, ed. Hymenaeus Beta, Scottsdale, AZ: New Falcon, 1992.

69 ———(received by). *The Holy Books of Thelema*. See (96) and (97).

70 ———. *Household Gods, a Comedy*. Pallanza, Italy: privately printed, 1912.

71 ———(editor and contributor). *The International: A Review of Two Worlds*. New York. Although Crowley was nominally contributing editor from August 1917 to April 1918 he became *de facto* editor, publishing much of his own work, often pseudonymously.

    71.a   *The International* XI(8), August 1917.

    71.b   *The International* XI(9), September 1917.

    71.c   *The International* XI(10), October 1917.

    71.d   *The International* XI(11), November 1917.

    71.e   *The International* XI(12), December, 1917.

    71.f   *The International* XII(1), January 1918.

    71.g   *The International* XII(2), February 1918

    71.h   *The International* XII(3), March 1918.

72 ———. *Jephthah: A Tragedy*. London: privately printed, 1898. 2nd rev. ed. *Jephthah and Other Mysteries, Lyrical and Dramatic*. London: K. Paul, Trench, Trubner, 1899. Reprinted in (57).

73 ———. *Konx Om Pax: Essays in Light*. London and New York: Walter Scott, and Foyers, UK: SPRT, 1907; facs. ed., Chicago: Teitan, 1990.

74 ———. *The Law is for All*, ed. I. Regardie. St. Paul, MN: Llewellyn, 1975; rpt. Scottsdale, AZ: New Falcon, 1991. Revised 2nd ed., ed. Louis Wilkinson and Hymenæus Beta, Scottsdale, AZ: New Falcon, 1996.

75 ———. [*Liber 418*.] *Liber XXX ÆRVM vel Sæculi sub figura CCCCXVIII. Being of the Angels of the Thirty Æthyrs the Vision and the Voice*. Without commentary as special supplement to (60.e). With commentary, Barstow, CA, 1952, and in (60.v).

• ———. *Liber 777*. See (85), (86) and (87).

76 ———. *Liber Aleph vel CXI. The Book of Wisdom or Folly*, ed. Karl Germer and Marcelo Motta, *The Equinox* III(6), Barstow, CA: Thelema Publishing Co., 1961; rev. 2nd edition, ed. Hymenaeus Beta, York Beach, ME: Weiser; New York: 93 Publishing, 1991.

77 ———. *Magick. Book 4, Parts I–IV*. (Co-authors: Mary Desti and Leila Waddell.) 1st one-vol. rev. edition, ed. Hymenæus Beta. York Beach, ME: Weiser, 1994; 2nd one-vol. ed., revised and enlarged, 1997.

78 ———. *Magick in Theory and Practice (being Part III of Book 4)*. The Master Therion [pseud.]. 4 vol. Paris: privately printed, 1929–30. 1 vol. subscribers ed. issued as *Magick in Theory and Practice*. London, 1930.

79 ———. *Moonchild*. London: Mandrake, 1929; rpt. York Beach, ME: Weiser, 1992.

80 ———. *Mortadello, or, The Angel of Venice: A Comedy*. London: Wieland, 1912; facs. rpt. Thame, UK and Edmonds, WA: First Impressions, 1992.

81 ———. *The Mother's Tragedy and Other Poems*. London: privately printed, 1901; rpt. Foyers, UK: SPRT, 1907; facs. rpt. Thame, UK and Edmonds, WA: First Impressions, 1992. Reprinted in *The Temple of the Holy Ghost* in (57).

82 ———. *Oz. Liber LXXVII*. 1st ed., London and Los Angeles, O.T.O., 1941; numerous reprints.

83 ———. *The Scented Garden of Abdullah the Satirist of Shiraz (Bagh-i-muattar)*. London, 1910; rpt. Chicago: Teitan Press, 1991.

84 ———. *The Scientific Solution of the Problem of Government* by Comte de Fénix [pseud.]. London: O.T.O., n.d. [c. 1937].

85 ———. *777 vel Prolegomena Symbolica ad Systemam Sceptico-Mysticæ Viæ Explicandæ, Fundamentum Hieroglyphicum Sanctissimorum Scientiæ Summæ*. London: Walter Scott, 1909.

86 ———. *777 Revised vel Prolegomena Symbolica ad Systemam Sceptico-Mysticæ Viæ Explicandæ, Fundamentum Hieroglyphicum Sanctissimorum Scientiæ Summæ*. London: Neptune, 1955; rpt. New York: Weiser, 1970; 2nd rev. ed. [Chico, CA]: O.T.O. [c. 1970].

87 ———. *777 and Other Qabalistic Writings*, ed. I. Regardie. New York: Weiser, 1977, rpt. York Beach, ME: Weiser, 1993.

88 ———. *[Shih I] Shih Yi*, ed. Helen Parsons Smith. [*The Equinox* III(7).] Oceanside, CA: Thelema Publications, 1971.

89 ———. *The Soul of Osiris: A History*. London: Kegan Paul, Trench, Trubner: Chiswick Press, 1901; facs. rpt. Thame, UK and Edmonds, WA: First Impressions, 1992. Reprinted with additions as *The Temple of the Holy Ghost* in (57).

90 ———. *The Soul of the Desert*, ed. Helen Parsons Smith. Kings Beach, CA: Thelema Publications, 1974.

91 ———. *The Star and the Garter*. Foyers, UK: SPRT, 1904.

92 ———. *The Sword of Song*. Benares [Paris], 1904; rpt. with additions in (57).

93 ———. *[Tao Te Ching.] The Tao Te Ching. Liber CLVII*, rev. ed., ed. Hymenæus Beta. *The Equinox* III(8), York Beach, ME: Weiser, 1995.

94 ———. *Temperance. A Tract for the Times*. London: privately printed by O.T.O., 1939.

95 ———. *The Temple of Solomon the King* (coauthored by J.F.C. Fuller), ed. Hymenæus Beta. Scottsdale, AZ: New Falcon, in press.

96 ———(received by). ΘΕΛΗΜΑ [*Thelema*], 3 vols. London: privately printed for members of A∴A∴, 1909.

97 ———(received by). [*Thelema*] ΘΕΛΗΜΑ: *The Holy Books of Thelema*, ed. Hymenæus Alpha and Hymenæus Beta. York Beach, ME: Weiser, 1983. *The Equinox* III(9).

Corrected 2nd printing, York Beach, ME: Weiser, and New York: 93 Publishing, 1990.

98 ——. *The Vision and the Voice.* See (60.e), (60.v) and (75).

99 ——. *Why Jesus Wept.* Paris: privately printed, 1904; rpt. in (57).

100 ——. *The World's Tragedy.* Paris: privately printed, 1910; 2nd ed. Phoenix: New Falcon, 1992.

101 Cunningham, Allan. *The Lives of the Most Eminent British Painters, Sculptors, and Architects.* 6 vols. London: Murray, 1830–1833.

102 Dickens, Charles. *The Posthumous Papers of the Pickwick Club.* London, 1836–1837; rev. ed., ed. Robert L. Patten, Harmondsworth, UK: Penguin, 1972.

103 Dunsany, Edward John Moreton Drax Plunkett, Baron. *Five Plays: The Gods of the Mountain, The Golden Doom, King Argimenes and The Unknown Warrior, The Glittering Gate, The Lost Silk Hat.* New York: Kennerley, 1914.

104 ——. *A Night at an Inn.* New York: Sunwise Turn, 1916.

105 Dumas, Alexandre. *Mémoires d'un médecin: Joseph Balsamo.* Nouv. ed., Paris, 1872; translated as *Memoirs of a Physician,* London: Routledge; New York: Dutton, 1879.

106 ——. *The Queen's Necklace.* New York: Limited Editions Club, 1973.

107 Eckartshausen, Karl von. *The Cloud upon the Sanctuary,* trans. Isabel de Steiger. London, 1903, 1919; rpt. Seattle: Sure Fire Press, 1991; rpt. Kila, MT: Kessinger, 1992.

108 Euripides. *The Bacchæ, and Other Plays,* trans. Philip Vellacott, rev. ed. Harmondsworth, UK; Baltimore: Penguin, 1972.

109 ——. *Bacchæ/Euripides,* trans. Richard Seaford. Warminster: Aris and Phillips, 1996.

110 Freud, Sigmund. *Beyond the Pleasure Principle,* trans. C. J. M. Hubback. London and Vienna: International Psycho-analytical Press, 1922.

111 ——. *Beyond the Pleasure Principle,* trans. James Strachey. New York: Norton, 1989.

112 Frazer, James George, Sir. *The Golden Bough.* 3rd ed. in 12 vols., London: Macmillan, 1911–15; 3rd ed. in 9 vols., New York: St. Martins, 1990; abridged 1-vol. ed., New York: Macmillan, 1922, 1960.

113 Fuller, John Frederick Charles. *The Star in the West: A Critical Essay upon the Works of Aleister Crowley.* London: Walter Scott, 1907; rpt. London: Atlantis, n.d. [c. 1980].

114 Gilbert, W. S. and Sullivan, Arthur. *The Mikado, or, The Town of Titipu.* London: Chappell, 1885.

115 Goethe, Johann Wolfgang von. *Faust,* trans. Bayard Taylor. New York: Modern Library, 1912.

116 ——. *Faust,* trans. Philip Wayne. Baltimore: Penguin, c. 1961.

• *The Greater Key of Solomon (Clavicula Salomonis).* See (130).

117 Grene, David, and Lattimore, Richmond, eds., *The Complete Greek Tragedies.* 4 vols. Chicago: University of Chicago Press, 1959.

118 Hæckel, Ernst Heinrich Philipp August. *The Riddle of the Universe at the Close of the Nineteenth Century,* trans. Joseph McCabe. New York; London: Harper, 1900.

119 Hartmann, Franz. *The Principles of Astrological Geomancy*. Boston: Occult Publishing, 1889.

120 Hooker, Denise. *Nina Hamnett: Queen of Bohemia*. London: Constable, 1986.

121 Hope, Anthony (Sir Anthony Hope Hawkins). *Rupert of Hentzau*. London: Macmillan, 1898.

122 Ibsen, Henrik. *Brand*, trans. Geoffrey Hill. London: Penguin, 1996.

123 ———. *The Complete Major Prose Plays*, trans. Rolf Fjelde. New York: New American Library, 1978.

124 ———. *Peer Gynt*, trans. Rolf Fjelde. 2nd ed. Minneapolis: University of Minnesota Press, 1980.

125 [*I Ching.*] *The Yî King. The Texts of Confucianism*, Part II, trans. James Legge, *Sacred Books of the East*, vol. 16. Oxford, 1882; 2nd ed. 1899; rpt. as *I Ching,* New York: Dover, c. 1990.

126 ———. *I Ching. The Classic of Changes*, trans. Edward L. Shaughnessy. New York: Ballantine, 1997.

127 James, William. *The Varieties of Religious Experience*. London, 1902; rpt. Cambridge, MA: Harvard UP, 1985; rev. ed. New York: Random House, 1993.

128 Jung, Carl Gustav. *Psychology of the Unconscious*, trans. Beatrice M. Hinkle. New York: Moffat, Yard, and London: Kegan Paul, Trench, Trubner, 1916. Revised and reissued as *Symbols of Transformation*, 2nd ed. Princeton, NJ: Princeton UP, 1970.

129 Keats, John. *The Complete Poetical Works of John Keats*, ed. H. Buxton Forman. New York: Oxford UP, 1934.

130 *The Key of Solomon the King (Clavicula Salomonis)*, ed. and trans. S.L. Mathers. London: Redway, 1888; facs. rpt., York Beach, ME: Weiser, 1972, rpt. 1994.

131 Kipling, Rudyard. *The Seven Seas*. London: Methuen, 1896.

132 Knorr von Rosenroth, Christian. [*Zohar.*] *Kabbala denudata*. 2 vol. (Salzbach, 1677–84). Partial translation in (133).

133 ———. [*Zohar; Kabbala denudata*, excerpts.] *Kabbala Denudata: The Kabbalah Unveiled*, trans. S.L. Mathers. First edition London, 1887: 2nd ed., 1926, rpt. 1971; rpt. York Beach, ME: Weiser, 1993; rpt. New York: Viking Penguin, 1991.

134 La Motte-Fouqué, Friedrich Heinrich Karl, Freiherr de. *Undine: A Romance*. London, 1818; Philadelphia, 1824; rpt. as *Undine: A Tale*, London: Sidgwick and Jackson, 1912; facs. rpt. Westport, CT: Hyperion Press, 1985; rpt. New York: Marlboro, 1990.

135 Lao-tzu. [*Tao Te Ching*, in] *The Texts of Taoism*, Part I, trans. James Legge, *Sacred Books of the East*, vol. 39. Oxford: Clarendon Press, 1881; rpt. Delhi: Motilal Banarsidass, 1988; rpt. New York: Dover, c. 1990.

136 ———. [*Tao Te Ching.*] Michael LaFargue. *The Tao of the Tao Te Ching: A Translation and Commentary*. Albany, NY: SUNY Press, 1992.

137 ———. [*Tao Te Ching.*] *The Tao Te Ching. Liber CLVII*, trans. Aleister Crowley, ed. Hymenæus Beta. *The Equinox* III(8). York Beach, ME: Weiser, 1996.

138 Lee, Marshall (ed.). *Books for Our Time*. New York: Oxford UP, 1951.

139 Le Sage, Alain René. [*Le diable boiteux*, 1707.] *Asmodeus; or, The Devil on Two Sticks*, trans. Joseph Thomas. New York: Doran, 1926.

140 Lévi, Éliphas. *La clef des grands mystères*. Paris; New York, 1861; rpt. Paris: Maisnie-Trédaniel, 1991. Translated as (143).

141 ———. *The Mysteries of Magic: A Digest of the Writings of Éliphas Lévi*, trans. and ed. A.E. Waite. London, 1886; 2nd rev. ed. 1897; rpt. Kila, MT: Kessinger, 1993.

142 ———. *Dogme et rituel de la haute magie*, 2 vol. Paris, 1854–56; 2nd 1 vol. ed., 1856; rev. 1 vol. ed., 1861; rev. ed., Paris: Bussière, 1967. Translated as (144).

143 ———. *The Key of the Mysteries*, trans. Aleister Crowley. London: Rider, 1959; rpt. London: Rider, and New York: Weiser, 1969, 1980. Also in (60.j).

144 ———. *Transcendental Magic: Its Doctrine and Ritual*, trans. A.E. Waite. London: Redway, 1896; rpt. London: Rider, 1913; 2nd rev. ed., London: Rider, and Philadelphia, McKay, 1923; rpt. London: Rider, 1968, and New York: Weiser, 1970; rpt. York Beach, ME: Weiser, 1993.

145 Lewis, Matthew. *The Monk, a Romance*, ed. Howard Anderson. [1st ed. 1795.] London: Oxford UP, 1973.

146 Longfellow, Henry Wadsworth. *The Song of Hiawatha*. London: David Bogue, 1855; Boston: Ticknor and Fields, 1856.

147 Lytton, Edward Bulwer-Lytton, 1st Baron. *A Strange Story*. Boston, 1862; rpt. Kila, MT: Kessinger, 1992.

148 ———. *Zanoni: A Rosicrucian Tale*. London, 1842; rpt. Blauvelt, NY: Spiritual Science Library, 1990.

149 Machen, Arthur. *The Angels of Mons: The Bowmen and Other Legends of the War*. London: Simpkin, Marshall, Hamilton, Kent, 1915.

150 ———. *Hieroglyphics: a Note upon Ecstasy in Literature*. New York: Knopf, 1923; rpt. London: Unicorn Press, 1960.

151 Marlowe, Christopher. *Christopher Marlowe's Doctor Faustus*, ed. Michael Keefer. Peterborough, Ont.: Broadview Press, 1991.

•   Mathers, S.L., see Knorr von Rosenroth, Christian.

152 Nordau, Max Simon. *Degeneration*, trans. George L. Mosse. Lincoln: University of Nebraska Press, 1993.

153 North, J. D. *Horoscopes and History*. London: Warburg Institute, 1986.

154 Paracelsus. *The Hermetic and Alchemical Writings of Aureolus Philippus Theophrastus Bombast, of Hohenheim, called Paracelsus the Great*, ed. and trans. A. E. Waite. London, 1894; rpt. Berkeley: Shambhala, 1976.

155 ———. *Samtliche Werke*, ed. Karl Sudhoff. Munich: Barth, 1922.

156 ———. *Selected Writings*, ed. Jolande Jacobi, trans. Norbert Guterman. Princeton, NJ: Princeton UP, 1951; rpt. 1989.

157 ———. *Werke: Theophrastus Paracelsus*, ed. Will-Erich Peuckert. Basel; Stuttgart: Schwabe Verlag, 1965.

158 Péladan, Joséphin. *Le vice suprême*. Paris, 1884; rpt. Geneva: Slatkine, 1979.

159 Pope, Alexander. *The Rape of the Lock*. London, 1896; rpt. New York: Dover [1968].

160 ———. *The Rape of the Lock, and Other Poems*, ed. Geoffrey Tillotson. 3rd rev. ed., London and New York: Methuen, 1971.

161 ———. *The Rape of the Lock*, ed. Elizabeth Gurr. Oxford: Oxford UP, 1990.

162 Rabelais, François. *Gargantua and Pantagruel*, trans. Burton Raffel. New York: Norton, 1990.

163 ———. *Gargantua and Pantagruel*, trans. Sir Thomas Urquhart and Pierre Le Motteux. New York: Knopf, c. 1994.

164 ———. *The Histories of Gargantua and Pantagruel*, trans. J. M. Cohen. Baltimore: Penguin, 1974.

165 ———. *Les Œuvres ... contenant cinq livres, de la vie, faicts, & dits heroiques de Gargantua & de son fils Pantagruel.* Lyon: Martin, 1558.

166 [*Rg-veda.*] *Rig-Veda Sanhita: A Collection of Ancient Hindu Hymns of the Rig-Veda*, trans. H. H. Wilson. New Delhi: Cosmo, 1977.

167 Robertson, John Mackinnon. *Pagan Christs: Studies in Comparative Hierology*. London: Watts, 1903; 2nd ed., 1911, rpt. 1928; rpt. New Hyde Park, NY: University Books, 1967; abridged ed. New York: Dorset, 1987.

168 Sabhapaty Swāmi, Srī Mahātmā Jñāna Guru Yogi. *The Philosophy and Science of Vedanta and Râja Yoga*, ed. S.C. Vasu. Bombay: Mandali, 1950.

169 Scott, Walter, Sir. *Ivanhoe*. Edinburgh, 1820; rev. ed., ed. A.N. Wilson, Harmondsworth, UK; New York: Penguin, 1986.

170 ———. *The Lay of the Last Minstrel*. London; Edinburgh, 1805. Oxford; New York: Woodstock, 1985.

171 Shelley, Mary. *Frankenstein: or, The Modern Prometheus.* 3 vol. London, 1818; rev. ed., ed. Maurice Hindle, Harmondsworth, UK; New York: Penguin, 1994.

172 ———. *Mary Shelley's Frankenstein*, ed. Harold Bloom. New York: Chelsea House, 1987.

173 Shelley, Percy Bysshe. *The Complete Poetical Works of Percy Bysshe Shelley*, ed. Neville Rogers. Oxford: Clarendon Press, 1972.

174 Sinnett, Alfred Percy. *The Mahatma Letters to A. P. Sinnett from the Mahatmas M. and K.H.*, ed. A.T. Barker. London: Unwin, 1923.

175 Sophocles. *The Dramas of Sophocles Rendered in English Verse, Dramatic and Lyric*, trans. Sir George Young. London; Toronto: Dent; New York: Dutton, 1913.

176 ———. *The Œdipus Trilogy*, trans. Stephen Spender. London and Boston: Faber and Faber, 1985.

177 Southey, Robert. *The Poetical Works of Robert Southey*. London, 1838.

178 Swinburne, Algernon Charles. *Collected Poetical Works*. New York: Harper [c. 1924].

179 ———. *William Blake: A Critical Essay*. London, 1868; rpt. London: Chatto and Windus, 1906; rev. ed., Hugh J. Luke, Lincoln: University of Nebraska Press [1970].

180 Symons, Arthur. *William Blake*. London: Constable; New York: Dutton, 1907; rpt. New York: Cooper Square Publishers, 1970.

181 Thackeray, William Makepeace. *The Memoirs of Barry Lyndon, Esq., of the Kingdom of Ireland*. London, 1856; rpt. Harmondsworth, UK; Baltimore: Penguin, 1975.

182 Thomson, James. *The City of Dreadful Night and Other Poems.* London, 1880; rpt. London: Methuen, 1932.

183 Underhill, Evelyn. *Mysticism: A Study in the Nature and Development of Man's Spiritual Consciousness.* London: Methuen, 1911; rpt. London: Methuen; Totowa, NJ: Rowman and Littlefield, 1977.

184 *The Upanishads*, trans. Swāmi Nikhilānanda. 5th ed., New York: Ramakrishna-Vivekānanda Center, 1990.

185 Villars, de Montfauçon, abbé de (Nicholas-Pierre-Henri). *The Count of Gabalis, or, The Extravagant Mysteries of the Cabalists*, trans. P. A. Gent. London, 1680.

186 ———. *Comte de Gabalis.* London: Brothers, 1913; rpt. New York: Macoy, 1922; rpt. Kila, MT: Kessinger, 1992.

187 Wagner, Richard. *Parsifal: ein Buhnenweihfestspiel*, trans. Margaret H. Glyn and Alfred Ernst. Mainz: Schott, c. 1926; rpt. New York: Dover, 1986.

188 Waite, Arthur Edward. *The Book of Black Magic and of Pacts.* London, 1898; rpt. York Beach, ME: Weiser, 1972, 1993.

189 Wordsworth, William. *Intimations of Immortality from Recollections of Early Childhood.* Boston, 1884.

190 Wordsworth, William. *Ode on Immortality, and, Lines on Tintern Abbey.* London; New York, 1885.

191 Yeats, William Butler. *The Letters of W.B. Yeats*, ed. Allan Wade. New York: Macmillan, 1954.

192 ———. *The Tables of the Law. The Adoration of the Magi.* [n.p.:] privately printed, 1897; rpt. Stratford-upon-Avon, UK: Shakespeare Head Press, 1914.

•   *Zohar.* See also Knorr von Rosenroth, Christian.

193 *The Zohar*, trans. Harry Sperling and Maurice Simon. London and New York: Soncino Press, 1984.

194 ———. *The Wisdom of the Zohar: An Anthology of Texts*, ed. F. Lachower and I. Tishby, commentary by I. Tishby, trans. D. Goldstein. Oxford: Littman Library and Oxford UP, 1989.

•   Zoroaster, see *Chaldæan Oracles.*

Index

A.˙.A.˙. 36-37, 88, 119
Aaron 115
Abbey of Thelema 163-165
    at Cefalù 126-134, 159
Abraham 31, 105, 150
Abraham the Jew 30
Abramelin 30
Abyss 173
Adam 84, 145, 147
Adams, Evangeline 91-95
ādi-buddha 116
Adonis 17
Adonis (Crowley) 112
Agamemnon 105
Agamemnon (Æschylus) 105, 106, 108, 111
Ægisthus 105
Agrippa, Henry C. 100
Aiwass 162, 165, 167
Ajax 105
Ajax (Sophocles) 111
ākāśa 87
ALHIM 158
Allāh 148
Allen, Charles Grant 17
Almaric de Bèna 65
Amaury of Bena, see Almaric
"Anactoria" (Swinburne) 109
Andrea, Johann Valentin 65, 122
Anti-Christ 151, 153
Aphrodite 108
Apollo 122
Apollonius of Tyana 65
Apuleius, Lucius 32
Archimedes 49
The Argonauts (Crowley) 112
Aristotle 176, 184

Artemis 108
Æschylus 25
As You Like It (Shakespeare) 111
Atalanta in Calydon (Swinburne) 112
The Atlantic Monthly 145
ātmadarśana 33
ātman 67, 148
"At the Fork of the Roads" (Crowley) 28
augœides 116
Augustine, Saint 162

Babalon 116
Bacchæ (Euripides) 17, 104, 111
Bacon, Francis, Sir 122, 176
Bagh-i-Muattar (Crowley) 73
Baker, Julian 27
Balzac, Honore de 20
Banville, Théodore de 20
Barnardo, Thomas John 84
Barry Lyndon (Thackeray) 22
Baudelaire, Charles 20, 115, 122
Beast, see Crowley
Bedlam 132
Beelzebub 30
Behemoth 130
Bell, Alexander Graham 121
Bennett, Allan 21, 23-24, 28, 33, 34
Bergson, Henri 78
Bernard, Saint, of Clairvaux 65
Besant, Annie 89-90
Bhāvanī 56
Bible 83, 84, 119, 206
    Acts 199
    Chronicles 150
    I Corinthians 162
    Ecclesiastes 150
    Exodus 62

Gospels 75, 98
  Matthew 74
  Psalms 150
  Revelation 39
Black Brothers 90, 118, 173
Black Lodge 28
Blake, William 65, 115-125, 203
  theory of O'Neil ancestry 117
Blau, Joel, Rabbi 145, 147
Blavatsky, Helena P. 21, 62, 65, 89
The Blind Prophet (Crowley) 112
Bluebeard 197
Boccaccio, Giovanni 85
Bœhme, Jacob 65, 75
Bolshevism 199
Bonaventura, Saint 65
The Book of Black Magic and of Pacts
  (Waite) 26
The Book of Lies (Crowley) 68, 147
The Book of the Law, see *Liber AL*
The Book of the Sacred Magic of Abramelin
  the Mage 30
Borgia, Roderic (Pope Alexander VI) 122
"The Bowmen" (Machen) 61-62
Bradlaugh, Charles 83
Brand (Ibsen) 111
Brothers of the Left Hand Path, see Black
  Brothers
Browning, Robert 98
Buddha 67, 107, 109, 148, 155, 161, 184
Buddhism 108
Buer 29
Būlāq Museum 156
Bulwer Lytton, Edward 22
Byron, Lord 123

Cagliostro 19, 22
cakras 56
Cambridge University 25
Campbell, Phyllis 62
Carroll, Lewis 85
Casanova 22
Catholic Church, Holy 45
Cefalù 126, 131, 159
The Chaldæan Oracles of Zoroaster 87
Chao, Duke of 99
Chesterton, G.K. 197, 201

Chogo Ri 70
Chokmah Nesethrah 119, 145
Christianity 45, 151, 153, 198
Christian Science 210
Chuang-tzu 43
The City of Dreadful Night (Thomson) 85
Clive, Robert, baron 129
The Cloud Upon the Sanctuary (Von
  Eckartshausen) 26
Coleridge, Samuel Taylor 123
Communism 164, 199
Comstock, Anthony 83
Comte de Gabalis (Henri) 21, 23
Corinna the Theban 120
Coriolanus (Shakespeare) 111
Crowley, Aleister 193
  as Ankh-f-n-khonsu the scribe 162,
    165
  as Baphomet 100
  as Frater Perdurabo 43, 68, 162, 167
  as the Beast 666 151
  as the Master Therion 88-90, 162,
    163, 165, 167, 177, 182,
    183, 186, 187, 188
  as Το Μεγα Θηριον 157, 166
  as V.V.V.V.V. 99
Crusades 200
"The Cry of the Modern Pharisee" (Blau)
  145

The Daily Chronicle 62
Dante 80
d'Aurevilly, Jules 20
Dee, John 16, 24, 65
Degeneration (Nordau) 59
Demeter 17
Derval, Philip, Sir 22
Descartes, René 176
Devil, the 23
dhāranā 27
Diable amoreux (Cazotte) 22
Diable boiteux (Lesage) 22
Dickens, Charles 204
Dionysus 65, 105, 115
A Doll's House (Ibsen) 111
Domnei (Cabell) 160
Du Bellay, Jean, cardinal 163

dukkhā 174

Eckartshausen, Karl von 26
Eckenstein, Oscar 49
Eckhart, Johannes 65
Edward III, King of England 120
Einstein, Albert 150
ekāgrata 74
El 17
Elias 105
Elias Artista 121
Elijah 123
Elizabeth of Schonau, Saint 65
Emerson, Ralph Waldo 65
An Enemy of the People (Ibsen) 111
Engers-Kennedy, Leon 97
The Equinox 38, 147
Euclid 44
Euripides 17
Eve 84
The Evening News (London) 59, 60, 62

The Fatal Force (Crowley) 112
Faust 13
Flamel, Nicholas 26
Fox, George 65
Francis, Saint, of Assisi 33, 65
Francis I, king 163
Franck, Sebastian 65
Frankenstein (Shelley) 22
Frazer, James G. 17
Freud, Sigmund 76, 78, 79, 152
Front-de-Bœuf, Reginald 202
Fu-hsi 51, 99
Fuller, J.F.C. 32
Fust, Johann 13

Gargamelle 80
Gargantua (Rabelais) 163
Gaugin, Paul 129
Gautama, see Buddha
Gautier, Théophile 20
George, Saint 61, 62
George III, King of England 125
Ghosts (Ibsen) 111
Gichtel, Johann G. 65
Gilbert, W. S. 128
God 44, 85, 165, 188

The Gods of the Mountain (Dunsany) 112
Goetia 28
Goncourt, Edmond and Jules de 20
Goodwin, Isabel 95
Graves, Robert 205
Great White Brotherhood 45, 88
Groot, Gerhard 65
Guyon, Jeanne Marie 65
Gyles, Althea 28

Hæckel, Ernst 41, 44, 45
Haldane, J.B.S. 204
al-Ḥallāj, Manṣūr 67
Halley's Comet 200
Hamlet (Shakespeare) 83, 111
Haraucourt, Edmond 20, 85
Hecuba 106
Hedda Gabler (Ibsen) 111
Heindel, Max 89
Heine, Heinrich 150
Henson, Hensley, Canon 62
Hera 80
Hermes Trismegistus 14, 18
Herod 115
"Hertha" (Swinburne) 123
Hertz, Heinrich 13
Hiawatha (Longfellow) 79
Hieroglyphics (Machen) 124
Hildegard of Binjen, Saint 65
Hiram 106
Hismael 17, 24
Hitler, Adolf 209
Holmes, Sherlock 58
Holy Ghost 206
Holy Guardian Angel 45, 116
Home, D.D. 34
Horace 155
Horton, Dr. 62
Household Gods (Crowley) 112
Hugh of St. Victor 65
Hunt, William Holman 204
Huss, John 193
Huxley, Aldous 194
Huxley, Thomas Henry 41, 194

Iacchus 89
Ibsen, Henrik 185
I Ching 99

Ingersoll, Robert G. 85
The International 88, 156
Iophiel 17
Isis of Corinth 120
Israel 151, 152, 153, 155
Issa bin Jusuf (Jesus son of Joseph), see
    Jesus Christ
Iśvara 64

Jacobs, Samuel Aiwaz 157
James, William 106
Jeheshua 23
Jehovah 198
Jephthah (Crowley) 105, 112
Jesus Christ 16, 17, 33, 75, 105, 106, 108,
    118, 121
    and Anti-Christ 153
    as Iesous the fish 166
    as Issa bin Jusuf 65
Joachim of Fiora 65
Joan of Arc 113-114, 197
Johannes, Abbot 59
John, Saint, of the Cross 65
John Bull 62
John the Baptist 115, 121
Jones, Charles Stansfeld 89
Jones, George Cecil (Frater Volo Noscere)
    27, 28, 29
Joseph 150
Julian (Flavius Claudius Julianus) 123
Julius Cæsar 209
Julius Cæsar (Shakespeare) 111
Jung, C.G. 76, 78-81, 152
Jupiter 17, 24
Jurgen (Cabell) 159, 160

Kanchenjunga 70
karma 88, 111
Keats, John 123, 129
Kelly, Edward 65
Kelvin, Lord 44
Kepler, Johannes 176
Key of Solomon 24
The Key of the Mysteries (Lévi) 20
Khayyám, Omar 115
King Lear (Shakespeare) 111
Kingsford, Anna 21
Knights Templar 79

Konx Om Pax (Crowley) 38
Kubla Khan (Coleridge) 123

Lamech 30
Lao-tzu 75
La peau de chagrin (Balzac) 22
Latimer, Nicholas 204
Law, William 65
Lazenby, Charles 88, 89
Lévi, Éliphas 18-22, 65, 122
liṅga 52
Liber 777 (Crowley et al.) 38
*Liber AL vel Legis sub figura 220, The Book
    of the Law* 78, 110, 146, 156-
    167, 173, 174, 179, 181, 187, 206
"Liber Trigrammaton sub figura 27"
    (Crowley) 99
Light 61
Livy (Titus Livius) 22
Loki 117
Lombroso, Cesare 44
Loyola, Ignatius, Saint 65
Luther, Martin 122
Lytton, Edward Bulwer 20

Macaulay 9
Macbeth (Shakespeare) 111
Machen, Arthur 60-62, 124
mahāliṅga 56
mahāthera 56
mahātmās 26
Maitland, Edward 21
Manet, Edouard 122
Manuel, Count 159, 160
Marconi, Guglielmo 13
Mars 113
Marxism 154
The Master Builder (Ibsen) 111
Master of the Temple 99, 118
Mathers, Samuel Liddell 21
Maximinus 122
McGraw, John Joseph 56
Meister Eckhart, see Eckhart, Johannes
Memoirs of a Physician (Dumas) 22
Merlin 122
Middle Ages 189, 198, 202
Milton, John 125
Mithras 17

Mohammed 67, 108, 129, 148, 151
The Monk (Lewis) 22, 124
Moon 24
More, Henry 65
Mortadello (Crowley) 112
Moses 122, 148, 150
The Mother's Tragedy (Crowley) 112
Mudd, Norman 158
Münzer, Thomas 65
Mussolini, Benito 209

Naaman 83
Napoleon 20, 184, 195, 196
Nasier, Alcofribas, see François Rabelais
neti neti 72
Neuburg, Victor Benjamin 65
The New Church Weekly 62
Newman, John Henry Cardinal 45
Newton, Isaac, Sir 44, 98, 176, 184
Newton's First Law 49, 98
Nicholas of Cusa 65
Nietzsche, Friedrich 185
A Night in an Inn (Dunsany) 112
nirvāṇa 57
Nordau, Max 59
Novalis 65
Nuit 123

Occult Review 60, 61, 62
"Ode to Psyche" ("To Psyche") (Keats) 124
Œdipus Rex (Sophocles) 111
O'Neil, see Blake
Ordo Templi Orientis (O.T.O.) 36-38, 79
    as Order of the Temple 100
Orestes trilogy (Æschylus) 111
Osiris 17, 106
Othello (Shakespeare) 111
Oxford University 133, 195, 198
Oxford University Poetry Society 193

Palestine 151
Palladino, Eusapia 44
The Pall Mall Gazette 62
Pan 79, 115, 124, 169
Pantagruel 80
Parabrahman 64
Paracelsus, Phillipus Aureolus 65, 121

Parsifal (Wagner) 15
Parzival 115
Pasteur, Louis 184
Paul, Saint 96, 150, 162
Peer Gynt (Ibsen) 111
Péladan, Joséphin 59-60
Pelops 80
Pentheus 104
Perdurabo, see Crowley
Pericles 184
Pickwick Papers (Dickens) 204
Pilate, Pontius 16
Plato 65, 176
plerōma 64
Plotinus 65
Poe, Edgar Allan 123
Poiret, Peter 65
Pope Alexander VI (Roderic Borgia) 122
Porphyry 65
Procrustes 128
Prometheus 115
Prometheus Unbound (Shelley) 124
Protestantism 163
Pythagoras 119

Qabalah 72, 119, 145
Qliphoth 210

Rabelais, François 85, 115, 122, 163-167
Rais, Gilles de 194, 196-204
The Rape of the Lock (Pope) 21
Rationalist Press Association 42, 43
Reformation 165
Rembrandt 71
Renaissance 163, 165
Reuss, Theodor (O.T.O. Frater Superior) 36
"The Revival of Magick" (Crowley) 156
Rg-Veda 81
Richard of St. Victor 65
Rickett, J.C., Sir 62
Ridley, Hugh 204
"Rime of the Ancient Mariner" (Coleridge) 124
rishi (ṛṣi) 47
Robertson, James Mackinnon 17
Rollinat, Maurice 20
Rome 151

Romeo and Juliet (Shakespeare) 111
Röntgen 121
Rosencreutz, Christian 21
Rosicrucians 18, 19
Rosmersholm (Ibsen) 111
Rupert of Hentzau (Hope) 80

Sabhapaty Swāmi, Śrī 75
Sachiel 17
Sade, Marquis de 109
Satan 113, 118, 123
The Scorpion (Crowley) 112
Scott, Walter, Sir 13, 198
Seb 123
"Sepher Sephiroth sub figura 500" (Crowley et al.) 102
Shakespeare, William 122, 124, 197
Shelley, Percy Bysshe 54, 67, 123
Shiloh 151
ShT 158
Shu 123
Simpson, Elaine 34
Sinnett, A.P. 62
Śiva 23, 47
śivadarśana 23
Smith, Bishop Taylor 62
Snowstorm (Crowley) 112
Society for Psychical Research (England) 62
Socrates 65, 116
soma 57
Southey, Robert 203
Spencer, Herbert 17, 80
Spinoza, Baruch 150
Spiritualism 210
St. Germain, Comte de 19
St. Martin, Claude de 65
The Star in the West (Fuller) 147
Stèle of Revealing (Stèle 666) 156
Stevenson, Robert Louis 201
Strange Story (Lytton) 22
Summers, Montague 203
Sunday, Billy 82-86
"The Surgeon's Warning" (Southey) 203
Suso, Heinrich 65
Swedenborg, Emanuel 65, 119
Swinburne, Algernon Charles 109, 119,

122, 123, 125
The Tables of the Law (Yeats) 123
Tahuti 13
tao 68, 72, 173
Taphthartharath 157
Tatham, Frederick 119
Tauler, Johann 65
Templars 200
Teresa, Saint 65
Thackeray, William Makepeace 22
Thèbes, Madame de 59
Thelemites 174
Theosophical Society 21, 88
Thoth 13
Trance of Sorrow 174
Tree of Life 119, 210
Truth 62
Twelfth Night (Shakespeare) 111
Tzadquiel 17, 157

Undine (La Motte-Fouqué) 21

Valentine, Basil 26
Van Ruysbroeck, Jan 65
Varley, John 120
Venus 113
Verlaine, Paul 20, 122
Verrall, A.W. 105
Le vice suprême (Péladan) 59
Viereck, George Sylvester 157
Villon, François 155
Virgil 80, 155
The Voice of the Silence (Blavatsky) 89
Volo Noscere, Frater, see Jones, George Cecil

Wagner, Richard 15
Waite, Arthur Edward 26
Wallace, Alfred Russell 44
Washington, George 184
Waterloo, Battle of 195-196
Watt, Charles 98
Watts, Charles 44
Weekly Dispatch 60
Weigel, Valentine 65
Weishaupt, Adam 123
Welldon, Bishop 62
Wellington, Duke of (Arthur Wesley) 195

Wên, King 99
Whistler, James 122, 125
Windram, James Thomas 102-103
Wordsworth, William 123
The World's Tragedy (Crowley) 38, 112
Wotan 117

yang 99

Yeats, William Butler 28, 119, 123
yin 99
yoni 52, 56

Zanoni (Lytton) 22
Zeus 32, 115, 123
Zion 145, 147, 151
Zoroaster 65

The letters O.T.O. stand for Ordo Templi Orientis — the Order of Oriental Templars, or Order of the Temple of the East. The O.T.O. is dedicated to securing the Liberty of the Individual, and his or her advancement in Light, Wisdom, Understanding, Knowledge, and Power. This is accomplished through Beauty, Courage, and Wit, on the Foundation of Universal Brotherhood. The O.T.O. is in sympathy with the traditional ideals of Freemasonry, and was the first of the Old Æon orders to accept *The Book of the Law.*

Many aspirants to the Great Work have a genuine need for information, guidance, fellowship, or the opportunity to assist their fellow aspirants and serve humanity. Such aspirants will find welcome in O.T.O.

The structure of the O.T.O., like that of Freemasonry and the ancient mystery schools, is based on a graded series of initiations, or Degrees. In these Degrees, the O.T.O. seeks to instruct the individual by allegory and symbol in the profound mysteries of Existence, and thereby to assist each to discover his or her own true Nature.

Every man and woman of full age, free, and of good report, has an indefeasible right to the introductory Degrees of the O.T.O.

The O.T.O. also includes the Gnostic Catholic Church (Ecclesia Gnostica Catholica), whose central public and private rite is "Liber XV," the Gnostic Mass.

The O.T.O. has active branches around the world, and issues numerous periodicals in many languages. In addition to the official O.T.O. instructions and the celebration of the Gnostic Mass, many national and regional O.T.O. Lodges, Oases and Camps offer classes and study programs to their members.

<table>
<tr><td>Ordo Templi Orientis
International Headquarters
P.O. Box 684098
Austin, TX 78768 USA</td><td>Ordo Templi Orientis USA
United States Grand Lodge
P.O. Box 10369
San Bernardino, CA 92423 USA</td></tr>
</table>